MODERN HUMANITIES RESEARCH ASSOCIATION
CRITICAL TEXTS
VOLUME 47

EDITORS
JUSTIN EDWARDS and CATHERINE MAXWELL

WILLIAM WEBBE
A DISCOURSE OF ENGLISH POETRY (1586)

William Webbe
A Discourse of English Poetry (1586)

Edited by
Sonia Hernández-Santano

Modern Humanities Research Association
2016

Published by

The Modern Humanities Research Association
Salisbury House
Station Road
Cambridge CB1 2LA
United Kingdom

© The Modern Humanities Research Association, 2016

Sonia Hernández-Santano has asserted her right under the Copyright, Designs and Patents Act 1988 to be identified as the author of this work. Parts of this work may be reproduced as permitted under legal provisions for fair dealing (or fair use) for the purposes of research, private study, criticism, or review, or when a relevant collective licensing agreement is in place. All other reproduction requires the written permission of the copyright holder who may be contacted at rights@mhra.org.uk.

First published 2016

ISBN 978-1-78188-125-5

Copies may be ordered from www.criticaltexts.mhra.org.uk

CONTENTS

Acknowledgements	vi
Abbreviations	viii
Introduction	1
1. Preliminary Considerations	1
1.1 Presentation of the Text and its Author	1
1.2 The Objectives of Webbe's Treatise	8
1.3 Structure	9
2. The Humanist Context of *A Discourse*: Roger Ascham's *The Schoolmaster* and Thomas Elyot's *The Governour*	10
2.1 Ascham's Humanist Principles in *A Discourse*	10
Matter and Form	11
Imitation	14
Translation	16
Versification	17
2.2 Thomas Elyot: *The Boke Named the Governour* (1531)	19
3. William Webbe and Cambridge Ideals: Canonizing Spenser's *The Shepherds' Calendar*	22
3.1 Webbe's Cambridge Background and Intellectual Relationships	22
3.2 Canonizing Spenser's *Calendar*	32
4. A Defence of the Quantitative Reformation of English Verse	37
4.1 Webbe's Remarks on English Rhyme and Rhymers	37
4.2 Humanist Implications of Quantitative Metres: Sophistication and Artificiality	39
4.3 Historical Overview of the Elizabethan Quantitative Movement: First Experiments, First Impediments	40
5. The Present Edition	49
The Epistle	57
A Preface to the Noble Poets of England	61
A Discourse of English Poetry	65
Textual Notes	141
Glossary	145
Bibliography	151
Index	160

ACKNOWLEDGEMENTS

This edition is principally indebted to the financial support provided by the former Spanish Ministry of Science and Innovation and now the Ministry of Economy through its programme 'Promoción General del Conocimiento', Project FFI2010-19279, 'English Poetic and Rhetorical Treatises of the Tudor Period'. This logistical support has enabled me to study the two extant copies of the first edition of Webbe's treatise, which are preserved in the Bodleian Library and the Huntington Library; it has also been fundamental for my attending conferences and seminars and for allowing us to enlarge the University of Huelva Library with specialised manuals on the topics we needed to research.

I also wish to thank all the members of this project: Attila Kiss, for working so closely on it from Hungary; Elena Domínguez and Lorena Laureano, for their constructive and encouraging comments; and I owe many and special thanks to the leader of the project, Zenón Luis, first for having entrusted me with this challenging work, and second for so many hours spent in his office, for the hundreds of e-mails and instant texting at any time of day on any day of the week, discussing all sorts of questions concerning difficult editorial decisions, sharing my concerns, and above all, raising my self-confidence at crucial moments.

I am especially grateful to all the scholars who attended the workshop 'Speaking Pictures: Poetry, the Arts of Discourse, and the Discourse of the Arts', held in Huelva in October 2014: Gavin Alexander, Sarah Knight, Michael Hetherington, György E. Szönyi, Rocío Sumillera, Manuel Gómez-Lara and Cinta Zunino. It is an honour to acknowledge my debt to Andrew Hadfield, whose comments on my presentation on Spenser and Webbe at the Sederi conference held at the University of Oviedo in 2014 were extremely helpful to my later rethinking of this issue. I am wholeheartedly grateful to Sarah Knight, who has always been present in one way or another, from our first academic meeting in Santiago de Compostela to her thorough supervision of the introduction to the edition. She deserves special recognition for her constructive comments and for her academic support and encouragement.

I owe many debts to the University of Huelva and its English Department, to the staff members of the Bodleian Library, Oxford, the Huntington Library in Los Angeles and The Newberry Library in Chicago.

I also wish to acknowledge my debt to the work of my predecessors in the editing of Webbe's treatise, from its first editors, Edward Arber and Joseph Haslewood, to the brilliant and solid edition provided by Gregory G. Smith.

I lastly owe many thanks to my supportive and patient husband, my parents, sister and friends for always understanding my reclusion, for their encouragement and love. I am also grateful to my closest colleague and friend, Beatriz Rodríguez, who has always encouraged me in everything I have done, with whom I have shared all my academic stages, and whose constant determination has been a model for me.

ABBREVIATIONS

This list includes frequently quoted sources, and the ones used in the Textual Notes.

A Discourse, Q	Webbe, William, *A Discourse of English Poetrie. Together, with the Authours iudgment, touching the reformation of our English Verse* (London: John Charlewood for Robert Walley, 1586)
Arb	Arber, Edward, ed., *A Discourse of English Poetrie. Together, with the Authours iudgment, touching the reformation of our English Verse* (London: English Reprints, 1815)
Brooks-Davies, SC	Spenser, Edmund, *The Shepherds' Calendar* (1579), in *Selected Shorter Poems*, ed. by Douglas Brooks-Davies (London: Longman, 1995)
Certain Notes	Gascoigne, George, *Certayne Notes of Instruction* (1575), in *Elizabethan Critical Essays*, ed. by Gregory Smith, 2 vols (London: Oxford University Press, 1904), I, 46–57
Defence	Sidney, Philip, *The Defence of Poesy* (1595), in *Sidney's 'The Defence of Poesy' and Selected Renaissance Literary Criticism*, ed. by Gavin Alexander (London: Penguin Books, 2004)
Governour, Gov	Elyot, Thomas, *The Boke Named the Gouernour* (London: Thomas Berthelet, 1531. 2nd edn London: Thomas East, 1580)
Hasl	Webbe, William, *A Discourse of English Poetrie*, ed. by Joseph Haslewood, *Ancient Critical Essays Upon English Poets and Poësy*, 2 vols (London: T. Bensley for Robert Triphook, 1815), II, 13–95
Letters	Spenser-Harvey correspondence in *The Works Of Edmund Spenser: A Variorum Edition. The Prose Works*, ed. by Edwin Greenlaw and others, 11 vols (Baltimore: The Johns Hopkins University Press, 1949), X
Meres	Meres, Francis, *Palladis Tamia* (1598), in *Elizabethan Critical Essays*, ed. by Gregory Smith, 2 vols (London: Oxford University Press, 1904), II, 308–24
OED	*Oxford English Dictionary* (Online edition)
Phaer	Phaer, Thomas, *The whole xii Bookes of the Aeneidos of Virgill* (London: William How, 1573) and *The xiii Bookes of Aeneidos* (London: William How, 1584)

Paradise	*The Paradyse of Daynty Deuises* (London: Henry Disle, 1576. 2nd edn 1578. 3rd edn 1580. 4th edn London: Robert Waldegrave, for Edward White, 1585)
$Q_1 Q_2 Q_3$	Spenser, Edmund, *The Shepheardes Calender Conteyning Twelue Aeglogues Proportionable to the Twelue Monethes* (London: Hugh Singleton, 1579. 2nd edn London: Thomas East for John Harrison, 1581. 3rd edn London: John Wolf for John Harrison, 1586)
Schoolmaster	Ascham, Roger, *The Scholemaster* (1570), in *English Works*, ed. by William Aldis Wright (Cambridge: Cambridge University Press, 1904)
The Art	Puttenham, George, *The Art of English Poesy*, ed. by Frank Whigham and Wayne E. Rebhorn (Ithaca: Cornell University Press, 2007)

For Carmen and Ángel

INTRODUCTION

1. Preliminary Considerations

1.1 Presentation of the Text and its Author

The present edition of William Webbe's *A Discourse of English Poetry* (1586) aims at refreshing scholars' interest in a Tudor treatise on poetry that has traditionally been eclipsed by the significant contributions to the literary theory of the sixteenth century of Puttenham's *The Art of English Poetry* (1589) and Sidney's *The Defence of Poetry* (c. 1580, printed in 1595). With this purpose in mind, this edition attempts, on the one hand, to integrate Webbe into the literary and academic context of Elizabethan times in order to determine to what extent his work constitutes a lively and committed response to the concerns raised throughout the period's continuing discussions on poetry. At the same time, this edition also aims to update and extend the so far unique editorial work carried out by Gregory Smith (1904) to provide readers interested in Webbe's treatise with a modern-spelling version which incorporates in its critical apparatus more recent scholarship and approaches to Elizabethan literary theory.[1]

The fact that George Gascoigne's *Certain Notes of Instruction* (1575) was published only as an annex to the quarto edition of his *Poesies*, and its scope limited to the presentation of sixteen practical suggestions for the improvement of the composition of rhymed verse, renders *A Discourse* the 'first extensive printed treatise to deal specifically with English poetry' (Pincombe, 329).[2] By the time of its composition, most likely during the summer of 1586, Sidney's *Defence* was already circulating in manuscript among his coterie of friends, but it seems that Webbe had not had the opportunity to read it, judging from his notable lack of engagement with Sidney's arguments. By the mid 1580s too, the enthusiasm about reforming English verse through the adoption of quantitative metre — which had been originally instigated by Roger Ascham in *The Schoolmaster* (1570) and widely discussed by Harvey and Spenser in their correspondence (*Letters*, 1580), two texts that significantly inform Webbe's approach to the English

---

[1] Philip Sidney's *The Defence of Poesy* (1595) in *Sidney's 'The Defence of Poesy' and Selected Renaissance Literary Criticism*, ed. by Gavin Alexander (London: Penguin Books, 2004); George Puttenham's *The Art of English Poesy*, ed. by Frank Whigham and Wayne E. Rebhorn (Ithaca: Cornell University Press, 2007); Webbe's *A Discourse of English Poetry* in *Elizabethan Critical Essays*, ed. by G. Gregory Smith, 2 vols (London: Oxford University Press, 1904), I, pp. 226–302.
[2] Michael Pincombe, "William Webbe", in *Dictionary of Literary Biography* (Detroit, Mi.: Gale, 1993), pp. 329–32.

hexameter — seemed to have cooled down as the latter poets, two of its main promoters, were now immersed in other professional projects. Therefore, despite Webbe's frequent acknowledgements of the modesty of his academic background and the mediocrity of his quantitative translations of Virgil's first two eclogues, his text should be valued as one of the first attempts to provide the bases for the consolidation of a coherent national poetic canon to stand as a model for contemporary and subsequent generations of poets. Webbe was aware that his ideas were not innovative (he was not the first in suggesting or attempting a reformation),[3] nor was he sufficiently endowed with the required academic or artistic skills to lead the regeneration of English verse. But he felt a responsibility to contribute to this process by supporting a revival of debates on the true nature of poetry and on the details of a much needed reformation which had apparently started to be forgotten by those who were extraordinarily qualified to be its artificers — the 'Noble Poets of England' to whom he addressed his vindication.

The text is preserved in two printed black-letter copies in quartos (84 pp.) which are located in the Huntington Library, California (Rare Books, 32084) and the Bodleian Library, Oxford (Malone collection, 708). Both copies have been inspected in these two locations and collated for the completion of this edition. None of the original copies contains revealing handwritten annotations other than references on their title-pages either to their provenance or to modern speculations about the dates of register and publication, as in the case of the Huntington copy, which includes a glued papercut-out of the entry of the book from the catalogue of Pearson's sale (1778). In both cases these annotations date from no earlier than 1781, as they allude to Thomas Warton's puzzling reference to a previous edition (1585) in *The History of English Poetry* (1774-81).[4] William Beloe's *Anecdotes of Literature and Scarce Rare Books* (1807: 233-35) is the earliest literary reference we find concerning the provenance of the two extant copies; he affirms that he 'never heard of but one copy' but specifies in a note below that 'Mr. Malone possesses another' (which corresponds to Malone collection 708 in the Bodleian). From William Oldys' *The British Librarian* (1738: 86-92), Beloe's *Anecdotes*, Joseph Haslewood's *Ancient Critical Essays Upon English Poets and Poësy* (1815: vol. 2, ii-iii) and the different sale catalogues which mention the book, we may almost entirely reconstruct the history of the Huntington copy. William Oldys, who had most likely worked with it, gives a copious abstract of the treatise's content, but does not explain where he happened

---

[3] 'Preface to the Noble Poets of England': 'Thus much I say, not to persuade you that are the favourers of English poetry, but to move it to you, being not the first that have thought upon this matter, but one that by consent of others have taken upon me to lay it once again in your ways ...' (p. 63).
[4] Thomas Warton, *The History of English Poetry*, 2nd edn, 4 vols (London: for Thomas Tegg, 1824; 1st edn 1774-81), vol. 3, p. 400, note q: 'For J. Charlewood. But there is another edition for Walley, 1585, 4to'.

to see it or if it belonged to the collection of his friend Peter Thompson, who had allowed him to use 'several *printed Books* which are more scarce than many Manuscripts' ('Postcript': 374). Sold by the Bibliotheca Westiana after James West's death in 1773, it belonged to Major Pearson's Library from that year until April 1778, when it was purchased by George Steevens for three pounds and five shillings; on May 19 1800 it was bought for the Duke of Roxburghe for eight guineas and sold again on June 2 1812 to the Marquess of Blandford for 64 pounds;[5] it became part of the collection of the White Knights Library, which auctioned it again as a result of the fall in fortunes of the Blandford family (headed by the fifth Duke of Malborough) in July 1819 (nº 4608).[6] The next record locates it in Craven Ord's sale in 1830 (nº 783),[7] but the Huntington Library purchased it at the Britwell Court Library's sale on February 1922 (lot 701): in the catalogue of this sale, which incorporates an illustration of its title page, it is described as 'one of the earliest volumes of criticism on English Poetry', featuring Webbe as a 'lavish and ungrudging admirer of Spenser'.[8]

A Discourse was printed jointly in 1586 by the prolific printer John Charlewood and by Robert Walley, son of the eminent John Walley, one of the founding members of the Stationers' Company; Robert Walley initiated his career with the publication of George Whetstone's *The Rocke of Regard* (1576) after his father had quitted the trade.[9] Although there is no evidence of any other editions than the one preserved, a double entry for the book — for 1585 and 1586 — in Joseph Ames' (1749) relation of John Charlewood's printings has led to some confusion.[10] Ames' first record excludes the subtitle concerning the reformation of verse and ascribes the printing exclusively to Walley, which seems to have led Warton to interpret that there had been a previous edition apart from that of 1586.[11] In his re-edition and extension of Ames' account, William Herbert's (1785) entry for 1585 mentions a licence instead of a printing;[12] but Arber's

---

[5] The Duke of Roxburghe's sale is recorded in *The European Magazine*, March 1813, vol. 63, p. 211 (http://hdl.handle.net/10689/14218).
[6] *White Knights Library. Catalogue* (London: W. Bulmer and Co., 1819), p. 216.
[7] *Catalogue of a Valuable Collection of Books of a Gentleman gone Abroad; Valuable Collection of Manuscripts of Craven Ord, Esq.*
[8] *Catalogue of a Further Selection of Extremely Rare and Valuable Books in Early English Poetry and other Literature from the Renowned Library formerly at Britwell Court, Burnham, Bucks* (London: Dryden Press, 1922), p. 112.
[9] For further information about John and Robert Walley see Charles Henry Timperley, *History of Printers and Printing* (London: H. Johnson, 1839), pp. 386–87.
[10] Joseph Ames, *Typographical Antiquities: Being a Historical Account of Printing in England* (London: by W. Faden, 1749), p. 370.
[11] See note 4 above.
[12] William Herbert, *Typographical Antiquities: Being a Historical Account of Printing in England. Begun by the late Joseph Ames. Considerably augmented both in the Memoirs and the Number of Books*, 3 vols (London, 1785), II, p. 1098.

(1875) transcription of the Stationers' Register only lists the 1586 edition, registered on September 4 that same year.[13] Haslewood (vol. 2: ii) concludes that this earlier licence may have prompted the belief that it was also then printed. A licence in 1585 might imply that the date of its composition was at least one year before the date of its printing in 1586.

In the dedicatory letter and the preface to the treatise, Webbe reveals most of the few details that are known about his identity and about the circumstances that surrounded the composition of *A Discourse*. In the mid 1580s he was working as a tutor of the two sons of Edward Sulyard, a squire to whom he dedicates the text as a token of his gratitude, owner of a country manor in Runwell, Essex; he twice mentions his geographical isolation from London literary circles to apologise for not having had physical access to some of the literary works he mentions, which he seems to know only from heard or read allusions, and for not including any of the outstanding contemporary poets. To justify the simplicity of the tract he argues that he has produced it as a gift to his patron and as an entertainment for the spare time that his duties as a tutor allowed him, especially during 'this summer evenings' ('Epistle': p. 58). Taking into account that it entered the register on September 4 1586, and that another licence for that year was also mentioned by Herbert, it would be most logical to consider that Webbe meant that same summer. Nevertheless, if we took into consideration that the title registered by Ames in 1585 is a shortened version of the definitive one, not including its subtitle, and that this copy seems to have been delivered to the stationers' office from Walley alone, would this mean that there was a licence for a first version that did not happen to be printed, a version which, being extended or corrected, was again licensed and printed one year later? As there is no evidence to prove these speculations, this edition accepts the summer of 1586 as the date of composition of the definitive version that has come down to us.

The biographical information about the author is largely restricted to these self-references in the text; he is introduced in the quarto title page as 'William Webbe. Graduate' and, according to the Cambridge records of students,[14] Webbe could have obtained his B.A. either in 1572–73 in St John's College or 1581–82 in St Catharine's. If he were the first one, he would have matriculated as a sizar around 1569. That means that, according to Andrew Hadfield's account of Spenser's college life (Hadfield 2012: 51–82), Webbe's days as a student in St John's would have overlapped with Spenser's at Pembroke Hall, where the author of *The Shepherds' Calendar* was serving Gabriel Harvey as a sizar too. In the latter case, his coincidence would have been with Abraham Fraunce, who matriculated

---

[13] Edward Arber, ed., *A Transcript of the Registers of the Company of Stationers of London, 1554–1640*, 5 vols (London: F.S.A., 1875), II, p. 211b.
[14] C. H. Cooper and T. Cooper, *Athenae Cantabrigienses 1586–1609* (1861), pp. 12, 542; J. Venn and J. A. Venn, *Alumni Cantabrigienses* (1927), part I, vol. IV, p. 355.

in St John's in 1575, was elected Fellow in 1580 and obtained his M.A. in 1583. Neither Cooper nor Pincombe (1993: 329) find sufficient evidence to identify our author with one or the other of the two Webbes, while Venn takes for granted that the writer of this treatise was the Webbe from St John's College, consequently assuming his friendship with Spenser. This edition follows Venn's identification, although with some reservations about the degree of acquaintance between Webbe and Spenser.

In the next sections of this introduction and in the footnotes to the main text, I will try to show that, in spite of the fact that Webbe avoids identifying Spenser as the author of *The Shepherds' Calendar*, there is evidence to think that he did not doubt this attribution and that his enthusiastic endorsement of a reformation of poetry is specifically addressed to Gabriel Harvey and Edmund Spenser; the tone of his comments concerning Harvey's and his two brothers' poetic skills denotes not only a wish to gain favour among these eminent personages in the Elizabethan cultural panorama, but also a sort of relative acquaintance, at least during the period of around 1570, when all of them would have coincided in Cambridge. Assuming that Webbe was in contact with Harvey would make it unlikely that he had not met Spenser at least casually, but the text does not offer evidence to prove actual links between them, only a fervent admiration on Webbe's part. All in all, the option of the second Webbe might not be completely discarded because the adulatory tone in which Webbe addresses these eminent poets of his time, which evinces his aspirations to be accepted as a member of the elite, seems to be more appropriate for a younger scholar in search of a position soon after having completed his degree. Notwithstanding, there is not as much evidence in the text for Webbe being the second person as there is for him being the first, as I will try to show below.

Apart from *A Discourse*, the translation into hexameters of Virgil's two first eclogues, and his rendering into Sapphic verse of Spenser's song to Elisa (*Calendar*, 'April') — all included in this volume — no other extant works by this author remain. Webbe also mentions that he presented 'another slender conceit' ('Epistle': p. 57) to Sulyard by 1582–1584,[15] by which he means a translation of the *Georgics* in 'that same English verse which other such works were in'. This may be interpreted as accentual or rhymed verse, considering that this is the metre previously used in 'other such works' he mentions, like Barnaby Googe's English version of Conrad Heresbach's *Foure Bookes on Husbandry* (translated in 1577), which included several passages of Virgil's *Georgics*.[16] In fact, Webbe

---

[15] It depends on whether we take 1585 or 1586 as the date of composition as Webbe affirms to have offered this other text to Sulyard 'two or three years since'. This also evinces that he had been serving the squire from at least that date.
[16] For Googe see note 71 in the main text.

describes the latter in these same terms: 'his witty translation of a good part of the *Georgics* of Virgil into English verse' (p. 104).[17]

Webbe is also the author of a commendatory letter printed in the edition of Robert Wilmot's *The Tragedy of Tancred and Gismond* (1591),[18] an updated version of the play *Gismond of Salerne*, composed in collaboration with other four members of the Inner Temple around 1566 and performed before the Queen at the Inner Temple in 1567. Webbe recalls in the letter that the performance had been highly celebrated by Elizabeth and by the general audience, but he does not provide any evidence in the text of his having personally witnessed it. The letter shows a Webbe still faithful to the poetic principles that he had acclaimed five years before; it corroborates his low esteem for rhyme and his conviction that its absence ennobles verse, at the same time that it recovers the recurrent idea in *A Discourse* — derived from Ascham —[19] that rhyme obeyed medieval mores and created an obsolete idiom for English poetics. Besides rescuing the manuscript from oblivion and having it printed, Robert Wilmot had also modernized the text by turning the rhymed quatrains into blank verse in sporadic combination with cross-rhymes. Webbe identifies these changes as the 'handsommes of fashion more answerable to these times' and praises Wilmot, using the metaphor of an orphan child, for 'disrobing him of his antike curiositie, and adorning him with the approoued guise of our stateliest Englishe termes'.[20] If there is an aspect in which Webbe's ideas seem to have departed from those displayed in *A Discourse*, it is his appreciation of blank verse as an appropriate device to provide English poetry with the prestige he had years before thought that only quantitative metres could achieve. In *A Discourse* Webbe, as Ascham had, tends to identify the absence of rhyme with unsuccessful attempts to achieve classical metres, as in the case of his judgment of Surrey's poems.[21]

The letter offers the last record we have about Webbe's whereabouts. He addresses it 'To his frend R.W.' and his signature as 'Guil. Webbe' is dated on August 8 1591 at Pirgo (Havering, London), the manor that Elizabeth I had granted John Grey in 1559, which was by then administered by his eldest son Henry Grey (cousin of Lady Jane Grey and father-in-law to Edward Sulyard) — to whose wife, Anne Grey, Wilmot's play is dedicated. Webbe could have quitted Sulyard's household in the late '80s and have taken up the position of tutor of the

---

[17] Webbe frequently means accentual verse (rhymed or not) when he alludes to 'our English verse' (pp. 84, 105), 'our English poetry' (p. 105), 'English verse' or 'English verses' (pp. 107, 112); whereas he usually refers to quantitative metre as 'reformed versifying' (p. 64) or 'true kind of versifying' (p. 117).

[18] For Robert Wilmot see note 77 in the main text.

[19] *The Schoolmaster*, pp. 289–90.

[20] 'To his frend R.W.', in Robert Wilmot, *The Tragedie of Tancred and Gismund* (London: Thomas Scarlet, 1592).

[21] See note 153 in the main text.

youths of the Grey family (mentioned by Wilmot in his dedicatory letter),[22] where he likely would have met the playwright.

A Discourse has not been treated as a major contribution to early modern poetics mainly due to the fact that original ideas concerning the definition and analysis of poetry are lacking and to its occasional want of academic rigour and precision; for instance, in his confusion about the chronology of ancient writers, the absence of a discussion of pioneering English poets such as Wyatt or his simplistic classification of poetic genres. It is obvious that Webbe's reflections are to a great extent informed by significant critical texts of the period which also set out the different aspects of a coherent treatise on English poetry, such as its origins and precedents, its role and contribution to the improvement of cultural identity, the list of authors who portray its canonical definition and the period's prosodic preferences. However, the true value of Webbe's text is not to be located in the scholar's capacity to innovate, but in his editorial labour and his enthusiasm in the defence of national letters. Taking into account that the lack of information about the author renders it an almost anonymous text, the intertextuality of the treatise becomes one of its most enlightening aspects when it comes to figuring out the nature of the literary spirit of a conventionally educated scholar of Elizabethan Cambridge. Mike Pincombe (1993: 330) splendidly synthesized the worthiness of this treatise when he affirmed that 'here is Tudor humanism in a nutshell'. The next paragraphs of this introduction will provide an overview of the main critical texts that inform A Discourse.

Webbe's conception and definition of poetry is primarily informed by Horace's Ars Poetica, a summary of which he annexes to the treatise in his own translated version of the German humanist Georg Fabricius' 'Canons' (De Re Poetica Libri Septem, 1565); Horace's principle of the instructive delightfulness of poetry is the unifying concept of Webbe's approach to all aspects of his poetic analysis in the sense that this idea sanctions the humanist trust in the potential of poetry not only to offer instruction in civil and moral values, but to embody a nation's cultural identity too. Related to the interests aroused by Webbe's job as tutor of two youths is the pervading presence of two pedagogical treatises by the two leading Cambridge scholars Thomas Elyot (c. 1490–1546) and Roger Ascham (1515–1568), which bring together several main concerns of Tudor educationalists. Ascham's The Schoolmaster (1570), a very influential text in 1580s Cambridge, provides Webbe with the appropriate discursive tools to hail literature as the principal idiom for the articulation of a mature cultural identity that would raise the English nation to the same status as the ancient empires, as

---

[22] Wilmot addresses Anne Grey and Mary Peter in his 'Epistle Dedicatorie': 'there is nothing more welcome to your wisedomes, then the knowledge of wise, graue, and worthie matters, tending to the good instructions of youths, of whom you are mothers'. These youths may have been the ones under Webbe's tutorship.

well as furnishing him with the arguments to define rhyme as a barbarous medieval and unsophisticated custom. Elyot's *The Boke Named the Governour* (1531) constitutes a primary source of arguments and textual examples for Webbe's defence of poetic didacticism, as well as lending authority to his choice of ancient poets who best serve instructive purposes. Along with these pedagogical works, Thomas Phaer's translation of the *Aeneid* (1573) provides Webbe with enlightening poetic *exempla* when it comes to demonstrating that the English tongue is capable of the rhetorical eloquence of classical texts. However, Spenser's *The Shepherds' Calendar* (1579) is rendered in *A Discourse* as the most outstanding evidence of poetic proficiency in their native tongue, whereas Webbe finds in it all sort of *exempla* so as to illustrate every aspect of his humanist definition of poetry; this introduction will further develop the analysis of Spenser's prominence in Webbe's *poetica*. As regards metrical issues, on the one hand, Webbe synthesizes the sixteen directions exposed in Gascoigne's *Certain Notes* (1575) into his own 'three special notes' (p. 107), which are aimed at conferring on rhyme a higher sophistication in order to release it to some extent from the charge of vulgarity. On the other, when it comes to offering a detailed account of the principles that should rule the reformation of English prosody according to the rules of ancient versification, Webbe's arguments and reflections may be interpreted as an attempt to contribute his own solutions to the principal controversies concerning the suitability of applying Latin rules of prosody to vernacular verse, which was the main subject of the debate raised by Harvey and Spenser in their *Letters* (1580). Regarding the nomenclature and description of metrical feet Webbe follows Audomarus Talaeus' *Rhetorica* (1552).

1.2 *The Objectives of Webbe's Treatise*

Webbe's treatise is primarily aimed at urging English poets, as the direct addressees of his preliminary letter and the implied interlocutors of the work as a whole, to keep on experimenting with quantitative metres so as to accomplish the reformation of verse that had become a craze among some Cambridge intellectuals for around two decades before it had started to lose steam by the mid 1580s. Upon this framework Webbe develops a manifesto that encompasses his project as a whole. Firstly, he offers a defence of poetry and of the natural ability of the English language and poets for attaining the poetic eloquence of the ancient models; secondly, he proposes a canon of ancient and English literary authorities that would function as models for contemporary writers, but above all that would evince, by rendering the latter as legitimate continuators of the achievements of the former, the rootedness of English literature in the Greek and Latin traditions. Finally, Webbe's treatise is conceived as a prescriptive manual on versification that provides practical instructions and examples so as to, on the one hand, contribute to the refinement of rhyme and, on the other, allow a coherent adaptation of Latin rules of prosody to English verse. All of Webbe's proposals aim at motivating English poetry to aspire towards consolidating a strong and competitive national literary idiom.

1.3 Structure

A *Discourse* is not such a rigorously structured *poetica* as is, for instance, Puttenham's, who exhaustively covers all aspects of the definition and description of poetry under book divisions and subheadings. Webbe's text is not conceived with such a technical perspective; his analysis delves into only those aspects about which he feels self-confident or that serve the purposes of his manifesto, and avoids entering into descriptions of issues that he fails to discuss systematically.[23] His reflections are structured as follows:

a) Dedicatory letter to Sulyard.
b) Preface urging English poets to abandon the habit of rhyme and work on a reformation of verse.
c) Definition of poetry, account of its value throughout history, and its origin and evolution from the perspective of its function.
d) Canon of poets according to the Horatian premise of delightful instruction; this section is divided into:
 — Catalogue of Latin authors who form the canon for imitation: Webbe shows that his knowledge regarding Greek literature is inferior to his formation as a Latinist, as he confesses on several occasions. All in all, his several mistakes about the chronology of Latin poets also demonstrate a general uncertainty among Elizabethan authors about the periodization of classical literature.
 — Catalogue of English authors from the Middle Ages to contemporary figures.
e) Description of poetry attending to the subdivision of matter (subjects) and form (versification):
 — Matter: In this section Webbe's principal concern is to elucidate the classical antecedents of each genre in order to legitimize English versions on the grounds of imitation. The generic classification of poetry is the weakest aspect of Webbe's discourse. He starts with a general classification under which he conceives only three genres: the 'comical', the 'tragical' and the 'historical'. Under the category of comedy he includes epigrams, elegies and

---

[23] For instance, in the case of the classification of literary genres which he restricts to comedy, tragedy and history; Webbe only develops in depth his analysis of pastoral poetry likely because it is the frame of Spenser's *Calendar* — whom he aims to proclaim the exponent of the maturity of English poetry.

other poems dealing with subjects more inclined to entertainment than instruction. Under the heading of 'tragical' he includes complaints and laments (as a more appropriate frame for elegies than the 'comical'). And the 'historical', apart from containing chronicles and epistles, integrates all subjects that he feels unable to classify under the previous or other headings or subheadings. Next, and as an introduction to a more detailed compilation of the English records of heroic poetry, eclogues and georgics — the two latter receiving sustained attention — Webbe introduces a digression which describes the function of poetry according to the Horatian premise of teaching while giving delight, which he builds upon arguments and textual *exempla* borrowed from Elyot's *Governour*. When it comes to describing heroic poetry, his acknowledgment that English literature has not produced any masterpieces in this genre ground leads him to depart again from his argumentative thread to demonstrate with examples from Phaer's translation of the *Aeneid* that English language does not lack the eloquence required for this genre. Then, the section on English eclogues focuses on hailing Spenser as the English Virgil for his *Shepherds' Calendar*, thus proclaiming pastoral poetry as the badge of national literary accomplishment; georgics also deserve a special mention in this section and put an end to his exposition on genres.

— Form: This section deals primarily with versification and is structured into a first compilation of instructions aimed at the refinement of rhymed verse according to the criteria exposed by Gascoigne in *Certain Notes* (1575), and a second part dedicated to the exposition of Webbe's account of quantitative verse.

f) Webbe's translations of Virgil's Eclogues I and II in hexameters together with his rendering into Sapphic verse Spenser's 'Song to Elisa' (from *Calendar*, 'April').

g) Appended translation of Georg Fabricius' 'Canons' on poetry as derived from Horace's *Ars Poetica*.

2. The Humanist Context of *A Discourse*: Roger Ascham's *The Schoolmaster* and Thomas Elyot's *The Governour*

2.1 *Ascham's Humanist Principles in* A Discourse

In his entry for 'William Webbe' in the *DLB*, Michael Pincombe offers a summary of the cultural value of *A Discourse* when he attributes its coherence to the fact that it agglutinates the founding principles of English humanism; as I have already mentioned, Pincombe states that in this treatise 'is Tudor humanism in a nutshell' (330). The motifs, on the one hand, that inform Webbe's rhetorical effort to persuade the poets of the need to reform English verse, as well as the argumentation by which he sustains that the English language and poets are prepared for such a modification of their instruments of expression, and, the methods, on the other, that Webbe considers the most suitable for attaining this reformation provide a comprehensive portrait of the spirit of humanist poetics in England, of which scholars and poets like Ascham, Spenser, Harvey (to mention those who most strongly influenced Webbe) are major exponents. Webbe presents his work as a modest and unambitious contribution to this cause; he takes up the task of motivating other scholars or poets better endowed than he to work towards it. But it is precisely his marginal position that renders *A Discourse* a valuable document in the sense that it offers a lively example of the extent to which Cambridge pedagogical interests from the 1540s[24] onwards informed the cultural ideology and aspirations of typical scholars.

In the particular case of Webbe, this humanistic perspective is considerably informed by Roger Ascham's *The Schoolmaster*, which was the principal instigator among the following generation of poets of the idea that rhyme belonged to medieval conceptions of culture and that it constituted the main obstacle to deprive the English nation from having a poetic idiom matching its political, religious and expansionist prowess. Besides being the pioneering promoter of the reformation of verse through the incorporation of quantitative metres — which was the main interest of the generation of Sidney, Dyer, Harvey and Spenser — Ascham's approach to pedagogy could be considered a manifesto of the fundamental premises of a Tudor humanism founded on Horatian poetics and Ciceronian rhetorical principles, remaining somewhat alien from the Ramist principles first acclaimed by Gabriel Harvey and widely assimilated by Abraham Fraunce in the Cambridge of the 1570s and 80s respectively.[25]

Matter and Form

Webbe's definition and defence of poetry is primarily founded on the Renaissance tendency to draw parallels between poetry and rhetoric, and informed by Ascham's philosophical conception of the latter. Influenced by the Ciceronian idea of the orator as a self-contained figure whose eloquence was a manifestation of his wisdom, civility and morality, Ascham's instructions for teaching Latin rhetoric accord with his aim to redefine English cultural and moral identity by imitating classical writers' civil, aesthetic and linguistic models. Latin rhetoric provided children with a discipline of learning that would contribute to shape their national selves according to the rarefied parameters of antiquity and at the

---

[24] This is primarily the period in which Roger Ascham, John Cheke and Thomas Watson were the intellectual leaders in Cambridge University.
[25] Harvey's *Rhetor* (1574) and *Ciceronianus* (1576) consecrated him as the leading exponent of Ramism in England; Fraunce's *The Lawiers Logike* (1588) was the first attempt to incorporate Ramus' logical theory to the study of law.

same time worked as a model for the refinement and embellishment of the native tongue, one of the principal constituents of national self-fashioning. Webbe assimilates Ascham's approach to rhetorical eloquence and transports its principles into the field of poetics. Style appears in *A Discourse* — using Debora Shuger's words — as 'the expression of national and class identity' (1999: 184).[26] In the preface to the noble poets, echoing the generalised complaint among Renaissance intellectuals about the deficient reputation of the English poetic idiom, and in order to persuade the poets not just of the need to give a new impulse to poetry, but also of the inherent potential of the English tongue to attain stylistic sophistication, he insists on the fraternal connections between poetry and rhetoric:

> Why should we think so basely of this, rather than of her sister, I mean, rhetorical elocution? Which, as they were by birth twins, by kind the same, by original of one descent, so no doubt, as eloquence hath found such favourers in the English tongue as she frequenteth not any more gladly, so would poetry, if there were the like welcome and entertainment given her by our English poets, without question aspire to wonderful perfection and appear far more gorgeous and delectable among us. (pp. 62–63)

The frequent use of the first person plural possessive pronoun when referring to 'our English poets', 'our English speech' (pp. 61, 62) and 'our English verse' (p. 84) denotes the conviction that the consolidation of the nation's poetic idiom constitutes a state affair to such an extent that a civilization would never achieve cultural maturity while its language and literary expression remained unrefined. Webbe insists on the fact that English rhetorical eloquence has already reached total ripeness — he mentions Lyly's euphuistic prose as evidence — indicates that the actual hindrances that poetry faces do not lie in the inherent mediocrity of their language, but in the insufficient labour and experimentation that national poets have historically applied to increase the sophistication of their style. As a consequence of Ascham's principle that labour and practice are the only means of attaining true acculturation, Webbe urges the noble poets of England (with the obvious intention of discriminating between the true poets and the mediocre ones) to keep up their efforts to reform poetic style, because the poetry destined to ennoble the cultural identity of their nation was not that produced in taverns with the aid of beer tankards, but that which was to be developed through a reasoned choice of perfect prosodic elements and which, consequently, would most effectively move readers to civic and ethical integrity in Horace's terms of teaching through delight.

---

[26] Debora Shuger, 'Conceptions of Style' in *The Cambridge History of Literary Criticism*, ed. by Glyn P. Norton, 9 vols (Cambridge: Cambridge University Press), III, pp. 176–86.

Working on this equivalence between rhetorical *elocutio* and poetic style, Webbe borrows the methods that Ascham proposes for the proper instruction of Latin rhetoric and applies them to literature. First of all, he is concerned with demonstrating that poetry has the same instructive potential as her sibling, and that, like rhetorical eloquence, poetic style becomes an inherent conveyor of moral and civic values. The scholar inherits from Aschamite Ciceronianism the idea that words are expressive incarnations of the aforementioned values and that as result form should accompany meaning. Hence, his endorsement of the theory that rhyme — a prosodic device he associated with rusticity and unlearned expression — was hindering style and preventing poetry from attaining that cohesion between matter and form to which Ascham ascribes the civilizing plenitude of classical texts. Webbe argues that the full acculturation of the English nation is therefore to be accomplished through the cultivation of prosody so as to make it converge with the traditional erudition of English literary subjects, thus enabling the desirable coherence between form and matter.

In contrast to Thomas Elyot's comments on how the Tudor period witnessed inferior levels of erudition in comparison with its ancient predecessors,[27] Webbe's humanist convictions lead him to argue that the prestige of learning in England has remained fully untouched since the times of the Norman conquest: 'although learning was not generally decayed at any time, especially since the conquest of King William Duke of Normandy, as it may appear by many famous works and learned books (though not of this kind) written by bishops and others' (pp. 76-77). In his historical overview of national poets, one of Webbe's main concerns is to demonstrate that knowledge has been a traditional attribute of English letters. He praises Henry I's 'good learning in all kind of noble studies', for instance intending to prove 'that learning in this country was not little esteemed of at that rude time' (p. 78). And he continues with allusions to John Gower as 'a singular well learned man' and to Geoffrey Chaucer's works as sources of 'delight and profitable knowledge', leading the reader to conclude that the origin of the poor condition of poetry was not due to a historical lack of erudition on the part of the poets, but to their accustomed attachment to rhyme, a barbarous device impeding any advances in the refinement of English versification. In this regard, *A Discourse* becomes a defence of the natural capability of English poetic style to be polished so as to attain the high level of learnedness that vernacular literature has steadfastly conveyed since its origins and so total cohesion between poetic matter and form would definitely communicate the cultural and ideological maturity of the nation.

---

[27] *The Governour*, 1.12 (Croft, I, p. 98): 'Nowe wyll I somwhat declare of the chiefe causes why, in our tyme, noble men be nat as excellent in lernying as they were in olde tyme amonge the Romanes and grekes'.

Imitation

Ascham proposes the study of Latin rhetoric not only as a didactic method aimed at improving students' proficiency in the understanding and reproduction of the Roman language, but also as a means of cultivating their native tongue. However, it is not as much a question of linguistic competence as a way of instilling in students the true judgement that characterizes the outstanding citizens of a mature commonwealth. Ascham's didactic method is therefore wholly grounded in the imitation of Greek and Latin texts, with a special emphasis on Roman rhetoric: 'This foresaid order and doctrine of *Imitation*, would bring forth more learning, and breed up trewer judgement, than any other exercise that can be used' (*Schoolmaster*: 301). Ascham's defence of imitation as a pedagogical method is founded on the conviction that what made the Latin language a superior artifact was its successful imitation of Greek diction. The fact that copying Greek linguistic behaviours had turned initial Latin rudeness into outstanding elegance made Ascham trust in the innate potential of all languages to attain considerable levels of sophistication through adequate polishing and refinement: 'the rudeness of common and mother tongues is no bar for wise speaking' (296). Accordingly, Webbe seems determined to release English poets from a traditional acceptance of their linguistic inferiority, which he suggests has been the cause of their attachment to such a simplistic device as rhyme, and of their passivity when it came to struggling to leave behind the rudeness of medieval prosody.[28] The scholar urges them to refashion their own national selves through imitating the idealized models of classical civilizations, arguing that if Latin poets attained perfection by following the Greek example, likewise, imitation of Latin metre would constitute the most efficient procedure to acquire their own poetic prestige.

Poetic imitation (with special attention paid to Latin writers) becomes one of the central topics of Webbe's theory, approached through a double emphasis. On the one hand, he intends to provide a canon of Latin poets to serve as models for English subject-matter and forms; and on the other, he strives to demonstrate that outstanding figures and works in English literary history were to a great extent inspired by classical precedents. Besides giving a (somewhat inaccurate) chronological catalogue of Greek and Latin authors, Webbe tends to introduce the sections that deal with any aspects of the history of English literature — whether descriptions of the most cultivated genres or lists of representative poets — with an overview of their Greek and Latin antecedents. His intention seems

---

[28] Webbe remarks: 'Surely the cankered enmity of curious custom which, as it never was great friend to any good learning, so in this hath it grounded in the most such a negligent persuasion of an impossibility in matching the best, that the finest wits and most divine heads have contented themselves with a base kind of fingering …' (p. 62). This is what Richard Helgerson calls 'this taint of cultural inferiority' which had been related to rhyme for decades before Webbe wrote his treatise; in *Forms of Nationhood. The Elizabethan Writing of England* (Chicago: The University of Chicago Press, 1992), p. 35.

to be to provide ancient models while asserting long-established cultural links between English and classical literature. His interest in presenting the ancients as the direct origin of national literature is such that, on one particular occasion, he dutifully justifies his digressions on Greek and Latin authors by arguing that the latter represent the head at the top of the body of English letters:

> ... though it may seem something impertinent to the title of my book, yet I trust the courteous readers will pardon me, considering that poetry is not of that ground and antiquity in our English tongue, but that speaking thereof only as it is English would seem like unto the drawing of one's picture without a head. (p. 87)

And a few lines later, as a general introduction to the sections dedicated to English poetic genres, each of which starts with an overview of its respective classical model, Webbe insists on praising imitation as an essential constituent of the national poetic canon: 'yet so as I must evermore have recourse to those times and writers whereon the English poetry taketh, as it were, the descent and propriety' (p. 87).

As a consequence, imitation becomes one of the main critical criteria for Webbe when it comes to legitimizing the authority of the English authors chosen to constitute the canon of national letters. He tends to allege their proficiency in imitating the Latin models in order to demonstrate the quality of their works. The clearest example in *A Discourse* of this approach to imitation as a defining virtue of some authors' works is precisely the detailed exposition of the parallelisms that exist between some of Spenser's and Virgil's eclogues; this discussion has no other purpose than to contribute to the proclamation of the former as the English Virgil (p. 102). And by discussing Virgil's influence on Spenser, Webbe seems to be at the same time answering Ascham's claim that teaching manuals should locate the places and methods in which Latin authors followed the Greeks, to provide students with a sort of commonplace book detailing what and how to imitate, although Webbe obviously transports this imperative to the terrain of the vernacular, his principal concern.[29] In any case, Webbe had already put forward Spenser's mimetic skills when the author first appeared in the treatise, as a sound argument to equate the English poet's artistic and intellectual stature with that of his ancient predecessors: 'Whose fine poetical wit, and most exquisite learning, as he showed abundantly in that piece of work, in my judgement inferior to the works neither of Theocritus in Greek, nor Virgil in Latin, whom he narrowly imitateth' (p. 68).

---

[29] *Schoolmaster*: II. 267: 'But if a man would take this paine also, whan he hath layd two places, of *Homer* and *Virgill*, or of *Demosthenes* and *Tullie* togither, to teach plainlie withall, after this sort. 1. Tully reteyneth thus moch of the matter, thies sentences, thies words ...'. See also his passage about Riccius, p. 272: 'But, if he had done thus: if he had declared where and how, how oft and how many wayes *Virgil* doth folow *Homer*, as for example the coming of *Vlysses* to *Alcynous* and *Calypso*, with the comming of *Aeneas* to *Cartage* and *Dido* ...'.

Translation

Besides imitation, Ascham also argues for double translation as an extraordinarily efficient method in the teaching of Latin rhetoric when compared with others not so appropriate for pedagogical ends, like paraphrasis, epitome (promoted by Quintilian, Ramus and Talaeus) or metaphrasis. Translation did not only favour the skilful imitation of ancient texts, but also contributed to the process of polishing and refining the native tongue. Likewise, inspired by the Ciceronian idea that the origin of the rhetorician's wisdom resided in his reasoned discernment of the appropriate words to sustain an argument, Ascham conceives of translation as a means of training young men's judgement by making choices among words which most efficiently expressed given ideas.[30] Translation therefore becomes a convenient method for the practice and assimilation of the skills required in an eloquent orator, because through translation 'is learned, easely, sensiblie, by litle and litle, not onelie all the hard congruities of Grammer, the choice of aptest wordes, the right framing of wordes and sentences, cumliness of figures, and formes, fitte for euerie matter, and proper for euerie tong …' (*Schoolmaster*: I. 245).

For Webbe, translation also constitutes illustrative proof for demonstrating poets' imitative skills and highlighting the relevance that the cultivating a poetic idiom in imitation of ancient literary criteria had for the consolidation of a national cultural self, as his commendations of Arthur Golding's rendering of Ovid's *Metamorphoses* (1567) suggest: 'for which gentleman surely our country hath for many respects greatly to give God thanks, as for him which hath taken infinite pains without ceasing, travelleth as yet indefatigably, and is addicted without society by his continual labour to profit this nation and speech in all kind of good learning' (p. 82). Webbe mentions Golding and Phaer as two of the main literary authorities who have contributed to the development of English poetic eloquence; and, along with imitation, represents translation in *A Discourse* as a telling method to vindicate the native tongue's natural potential for eloquence.

Webbe seems to react once more to Ascham's assertion of the usefulness of offering an analytical comparison between original English works and the classical models they follow when, to demonstrate that the English language is inherently capable of attaining the eloquence of the ancients, he compares in detail Thomas Phaer's translation of the *Aeneid* and Virgil's Latin original, quoting for this purpose long relevant passages from both texts:

> But a more nearer example to prove my former assertion true (I mean the meetness of our speech to receive the best form of poetry) may be taken by conference of that famous translation of Master Thomas Phaer with the copy

---

[30] Ibid. II. 239: 'Here his witte shalbe new set on worke: his iudgement, for right choice, trewlie tried.'

itself, whosoever please with courteous judgement but a little to compare and mark them both together, and weigh with himself whether the English tongue might by little and little be brought to the very majesty of a right heroical verse. (p. 96)

Versification

The metrical principles displayed in this treatise are derived from Ascham's definition of rhyme as a popular and unrefined prosodic device as well as from his association of the classical quantitative metres with a cultural elite's instrument of versification; in other words, rhyme is made to seem vulgar because of its simple, obvious mechanisms within reach even of the vast majority of mediocre rhymers, while use of the hexameter denotes artificiality and is regulated by complex rules unlikely to be recognizable by common readers. As I have already mentioned, the humanistic pedagogical precepts displayed in *The Schoolmaster* put special emphasis on reasoned labour and on practice, thus valuing to a greater extent those students to whom Ascham refers as 'hard wits' — individuals whose abilities or skills are mainly due to effort and perseverance, in contrast to 'quick wits' — those with an innate predisposition to easily gain shallow knowledge unsuitable for turning them into the efficient citizens or clerks with which Ascham intends to fill the nation (*Schoolmaster*: I. 188–92). This preference for quantitative metres is obviously associated with the humanist appreciation of labour and hard work over natural disposition as a symptom of intellectual and cultural maturity.[31] As for the Ciceronian rhetorician, innate wit is not enough for the poet to attain either the prosodic sophistication or the civilizing knowledge that would enable him to achieve the idealised cohesion between form and matter; by associating learning with good judgement, Ascham was once again relating study and intellectual formation to civic and moral values. His support of quantitative metres implies the long-standing Tudor conviction that quality of poetic style corresponds directly to a nation's virtuousness. This humanist emphasis on the ideological connotations of style is what leads Tudor quantifiers to advocate the reformation of metre as a definitive step towards the total acculturation of England.[32]

---

[31] Ibid. II. 294: 'For, quicke inuentors, and faire readie speakers, being boldned with their present habilitie to say more, and perchance better to, at the soden for that present, than any other can do, vse lesse helpe of diligence and studie than they ought to do: and so haue in them commonlie, lesse learning, and weaker iudgement, for all deepe considerations, than duller heades, and slower tonges haue'.

[32] Helgerson (1992: 23): 'Having a distinctly national poetry and a distinctly national legal system was then thought, as it is still thought today, to be fundamental to a nation's sovereignty. But neither poetry nor law could be conceived apart from the forms in which each had been embodied elsewhere. Certain rules of verse, certain poetic genres ... provided the recognized

In his famous account in *The Schoolmaster* of the origin of rhyme in Europe, a section which contributed significantly to forging English poets' assimilation of the ideological connotations of prosodic questions, and which Webbe cites in the treatise (p. 77), Ascham traces rhyme to its barbarous and medieval origins. Ascham explains that it was introduced into Europe by the Huns and Goths, and was extended through Italy towards France and Germany (*Schoolmaster*: II. 289). Therefore Ascham both links rhyme to a barbarous parentage from which he intends to disconnect humanist England and takes the opportunity to ascribe its dissemination throughout Europe to Popish literary preferences; his treatise contains a harsh attack on the noxious influence of Catholic cultural ideology in the education of English youths who have travelled to Italy ('*Circes* court', I. 250) to continue with their education and came back transformed into hybrid monsters with no moral principles ('*Englese Italianato, e un Diabolo incarnato*', I. 252). Accordingly, Webbe puts the blame for the consolidation of rhyme in England on the medieval bishops' disdain for poetry in the times of William the Conqueror as implied by the records of 'their rude versifying, which of long time was used (a barbarous use it was) wherein they converted the natural property of the sweet Latin verse to be a bald kind of rhyming, thinking nothing to be learnedly written in verse, which fell not out in rhyme' (p. 77).

In addition, Ascham attributes the consolidation of rhyme in England to the vulgar poets' idleness (instead of labouring towards perfection) and ignorance (contempt for learning), to those who find enough satisfaction in 'pleasing the humor of a rude multitude' and invade the bookshops with their 'lewd and rude rymes' (II. 329). Accordingly, in his 'Preface', Webbe reproduces Ascham's discrimination between rustic and popular composition and what he considers 'true poetry' (p. 62). In fact, seldom in the treatise does he refer to rhymed verse as 'poetry', preferring euphemistic denominations like 'rhyme', for example, and generally making a distinction between the 'rude multitude of rustical rhymers' (p. 61) or 'rhyming ballet makers' (p. 85) and the 'Noble Poets of England' ('Preface'); likewise, he generally reproduces Ascham's parameters of naturalness versus artificiality, ignorance versus learning, and popularity versus elitism, though applied specifically to prosody. In the fourth section of this introduction I will develop further the significance of Webbe's position regarding versification.

---

models of civility and barbarity against which English writings were inevitably measured'. For Debora Shuger there was among the Elizabethans a 'feeling for style as the expression of national and class identity', in 'Conceptions of Style', in *The Cambridge History of Literary Criticism*, ed. by Glyn P. Norton, 9 vols (Cambridge: Cambridge University Press, 1999), III, pp. 176-86, 184.

2.2 Thomas Elyot: The Boke Named the Governour (1531)

As has been previously mentioned, Webbe's theory of poetry and his claim for a reformation are principally grounded on Ascham's approach to Latin rhetoric as a civilizing instrument to instill in students the ethical and civic values embodied by Ciceronian orators through the acquisition of Latin linguistic skills which function as a training toward the dignifying their native tongue. Webbe exemplifies the Renaissance tendencies to assume a sisterhood between rhetoric and poetry and to import the didactic mechanisms proposed by Ascham for rhetorical instruction with the aim of refashioning poetry according to these same humanistic principles, which results in his emphasis on imitation and translation as the two principal means of dignifying English poetry and of providing criteria for the assessment of canonical poets. However, Webbe seems to find some gaps in *The Schoolmaster* when it comes to deepening his vindication of poetry as an instrument used for pedagogical aims in itself, as Ascham treats it merely in relation to rhetorical eloquence. Webbe cements his trust in the civilizing role of poetry, which derived from the traditional association of poetic creation with the power of persuasion, as represented in the myth of Orpheus, a mythical emblem of poetic didacticism. Therefore, when developing his arguments for a specific defence of the instructive potential of poetry, Webbe finds in Thomas Elyot's *The Governour* a central source of thought and textual examples. Webbe's editorial merits should be acknowledged here because his selective use of sources to fashion his particular theory of poetry evinces a scholarly, mature and well defined criterion.

Elyot's presence in Webbe's treatise is central in two of its main aspects: first, as I have already mentioned, in the general defence of the instructive potential of poetry, communicated in particular through the author's pervasive emphasis on offering moralised interpretations of the works of pagan poets, especially epigrammists and comedy authors, supposed to be those who do not deal with 'grave' or 'serious' matters (pp. 66, 71). Second, Webbe takes Elyot's side in the humanist debate about the methods and objects of imitation, which was most evidently manifest at the time in what is known as the 'Ciceronian controversy'.[33] Whereas Ascham was a declared Ciceronian, that is, not as radical in his adherence to strict formalism as in his defence of Cicero's exclusive centrality as a model for imitation, Elyot represented Erasmian eclecticism, by proposing a wide diversity of authors as literary models.

Webbe's defence of poetry is principally informed by the tenth and thirteenth chapters of the first book of *The Governour*; here, Elyot provides his particular interpretation of each of the lessons that the works of Greek and Latin poets like

---

[33] See John Monfasani, 'The Ciceronian controversy', in *The Cambridge History of Literary Criticism*, 1999, pp. 395–401.

Homer, Virgil, Ovid, and a complete syllabus of authors can offer to young students in terms of moral, ethical, civil and even martial instruction. Although Elyot takes eloquence as a fundamental requirement when it comes to judging the pedagogical utility of Latin authors, he also places special emphasis on the morally profitable nature of the subjects they treat. Thus, he considers that those who cultivated prosody but neglected subject-matter were not to be called poets, but simply 'versifyers' (1.13: 120). Webbe seems to have used Elyot's treatise mainly as a manual for his own pedagogical instruction; his main objective appears to be to seek enlightenment about how each author is suitable for teaching, since the intertextuality between *A Discourse* and *The Governour* is precisely concentrated on the passages which reveal the value for teaching of specific classical works. Webbe, for instance, shares Elyot's conception of Homer as the universal example of perfect harmony between 'eloquence and lernyng' (*Governour* 1.10: 58) and borrows Elyot's commentaries illustrating the specific lessons that his *Odyssey* and *Iliad* may provide to the youth. Similarly, Webbe echoes Elyot's proclamation of Virgil as the direct heir of Homer's eloquence and instructive values. In general, Webbe's catalogue of Latin authors is greatly informed by Elyot's manual and by his approach to poetic didacticism; the former primarily founds his selection of English canonical poets on this combination of eloquence and learning and tried to establish the criteria to tell the vulgar 'versifiers' from the true poets, attending not only to questions of versification but also to the instructive value of a text's contents.

Webbe dedicates a section after the catalogue of authors to his reflections on the function of poetry according to the Horatian terms of teaching while giving delight, which is fundamentally informed by Elyot's defence of the didactic nature of the works of Latin comedy writers and epigrammists like Plautus, Terence, Ovid or Martial. For this section Webbe practically reproduces *verbatim* Elyot's argumentation and borrows his original translations of a few excerpts of the works of the classical poets, which Elyot had provided as *exempla* of their didactic value and had glossed with his particular moralising interpretations.[34]

In his critical commentaries on the works of ancient authors, Elyot tends to classify the subjects according to their sobriety into 'good and wise mater' or 'lite mater', while alluding to the Latin epigrammists as 'wanton poets' (1.13: 129); this distinction is made in relation to the didactic use of the subjects or their status as merely entertaining works. Elyot makes a defence of the instructive potential of the works of the pagan poets and attributes their dubious reputation to the wicked interpretations of vicious readers. He develops the metaphor of the garden in which, in order to enjoy the beauty of blossoms, one has to be aware of the

---

[34] See *The Governour*, 1.13 and *A Discourse*, pp. 91–94.

nettles and be able to weed them out.³⁵ Similarly, the occurrence of 'wanton maters' in these works does not hinder the general profitableness of the texts and is therefore no reason to discard these poets from the syllabi of grammar schools: 'Wherefore sens good and wise mater may be picked out of these poetes, it were no reason, for some lite mater that is in their verses, to abandone therefore al their warkes'. This argument, including the garden metaphor, is copied by Webbe in the section dedicated to the defence of the instructive nature of all kinds of literary works authored by Greek and Latin poets: 'the works themselves do not corrupt, but the abuse of the users, who, undamaging their own dispositions by reading the discoveries of vices, resemble foolish folk who, coming into a garden without any choice or circumspection, tread down the fairest flowers and wilfully thrust their fingers among the nettles' (pp. 91–92). But Webbe's argumentation in defence of poetry becomes quite emotional and even virulent when it comes to refuting the rumours that identify Spenser's eclogue for 'January' with a manifesto on pederasty;³⁶ his defence of Spenser develops into an ardent attack on those who approach poetry with a suspicious attitude, and ends in a vindication of the artistic freedom of poets: 'We must prescribe to no writers (much less to poets) in what sort they should utter their conceits'. Regarding, therefore, the combination of wanton and serious matters discussed by Elyot, Webbe seems to link the presence of the former in a poetic work with the necessary component of entertainment that should accompany instruction through literature, just as Elyot argues that allusions to hunting or to fantastic beings make Virgil's *Georgics* and *Aeneid* more attractive for children, and thus increase the efficacy of the moral lesson contained within (1.10: 64–65). Like Elyot, but differing from Ascham, Webbe proposes that no Latin author should be excluded either from grammar school syllabi or from the catalogue of canonical models for English poets to imitate.

Webbe therefore shares Elyot's determination to unveil the instructive lessons contained in ancient literature and employs the same strategy to legitimize the incorporation of works by outstanding English poets into the national canon, with a special emphasis on Spenser's *Calendar*.³⁷ His intertextual reliance on

---

³⁵ 'Wherfore sens good and wise mater may be picked out of these poetes, it were no reason, for some lite mater that it is in their verses, to abandone therefore al their warkes, no more that it were to forbeare or prohibite a man to come into a faire gardein, leste the redolent sauours of swete herbes and floures shall meue him to wanton courage, or lest in gadringe good holsome herbes he may happen to be stunge with a nettle. No wyse man entreth in to a gardein but he soon espiethe good herbes from nettles, and treadeth the nettles under his feete whiles he gadreth good herbes ... Semblablye if he do rede wanton mater mixte with wisedom, he putteth the warst under foote and sorteth out the best.' (1.13: 129).
³⁶ See note 146 in the main text.
³⁷ He dedicates a passage to display in detail the 'many good moral lessons' which are contained in each of the eclogues; see pp. 102–03.

Elyot's *The Governour* is therefore made manifest by frequent copies *verbatim* of entire sections or by Webbe's emphasis on the moral profitableness of poetry by offering moralising interpretations. Yet Webbe's use of Elyot's text does not always consist of slavishly copying it; he occasionally amplifies Elyot's reasoning (as in those observations on whether the Latin poets are appropriate for children at too young an age),[38] or modifies the tenor of his predecessor's observations, as, for instance, when he slightly transforms the garden metaphor to confer on it a harsher tone that better suits his outraged charge against wicked readers.[39] And eventually Webbe disagrees with Elyot's view, confirming that he has his own criteria regarding certain issues, as in, for example, the case of his characterising Ovid's *Metamorphoses* as a quite profitable text for teaching children if properly interpreted, which contrasts with Elyot's opinion that the teaching of Ovid, since it contains 'litell other lernyng', only needs a one-day lesson (1.10: 67).

3. William Webbe and Cambridge Ideals: Canonizing Spenser's *The Shepherds' Calendar*

3.1 Webbe's Cambridge Background and Intellectual Relationships

As I mentioned in the preliminary section, we have only a few facts to shape the biographical profile of William Webbe, apart from his appearance in the Cambridge student records,[40] corroborated by his not very revealing signature on his title-page as 'Graduate', which leaves the nature of his academic degree unspecified. Moreover, the coexistence in Venn's and Cooper's records of two Webbes who graduated respectively either in 1572/73 or 1581/82, hinders the identification of our author as to his belonging to Edmund Spenser's generation, or to the slightly later one of Abraham Fraunce. Other casual personal allusions in the text, such as a reference to his current tutorship of Sulyard's sons in the 'Dedicatory epistle' (which accounts in part for his interest in humanist pedagogy), his mention of the 'summer evenings' of leisure (which suggests the approximate date of composition), or his geographical distance from the literary circles of London while he was living in Sulyard's manor in Runwell (which he alleges as an apology for his difficulties in giving a precise overview of contemporary authors) constitute the only objective, factual information which has reached present readers about the author of the first published treatise exclusively dedicated to the theory of poetry. However, despite their vagueness, these details should not be undervalued: they may be seen as key evidence in better contextualizing the nature of the treatise and the cultural and personal

---

[38] Contrast *Governour*, 1.13:131 and *A Discourse*, p. 94.
[39] See note 101 in the main text.
[40] See note 14 in this introduction.

aspirations of its author, particularly when set against the literary ideals this text endorses and its author's discursive strategies.

This section of the introduction therefore aims to shed more light on Webbe's identity by attending simultaneously to two parallel, interrelated aspects of his discourse. First I will analyse the personal dimension implicit in his comments and documentary allusions to contemporary poets and scholars, especially Spenser, Harvey and those integrated within their coterie; this enables us to infer the nature of Webbe's relation with Cambridge literary circles of 1570s and 1580s, along with his particular interests in getting the treatise published. Second, by interpreting the text through its use of literary exemplification, I will focus specifically on how Webbe hails Spenser as the pinnacle of English poetry and uses his *Calendar* as an almost exclusive source of examples, to illustrate humanist literary ideals that had for several decades forged the intellectual identity of scholars at Cambridge. Studying the *Calendar*'s presence in Webbe's text will allow us to explore not only Webbe's total endorsement of poetic ideals first shaped at Cambridge, which Abraham Fraunce would also find incarnated in Spenser's eclogues,[41] but also his personal interest in making public his admiration for the new poet (if not his acquaintance), which places Webbe at the periphery, at least, of certain nuclear circles of Tudor scholarship and literary creativity. An analysis of the use of the *Calendar* in *A Discourse* provides a closer approximation to the author's situation in relation to these intellectual circles first formed at Cambridge.

Webbe's close connections with Cambridge, manifest in university records, are also made clear by the treatise's distillation of the common intellectual and literary concerns shared by the most prominent of its figures such as Spenser, Harvey, Fraunce, Drant, or Dyer among others. The university can be seen as the cradle of demands for metrical reform based on Ascham's censure of rhyme and exhortation to adopt classical hexameter, and in addition one of its principal educational strengths was the central pedagogical position occupied by literature in the teaching of languages, rhetoric, and civil values. Webbe's treatise may traditionally have only been considered as a compendium of ideas borrowed to a greater or lesser extent from canonical works by his contemporaries, but it is nonetheless evident that his editorial and selective work obeys a coherent personal conception of the English poetic panorama forged in the light of such Cambridge ideals. In Kathrine Koller's (1940: 119-20) illustrative account of the extent to which Abraham Fraunce's works represented the spirit of the Penhurst group, we can also find an eloquent description of Webbe's poetic ideology. In fact, in her influential article on Fraunce, she establishes interesting and revealing common traits between Spenser's protégé and our author, the most evident being

---

[41] See Kathrine Koller, 'Abraham Fraunce and Edmund Spenser', *ELH*, 7.2 (1940), 108-20.

that both use the *Calendar* extensively to illustrate their theories and make praise of Spenser a literary commonplace. Koller observes that 'a study of the works of Fraunce helps us to understand that Penhurst group who were actively concerned in improving English poetry, writing "usual" English, the common speech, in trying new forms, and who never stopped believing in the high function of poetry' (120). It seems obvious from the tone of his treatise — that of an aspirant, not an established figure — that Webbe was not a full member of the Penshurst circle; however, it is also evident through an analysis of his work that he shared with this elite all the concerns and perspectives regarding poetics outlined in the previous section of this introduction. If we compare each of Koller's statements which define the Penshurst group's literary ideology with Webbe's approach to poetry, we find that her description summarises many of the main concerns of *A Discourse*. It is for instance palpable that Webbe's central objective is to urge the 'learned poets' of England[42] to do all they can to raise the dignity of English letters, with the ulterior concern to consolidate a nobler national poetic idiom than that being widely disseminated by a profusion of 'rustical rhymers' and 'bad' writers whose works 'pestered' and 'stuffed' the bookshops ('Preface'). Webbe's activism in this regard constitutes the main purpose of his treatise, as he states in the preface; aware that he was not sufficiently skilled for such a large enterprise, he was eager to make at least a contribution through his humble directions to establish the difference between good and bad poetry, and, above all, to encourage and supplicate the best poets of the country to keep on working to that purpose. He makes a modest attempt himself in his rather extravagant translation of Virgil's two first eclogues, although his intention seems to be not as much artistic as strategic, that is, to offer it as an example and thereby to challenge others to try writing hexameters. I will come back to the relevance of the preface for the identification of Webbe's biographical connections later in this section.

Regarding the preference for the use of ' "usual" English' and the value of 'common speech' that Koller ascribes to elite Cambridge poets, we are led to set Webbe's perception of poetic language against the apology for the 'natural rudeness' and 'good and natural English words' articulated by E.K. in his 'Dedicatory Epistle' to Spenser's *Calendar* (Brooks-Davies: 20-21), which, as I will explain in more detail later in this section, is one of Webbe's main sources of inspiration. His enthusiastic praise of the eclogues shows that Webbe shares with the Spenser-Harvey circle this conception of the pastoral register as a means of supporting the humanist values endorsed in his treatise. Moreover, Webbe positions himself within that branch of Tudor criticism that argued for the linguistic value of Skelton's works, whose prestige was questioned by some Elizabethans like George Puttenhan or Francis Meres,[43] but which were highly

---

[42] He addresses his preface 'To the Noble Poets of England'.
[43] See note 64 in the main text.

appreciated at Cambridge and evidently acted as inspiration for Spenser's character Colin Clout. The prominence placed on people's everyday language is likewise reinforced by Webbe's emphasis on Chaucer's unquestionable role as promoter of English as a literary language. As further evidence of Webbe's interest in popular language, I have previously pointed out in this introduction his concern with the translation of Latin texts, not only as a means of making these more accessible to common readers, but as part of the process of promoting the vernacular as the national poetic idiom.

The Cambridge group's fondness for new poetic forms is also made manifest in various aspects of *A Discourse*. Besides Webbe's active campaign to support the promotion of classical hexameters, he takes special pains in his section on formal questions to provide examples of experimental uses of lines and stanzas, mainly taken from Spenser's eclogues and, occasionally, from other sources, such as William Hunnis' poem 51 in *The Paradise of Dainty Devises* (in the 1578 and 1585 editions).[44] Webbe's fascination with formal innovation is also demonstrated by the pervasive presence of such a varied, experimental anthology as *Paradise* (1576), which he seems to have had in front of him while he was working on the treatise. Besides being the origin of Hunnis' poem, and, most likely, the collection that inspires his brief summary of the many possible combinations of rhyme patterns,[45] *Paradise* is also an important source for Webbe's catalogue of contemporary poets, although most of them seem to be unknown to him, as he only provides their initials exactly as they appear in the signatures of many of the original poems. However, Webbe does not just show his interest here from the position of literary theorist; he also dares to try his skill as a poet experimenting with the English hexameter by translating Virgil's two first eclogues and transcribing Spenser's 'April' into Sapphic verse.

The high consideration of poetry that Webbe shared with members of the Penhurst group and with many Cambridge contemporaries, alluded to by Koller, as we have seen, in her last statement about Fraunce, does not need to be exposed here as it has already been widely discussed in the previous section of this introduction, where I examined *A Discourse* from the humanist perspective and concluded that Webbe approaches poetry as a key moral, civilising and political instrument for the consolidation of English as the poetic idiom that corresponds to a great nation such as theirs.

Given how scarce the biographical information is that we have about Webbe, figuring out the concrete degree of integration in or even acquaintance with other

---

[44] See notes 201 and 209 in the main text.
[45] 'Now the sundry kinds of rare devises and pretty inventions which come from the fine poetical vein of many in strange and unaccustomed manner, if I could report them, it were worthy my travail: such are the turning of verses, the enfolding of words, the fine repetitions, the clerkly conveying of contraries, and many such like' (pp. 115-16).

Cambridge poets and scholars is rendered impossible. Nevertheless, if the tenets outlined in his *poetica* attest to his university training, his personal links with Cambridge are also intimated when it comes to analysing the selection of figures included in his catalogue of contemporary poets as well as the nature of his critical commentaries about them. The commentaries usually denote a special interest in demonstrating his awareness, although mostly very limited, of the activities in which poets related to Cambridge were engaging, and show that, despite his marginalised geographical location when composing *A Discourse*, he did his best to be up to date with any innovations produced within that literary context. Present in Webbe's work are Cambridge reminiscences dating back four decades before its composition, that is, from the period when Ascham, Cheke and Watson were leading figures in the university. Besides quoting 'Master Ascham' for his account of the historical provenance of the barbarous custom of rhyme (p. 77), Webbe also pays homage to his and Ascham's alma mater (St John's College) by hailing as the perfect accomplishment of quantitative verse two lines from the *Odyssey* that 'one Master Watson, fellow of St John's College in Cambridge' (p. 122) had translated out of Horace's Latin version. That said, Webbe most likely knew about these lines from their citation in *The Schoolmaster* (I. 224), and the name of 'one Watson' (referring to Thomas Watson) would have probably seemed much more remote to him if it had not been for Ascham's references.

The design of Webbe's account of contemporary poets seems to follow neither a rigorous chronology nor the criteria of literary genre, although he notes the difference between the works of translators (he mentions Phaer and Golding as the most relevant) and those of the original composers, but in general his structure appears somewhat spontaneous or improvised. Webbe tends to glance over those contemporary poets that he apparently treats as minor or peripheral, integrating them in mechanical lists of names mainly borrowed from the authors who contributed their poems to the popular collection *The Paradise of Dainty Devices*, and for some of these, as I have mentioned, he only reproduces their initials as they appear in the first editions of the anthology. Several of these poets had also published in other popular collections, such as William Hunnis, who had some poems in *A Handful of Pleasant Delights* (1584), another anthology that seems to have inspired Webbe in his mentions of different popular tunes.[46] Others, like Churchyard, Vaux and Heywood, also contributed a few poems in *Tottel's Miscellany* (1557), but this anthology is strangely ignored by Webbe, and he makes no allusion either to it or to Thomas Wyatt in *A Discourse*. Surrey appears in this section with no special commendation but Webbe later ascribes to him the first attempt to compose English hexameters in his translation of the

---

[46] He mentions 'Rogero', 'Trenchmore', 'Downright Squire', galliards, pavans, jigs and brawls (p. 112).

Aeneid, mistaking blank verse for quantitative metre and thereby reproducing Ascham's misinterpretation (*Schoolmaster*: II. 291).

There are particular occasions when Webbe seems intentionally to give special mention or to linger on the commendations of poets who happen to be significantly connected with Cambridge, or with the two figures who become the main targets of Webbe's panegyrical efforts and most enthusiastic praise: I mean, of course, Edmund Spenser and Gabriel Harvey, whose presence hovers over the pages of *A Discourse* from the start, and whose commendations in the catalogue of authors Webbe postpones to the final paragraphs with the intention of hailing them as the paradigms of English poetry. Out of this group of Webbe's most admired poets, he dedicates a prominent position to George Gascoigne; educated at Trinity College, Cambridge, Gascoigne had been an influential member of the literary coteries of Gray's Inn for around a decade and a half (until 1569), and was greatly admired by the poets of the Cambridge circle during the mid 1580s. Philip Sidney's appreciation of him was widely known, as was the special consideration that Harvey and Spenser had shown for his poems. According to Gillian Austen (2008: 9–10), eighteen months after Gascoigne died in October 1577, Harvey wrote one of the two known elegies on his death, ranking him with Chaucer and Surrey, a poem that is unfortunately not extant.[47] George Whetstone, who, according to Austen, may have known Gascoigne through the Inns of Court, was the author of the other poem lamenting his death (*A Remembraunce*, 1577). And, although there is no direct evidence of this relationship, Spenser may have been personally acquainted with him for he included an enthusiastic recognition of his literary merits in E.K.'s gloss to 'November' (Brooks-Davies: 185) which Webbe reproduced *verbatim*, without specifying the source, seven years later, thus helping to revitalize Gascoigne's popularity. By copying E.K.'s words, Webbe seems to follow two personal impulses at the same time: first, to show his faithful adherence to the worship that Spenser and Harvey (for Webbe, as we have seen, the intellectual leaders of the moment) professed for Gascoigne, avoiding the risk of understating Gascoigne's worth which had been so intensely articulated by E.K., and, presumably, by Harvey in his lost elegy; and second, to profess his oath of allegiance to the poetic criteria outlined by the author of the glosses, whether that was Spenser himself, the enigmatic 'E.K.', or Harvey. This would not be the only occasion on which Webbe reproduces *verbatim* from E.K. a critical commentary on an author, and it also occurs with the commendations of Spenser in the 'Dedicatory epistle' of the *Calendar* (Brooks-Davies: 19, ll. 22–28). It seems that Webbe does not trust his own laudatory skills when it comes to commending key figures in his contemporary literary world, or that he desires to raise E.K.'s critical

---

[47] Gillian Austen, *George Gascoigne* (Cambridge: D. S. Brewer, 2008).

views to the status of official literary theory. Webbe's judgement of Gascoigne as poetic authority is finally corroborated by his adoption of Gascoigne's *Certain Notes of Instruction* (1575) as the guiding text for his own suggestions about the methods to follow to confer sophistication on English rhyme.

The remainder of Webbe's allusions to contemporary writers which offer any kind of brief commentary — generally, vague compliments with no elaborate critical assessment — all illustrate to some extent Webbe's apparent interest in pleasing addressees connected with various political spheres, like the Earl of Oxford, or in showing his prevailing attachment to the literary world of Cambridge by praising figures who either had been intellectually nurtured there, were eminent in the composition of pastoral, or were particularly linked with the Spenser-Harvey circle in particular and with university coteries in general. Some examples are Barnaby Googe, whose eclogues in the style of Mantuan had a great influence on Spenser's *Calendar*;[48] Abraham Fleming, who was a sizar in Cambridge from 1570, where he could have coincided with Webbe provided that the latter were identified with the first of the two Webbes who appear in the university records of that period;[49] George Whetstone, who was acquainted with Churchyard and Gascoigne and had appended some of Fleming's Latin poems to his *Rocke of Regard* in 1576; and Abraham Fraunce, who Webbe mentions obliquely without explicitly uttering his name, and who is urged to publish his poetical experiments, which Webbe knew were circulating among the former's friends.[50] In addition, some of these allusions seem to aim at letting the reader realize that Webbe's disconnection from literary activity was not absolute despite the fact that he alleges his geographical isolation on two occasions as an apology for his ultimately inaccurate data. When Webbe refers to Anthony Munday, too, he interestingly appeals to the reader's sense of complicity when, by ascribing to Munday the witty epithet of 'an earnest traveller', he refers at the same time to the poet's passion for travelling and defends Munday's innocence in a legal conflict with his master John Allde.[51] The reference to Abraham Fraunce happens to be a similar wink to the reader: Webbe dedicates to him one of his less vague and most emphatic commendations, despite the fact that he neglects to mention his name or the title of the 'dainty morsels and fine poetical inventions' that he urges him to publish, undoubtedly meaning Fraunce's first experiments with English hexameters in his translation of Thomas Watson's Latin poem *Amyntas*, which, although they were not published with the title of *Lamentations of Amyntas* until 1587, Webbe seems to suggest that he had already read (May, 2010: 34).[52]

---

[48] See note 71 in the main text.
[49] See notes 72 and 151 in the main text.
[50] See note 73 in the main text.
[51] See note 76 in the main text.
[52] Stephen W. May, 'Marlowe, Spenser, Sidney and — Abraham Fraunce?', *The Review of English Studies*, New Series 62 (2010), 30-63.

Although Steven W. May (38) has stated that the circulation of original manuscripts in advance of publication was not as carefully restricted to coteries closely linked with the authors as has commonly been assumed, the fact that Fraunce's manuscript could have reached Webbe while he was living in Runwell, as well as the tone of his affectionate reproach for keeping them private, imply that Webbe enjoyed some acquaintance with Fraunce or other members of his circle, despite the evidence that they did not coincide at Cambridge. We should not underestimate, too, the fact that Fraunce was Sidney's protégé until the latter's death in October 1586, and that he had tight connections with Gabriel Harvey and presumably with Spenser, which also made him an influential figure within the circles Webbe seems to have admired. In fact, Fraunce would become one of the most enduring advocates of the hexameter once Harvey and Spenser had lost their interest in this enterprise by the mid 1580s. Likewise, in his commendation of Abraham Fleming (p. 104) as a translator of Virgil, Webbe shows once again his interest in being up to date with the publications of one of his Cambridge colleagues, as he wonders if Fleming would have fulfilled the commitment he had made in the preface of the *Eclogues* (1575) of translating the *Georgics* too, an enterprise he would finally complete in 1589.[53]

The special attention paid to these poets in particular may allow us to view more clearly Webbe's profile up to the moment of the composition of *A Discourse*. He appears as a scholar who enthusiastically represented ideals of poetry associated with contemporary Cambridge, although in a private rather than public sphere, and strove to maintain, despite geographical impediments, the usual associations preserved by those who came from the university. The strenuous defence of literature displayed in his treatise portrays a Webbe who shared with his Cambridge colleagues that 'enduring interest in poetry' which characterised the former students of St John's (May: 38), and who sought to maintain a due awareness of his Cambridge contemporaries' poetic accomplishments. If we accept these facts, the question now should be what motivated him to compose the first published theory of English poetry. Webbe's commentaries do not seem to be a neutrally descriptive catalogue of contemporary literary authorities; instead, from most of them the reader may infer Webbe's desire to be noticed by those to whom he alludes, both by publicly recognising their merits, and by displaying his remaining links with the Cambridge world. Whether he intended to obtain patronage and to be accepted at an Inn of Court,[54] or simply

---

[53] See note 151 in the main text.
[54] He also dedicates a general mention to the poets of the Inns of Court and of the universities. If he was an aspirant to enter in an Inn of Court, judging by the emphasis he gives to the Earl of Oxford, Gascoigne or Fraunce it would likely be Gray's Inn, in which the former was a honorific member and Gascoigne had become very influential during fourteen years until 1569; and since the latter's enrolment there in 1583 had contributed considerably to increase his prestige.

aspired to be accepted by the literary elite at whose apex he situated Harvey and Spenser is difficult to ascertain, although the following paragraphs may make the reader consider more carefully the second option.

As I have previously argued, and as Webbe explicitly states, he 'purposely' reserves the final section of his catalogue to the author of *The Shepherds' Calendar* in order to proclaim that he alone deserved the title of 'the rightest English Poet' (p. 84). In his three direct allusions to Spenser in the treatise, Webbe avoids, in one instance more subtly than in the others, mentioning the name of the author of the *Calendar* in order to conceal his identity, as it was still the wish of the author not to make it public until his name appeared in the edition of 1589.[55] Despite Webbe's various protestations of ignorance, there is no reason to question his knowledge of Spenser's identity, given that his three allusions to him slyly hint at this and that the identity seems to have become by then an open secret.[56] This section of the introduction will analyse in depth Webbe's discursive strategies regarding the author of the *Calendar* and the significance of the use Webbe makes of the eclogues in particular.

But for the moment I should call the reader's attention to the revealing manner in which Webbe refers to Gabriel Harvey as the second in prominence among the English poets, as well as his two brothers, Richard and John, in this final passage of his catalogue of poets. Webbe introduces him as someone who, although 'now long since occupied in graver studies (Master Gabriel Harvey), yet as he was once his [*Spenser's*] most special friend and fellow poet' (p. 84). As in the case of some of the aforementioned poets, Webbe demonstrates that he knows first-hand about Spenser and Harvey's friendship, and not just through E.K.'s allusion in the 'Dedicatory Epistle' to the *Calendar*; this perhaps runs contrary to how we may interpret his reference to their relationship in the exact terms used by the enigmatic glosser of the eclogues: 'Now I trust, Master Harvey, that upon sight of your special friend's and fellow-poet's doings ...' (Brooks-Davies: 25, ll. 201–02). Although the treatise provides evidence that he had read their famous *Letters* (1580) and, therefore, this could be the source of his reference to their friendship, the usage of the adverbial 'once' shows that not only had he known about their past connections, but that he had never lost the thread of their relationship. His use of 'once' implies that at the moment of the composition of *A Discourse* Webbe was quite aware of the separate paths their careers had led them to take. In 1586 Harvey was qualified as Doctor of Laws in Trinity Hall,

---

[55] Although in the first one he refers to him as 'our late famous English poet who wrote *The Shepherds' Calendar*' (p. 67), in the second he speculates with the initials 'Sp.' and with Pembroke Hall as his academic origin (p. 84), and in the third one he has definitely assumed the authorship of 'Master Sp.' (p. 101).

[56] Koller (113) affirms that in Fraunce's and Webbe's works there is evidence of their awareness of Spenser's authorship.

and, as Andrew Hadfield points out (2012: 70),[57] at the time Webbe wrote his treatise, he had probably left Cambridge and had settled in London; when Webbe utters that Harvey was by that time 'seriously occupied in graver studies', he is no doubt referring to this situation. As for Spenser, who had first moved to London in 1578 — when he became secretary of Bishop John Young (Hadfield: 83; Hamilton: 669) —[58] he had been appointed private secretary to Lord Grey of Wilton, the new lord deputy of Ireland in 1580 (Hadfield: 105; Hamilton: 670), and so by 1586 he was living in the colony, where he would remain until the end of his life. Webbe's main concern about this new situation seems to be that the enthusiasm for the English hexameter that they had deployed in the years before their correspondence seemed now to have cooled down. In fact, according to Hadfield (109), those letters suggest that they were already disappointed with the quantitative project. After highlighting the great efforts Harvey had made 'not only in his Latin poetry', but especially in his attempts 'to reform our English verse and to beautify the same with grave devices' (obviously referring to his hexameters, which were never published and have not survived),[59] Webbe's discourse acquires a tone of paternalistic reproach regarding two issues: first, that his experiments with verse 'lie hid in hateful obscurity' (that is, unpublished); and second, that he had not done as much as his poetic skills would have enabled him to do in successfully developing this new kind of versification, but conversely had handled it 'but with half that skill which I know he could have done', and had 'poured it forth at a venture as a thing between jest and earnest'. As Webbe states in the preface to the 'Noble Poets of England', one of his main motivations in composing this *poetica* is to urge the leading poets of his time to keep on trying to incorporate Latin metres into English verse, and that is precisely why Webbe directs his exhortations to publish their works to Spenser, Harvey and Fraunce throughout the treatise, since he considers these texts to be fundamental models for subsequent generations of poets.

As for Spenser, in this same passage, although he abandons the affective tone of reproach he used for Harvey and adopts an almost supplicatory attitude, Webbe nonetheless requests him ('the other Gentleman') or 'his friends' to let his 'excellent poems, whereof I know he hath plenty, come abroad, as his *Dreams*, his *Legends*, his *Court of Cupid*, his *English Poet*, with other ...' (p. 85). Webbe clearly feels the need to explain that the reason for treating them jointly is that they are the only national poets able successfully to achieve the reformation of verse. Therefore, he verbalizes his wish that they should continue their poetic experiments 'if their high dignities and serious businesses would permit',

---

[57] Andrew Hadfield, *Edmund Spenser: A Life* (Oxford: Oxford University Press, 2012).
[58] A.C. Hamilton, ed., *The Spenser Encyclopaedia* (London: Routledge, 1996; 1st edn Toronto: University of Toronto Press, 1990).
[59] We only know about them from Spenser-Harvey's *Letters*.

obviously referring to their new professional occupations mentioned in the previous paragraph. His insistence on ascribing to them both the national responsibility to strive to refine English poetry, along with his apparently reproachful reference to their being occupied in more 'serious businesses' (could this be interpreted ironically?) may lead us to infer that the preface that Webbe dedicates to the 'Noble Poets of England', soliciting their active involvement in the reformation of poetry, is most likely addressed to these two leading exponents of the Cambridge quantitative movement. In fact, in this introductory passage, Webbe sets out the same idea that he articulates at the end of the catalogue of poets: namely, that the reasons why the total refinement of English poetry had not been yet accomplished were, on the one hand, that the only national poets enabled to do it had kept their works private ('those that can, reserving their skill to themselves', p. 62), and on the other, that the same individuals had given up this enterprise and were at that moment embarked in their 'divine cogitations', most likely an allusion either to Harvey's Doctorate in Law or to Spenser's secretarial role for Lord Grey. Be that as it may, Webbe lays this matter 'once again' in the way of these eminent poets intending to make them 'stumble upon it', and invites them 'to look so low from your divine cogitations, when your muse mounteth to the stars and ransacketh the spheres of heaven'. Is Webbe here using the same ambiguous tone between ironic reproach and respectful recognition with which he seems to address Harvey in the catalogue of poets? Because, if we assumed in Webbe's tone this inclination to ironize, would it not imply a certain acquaintance with these two poets or, at least, with their coterie that allowed him almost to reprimand them in these affective but sarcastic terms, simultaneously celebrating their rare abilities and recriminating them for their inactivity? If we return to the passage which closes the account of contemporary literary personages, what makes Webbe's wish to compliment Gabriel Harvey even more obvious is his inclusion of the poet's two brothers, Richard and John ('the one a godly and learned divine, the other a famous and skilful physician', p. 85).[60] In the final passage dedicated to Spenser and Harvey, Webbe not only signals the latter's siblings as being extraordinarily able to accomplish the incorporation of Latin metres, but also demands of them a more appropriate use of their literary skills in favour of poetry.

3.2 *Canonizing Spenser's* Calendar

During the Elizabethan period the backwardness of English poetic eloquence was a frequently assumed fact; Webbe ascribes it to widespread underestimation of their own skills that had led the 'finest wits and most divine heads' to be satisfied

---

[60] For further details on the Harveys' careers and writings see note 82 in the main text.

with the rustic device of rhyme ('Preface'). His humanist convictions encourage him to foster the idea that the natural wealth of the English tongue, along with the skill and effort of true English poets, would render prosodic perfection both a reality and the badge of the cultural grandeur of their people. Poetry is consequently treated as a national issue, a question of state, and Webbe demands from national poets a commitment to the task of adorning their country through the development of a dignified poetic idiom. This is exemplified, for instance, in his recognition of Arthur Golding's patriotic contribution through 'his continual labour to profit this nation and speech in all kind of good learning' (p. 82). *A Discourse* therefore becomes both a propagandistic defence of national letters and poets and a manifesto of the quantitative movement as well as a prescriptive manual of the humanist ideals of poetry described in previous sections.

In this context, then, Webbe declares *The Shepherds' Calendar* to be the paradigm of all premises which shape his definition of poetry, and — like Abraham Fraunce in his *Shepheardes Logike* (composed before 1585) and in his *The Lawiers Logike* (1588) — he finds in Spenser's eclogues an exclusive source of examples used in his discussions of content, form and poetic function.[61] Spenser, whose authorship Webbe does not openly assume, is extolled both as an innovator (in fact, he is referred to as 'the new poet') and as a consolidator of the canon of English national poetics, equated in this regard to Virgil for his success in transforming his vernacular language into a dignified instrument of poetic expression.

The presence of Spenser and the *Calendar* pervades most of *A Discourse* and occurs in many, varied discursive forms either through the usage of E.K.'s editorial commentaries (whether from the 'Dedicatory epistle', the introductory 'arguments' to each eclogue and, to a greater extent, from the glosses) or through the poetic material from the eclogues. Webbe incorporates content borrowed from E.K. into his argumentation through two main strategies: either by means of explicit quotations which openly refer to the source, or through a tacit *copia* of ideas (sometimes reproduced *verbatim*), mainly to do with historical accounts of poetry or information about the author and his unpublished works. As for the intertextuality of the poems, their function is primarily to provide literary *exempla* of the perfect use of poetry as well as models for imitation.

---

[61] Kathrine Koller associates Webbe's and Fraunce's works for their similar use of examples from Spenser's eclogues in order to illustrate their common conception of poetry: 'This attitude towards *The Shepheardes Calendar* is not limited to Fraunce. William Webbe bases the larger portion of his *Discourse on English Poesie* (1586) on Spenser's poem. Here again both content and form of the eclogue serve as illustrations of the power of pastoral poetry to delight and to instruct, and here Webbe finds examples of all forms of English verse' (1940: 113).

In addition, direct references to the figure of the author with commendatory and panegyrical aims occur three times across the treatise at apparently strategic moments. The first appears in the introductory section dedicated to the definition of poetry in terms of divine inspiration, where Webbe introduces a quotation from Ovid's *Fasti* inspired, incidentally, by Cuddy's emblem for 'October' (Brooks-Davies: 66) to support his belief in the 'celestial instinction' (p. 67) of poetry, and underlines his reasoning with 'the authority of our late famous English poet' by quoting two lines from Spenser's 'October' eclogue. This first allusion presents the new poet and anticipates the central role that he and his work will play in the treatise. At this stage, Webbe already declares Spenser the national poet *par excellence* by referring to him as a literary authority. One of Webbe's main arguments which generally legitimates Spenser's privileged position in the treatise is that the poet has convincingly demonstrated his status as heir to the classical poets through his absolute mastery of imitation — on this occasion Webbe cites Theocritus and Virgil, who Spenser 'narrowly imitateth'. Following Ascham's humanist conception of imitation as the only means to attain perfect eloquence, Webbe frequently resorts to Spenser's mimetic skills to raise the poet to the standards of classical literature, without overlooking his capability even to surpass them, if it were not for his attachment to rhyme. In this introductory allusion to the poet, Webbe also refers for the first time to Spenser's unpublished *English Poet*, which he says he came to know through 'his friend E.K.',[62] who in the *Calendar* had expressed his intention to publish it (Brooks-Davies: 159); Webbe acknowledges that he does not know whether E.K. had by then fulfilled his commitment. Consequently, this initial mention introduces all of the aims Webbe has in mind in relation to Spenser, which recur throughout the treatise: to consolidate his position as the best national poet, to legitimate him as the incarnation of a revival of the ancient canon and to demand the publication of his other works.

I have already discussed the second direct allusion to Spenser which appears at the end of the catalogue of poets and its implications for how we might interpret Webbe's connections and aspirations regarding the Cambridge circle; this is when Webbe refers to him as 'Master Sp.' and pretends not to be certain of whether he is the author of the eclogues although, in any case, he assumes that the author must be someone from Pembroke Hall (p. 84). As for the last direct allusion, which we find in the section on the history and relevance of the eclogues as a literary genre (p. 101), Webbe's forced caution concerning the preservation of Spenser's anonymity seems to have relaxed to some extent because the scholar now assumes that 'Master Sp.' — whoever he might be — is definitely the author of *The Shepherds' Calendar*. In this section Webbe places special emphasis on

---

[62] See note 29 in the main text.

Spenser as heir and imitator of the Greek and Latin pastoral tradition, and, as in the aforementioned case of his commendations of Gascoigne, E.K.'s famous passage describing the poet's literary virtues is quoted *verbatim*, thus showing once more Webbe's comprehensive adherence to this work and to the literary view of its author and glosser.

The *Calendar*'s pastoral poems provide Webbe with material to canonize Spenser on the basis of three main aspects of his theory of poetry: imitation as a means of ennobling the English literary idiom; the instructive nature of poetry; and the civilizing effect of decorum as conveyed by the cohesion between matter and form. Firstly, as if he were following Ascham's request for catalogues of topics and places of imitation (*Schoolmaster*: 268)[63] Webbe develops a parallelism between Virgil's and Spenser's eclogues concerning their content and intention; however, the study demanded by Ascham additionally motivates Webbe to prove the extent to which Spenser's work is a sophisticated imitation of Virgil's, thus evincing both the Elizabethan writer's success in attaining the poetic proficiency of the ancient poets and his capability to improve the quality of their inventions: 'What one thing is there in them so worthy admiration, whereunto we may not adjoin something of his of equal desert? Take Virgil and make some little comparison between them, and judge as you shall see cause' (p. 102). Webbe's praise of Spenser for his assimilation of the Virgilian tradition derives from his humanist conception of imitation as a tool for boosting individual as well as collective erudition; he strives to demonstrate that Spenser's subjection to the customary device of rhyme is widely compensated by his exceptional learning which distances him from the rusticity that rhyme represents. This quality is also underlined in the passage in which Webbe offers a detailed analysis of the sophistication of Spenser's rhymed verse.

For a proper exposition of the mechanisms through which Webbe tries to prove the uniqueness of the *Calendar* in terms of moral instruction and perfect eloquence (the latter understood as the close cohesion of matter and form), we should recall E.K.'s famous account of Spenser's merits which Webbe quotes in his third direct allusion to the new poet:

> I think no less 'deserveth' (thus saith E.K. in his commendations) 'his wittiness in devising, his pithiness in uttering, his complaints of love so lovely, his discourses of pleasure so pleasantly, his pastoral rudeness, his moral wiseness, his due observing of *decorum* everywhere, in personages, in seasons, in matter, in speech, and generally in all seemly simplicity of handling his matter and framing his words'. (p. 102)

This quotation not only celebrates Spenser's skills, but also acts as a manifesto for pastoral poetry in terms both of subject-matter and style, and chimes with

---

[63] See note 29 of this introduction.

Webbe's advocacy of this genre's virtues some lines earlier on: 'Although the matter they take in hand seemeth commonly in appearance rude and homely, as the usual talk of simple clowns, yet do they indeed utter in the same much pleasant and profitable delight' (p. 101). After a general interpretation of the instructive function of the *Calendar*,[64] Webbe extends E.K.'s brief allusion to Spenser's 'moral wiseness' by providing his own moralised readings of some of the eclogues such as 'February', 'May', 'July', 'September' and 'October', although in the case of 'July' and 'September' he is silently copying EK's introductory 'arguments' (p. 102; Brooks-Davies: 113, 141).

This exposition of the didacticism of Spenser's eclogues gives way to a rapturous defence of poetry and poets' creative freedom in answer to the accusations of immorality that 'some curious heads' (p. 103) have poured onto the love between Hobbinol and Colin ('June'); Webbe seems to have known about this questioning of Spenser's integrity from E.K.'s gloss to 'January' (Brooks-Davies: 36), where the glosser reveals that the relation between these two characters had been interpreted by some as the poet's endorsement of pederasty. Webbe's defence of poetry in this passage turns into one of the most eloquent and vehement speeches in the treatise and is in tune with Sidney's view that corruption does not reside in poetry itself, but in the wicked minds of malicious readers (*Defence*: 35). This issue seems to have become a frequent subject of discussion in contemporary literary circles as Webbe declares to 'have often answered' these allegations in two ways: first, stating that Spenser's recreation of the friendship between elder and younger shepherds imitates a pastoral topic that has its origin in classical literature; and second, by displaying his own moralising interpretation. Once again he resorts to imitation as a guarantee of the legitimacy of early modern poetry, and Webbe's self-fashioning as a public defender of Spenser may be also understood as one more deliberate reference to his links with literary circles, this time in particular with his active participation in literary debates.

Meanwhile, the observance of the cohesion between matter and form leads Webbe to structure the second part of the treatise into the study of poetic genres (matter), and a description of the most representative examples of lines and stanzaic structures (form). Following the emphasis that E.K.'s commendation of Spenser places on the poet's mastery of 'decorum', understood here as the harmony between what is meant and how it is expressed, Webbe employs the eclogues as his main source of examples to illustrate the sophistication of English verse forms in these terms. Within this context, Webbe's main contribution is not his selection of specific excerpts to exemplify the originality of verse

---

[64] 'The occasion of his work is a warning to other young men, who being entangled in love and youthful vanities, may learn to look to themselves in time and to avoid inconveniences which may breed if they be not in time prevented' (p. 102).

structures, but his concern to pinpoint how these forms suit the emotions or matters they convey, thus displaying an absolute proficiency in Ciceronian decorum. He cites, for instance, 'January' for ten-syllable lines, 'February' for nine, 'March' for seven and eight, 'April' for the complicated rhyme scheme which he calls — borrowing Hobbinol's words — 'the tune of the waters fall' (Brooks-Davies: 271), and so forth. And in most of these instances he tries to demonstrate how these forms accompany the moods of the characters as, for example, in the case of 'February': 'The second sort hath naturally but nine syllables, and is a more rough or clownish manner of verse, used most commonly of him if you mark him in his satirical reprehensions and his shepherds' homeliest talk' (p. 110).

4. A Defence of the Quantitative Reformation of English Verse

4.1 Webbe's Remarks on English Rhyme and Rhymers

At this point of the introduction I have generally outlined the cultural connotations and aspirations that led the quantitative reformers in general and Webbe in particular to rail against the tradition of rhyme and to consider the incorporation of classical metres as the only way of accomplishing the perfect emulation of Latin verse. All of these men seemed firmly to believe not only in the possibility, but also in the necessity of applying Latin prosody to English verse to dignify the impoverished state of national poetry, which was a generalised assumption among Tudor intellectuals. Despite the practical difficulties they found in adapting English words to Latin rules of prosody, they based their confidence on the precedent of Virgil, who had been able to contribute to the advancement of Latin poetry by modifying Greek rules according to the linguistic requirements of his own tongue.[65]

Before starting my exposition of Webbe's contribution to the promotion and actual incorporation of Latin rules of prosody, I should first offer a brief account of what is apparently a self-contradictory approach in Webbe's treatise. Being,

---

[65] 'For why may I not think so of our English, seeing that among the Romans a long time, yea even till the days of Tully, they esteemed not the Latin poetry almost worth anything in respect of the Greek, as appeareth in the oration *Pro Archia Poeta*, yet afterwards it increased in credit more and more, and that in short space, so that in Virgil's time wherein were they not comparable with the Greeks? So likewise, now it seemeth not current for an English verse to run upon true quantity and those feet which the Latins use because it is strange, and the other barbarous custom, being within compass of every base wit, hath worn it out of credit or estimation. But if our writers, being of learning and judgement, would rather infringe this curious custom than omit the occasion of enlarging the credit of their native speech and their own praises by practising that commendable kind of writing in true verse, then no doubt, as in other parts of learning, so in poetry should not stoop to the best of them all in all manner of ornament and comeliness' (pp. 117–18).

on the one hand, a fervent opponent of rhyme who continually highlights the distinction between 'rhymers' and 'poets' and, on the other, a vindicator of English poetic tradition, especially when it comes to placing Spenser's rhymed *Calendar* at the top of the national poetic canon, Webbe's own discursive aims force him to resolve an argumentative tension between these two apparently opposed claims. In the preface he first expresses his concern with being misinterpreted as a betrayer of his own national tradition, despite its imperfections or lack of refinement: 'not that I mean to call in question the reverend and learned works of poetry written in our tongue by men of rare judgement and most excellent poets' (p. 63). He seems to anticipate here the rhetorical mechanisms that will later allow him to reconcile his choice of Chaucer or Skelton as pioneers of the vernacular literature as well as his canonization of Spenser's *Calendar*, with the Aschamite indictment of the rusticity of rhyme and its association with barbarous traditions. Webbe's discourse in this regard showcases a radicalism that does not correspond with the actual treatment he gives to the English poetic tradition in the treatise. He borrows the harsh discourse of E.K. to scorn bad rhymers: 'I scorn and spew out the rakehelly rout of our ragged rhymers (for so themselves use to hunt the letter) which without learning boast, without judgement jangle, without reason rage and foam' (p. 86);[66] but at the same time acknowledges that such a feature has become part of the idiosyncratic essence of English poetry: 'This brutish poetry, though it had not the beginning in this country, yet so hath it been affected here that the infection thereof would never (nor I think ever will) be rooted up again' (p. 77). And what is more, he is realistic about the damage that a blatant refutation of rhyme would cause to the cultural identity of the nation, in that it could erase the tradition out of which it had grown: 'Yet, being so engraft by custom and frequented by the most part, I may not utterly disallow it, lest I should seem to call in question the judgement of all our famous writers which have won eternal praise by their memorable works compiled in that verse' (pp. 105–06). Therefore, in practical terms, Webbe nuances his rejection of rhyme by focusing on a question of quality rather than propriety, thereby abandoning the absolutist position that would prevent him from coherently justifying his idolatry of *The Shepherds' Calendar*. He states in his preface that he aims to equip readers and poets to distinguish between good and bad poetry. Consequently, his declaration of contempt for rhyme is in practice moderate, concerned only with 'the uncountable rabble of rhyming ballet makers and compilers of senseless sonnets' (p. 85) who do not embody the Aschamite premises of learnedness and erudition. The bases of this distinction — and likewise of his quantitative aspirations — are to be found in the Elizabethan tendency to worship artificiality as an aesthetic feature identified

---

[66] In 'Dedicatory Epistle' (Brooks-Davies: 22, ll. 118–26).

with the poetic elites in contrast to vulgar verse. The composition of good poetry could not be within the reach of common or mediocre writers, let alone to be considered a spontaneous and natural process; Webbe continually rails against those 'copper noses' (p. 86) whose prolific production of vulgar verses derives from the inspiration that beer tankards provide under the patronage of tavern owners (a clear allusion to the popular ballad-writer William Elderton).[67]

In tandem with the effectiveness of instruction through delectation, artificiality becomes one of the main arguments Webbe uses to reconcile his adherence to contemporary anti-rhyme discourse with his genuine praise of some of the key poets exemplifying earlier English traditions, and, above all, of the new poet Spenser. With the main purpose of encouraging the 'noble poets' to make this barbarous device 'more artificial, according to the worthiness of our speech' (p. 106), Webbe summarises Gascoigne's guidelines for rhyme and proposes to bestow on this device a rhetorical component; he recommends exercises of memory (the fourth part of classical rhetoric), based on elaboration and learning by heart long lists of rhyming words that the poet would recall when rhyming *extempore*. This activity appears to reproduce the method used by school students to prepare their oral rhetorical exercises, consisting of memorizing beforehand arguments for and against diverse topics from commonplace books, the basic manuals of learning in Elizabethan grammar schools. In addition, the copious use of examples of a wide range of stanzaic patterns from the *Calendar* highlights the high degree of sophistication that rhyme may attain when practised by the best of the learned poets of England, although Webbe elsewhere laments that Spenser is attached to such an extent to this 'custom which he would not infringe' (p. 102).

4.2 Humanist Implications of Quantitative Metres: Sophistication and Artificiality

When in *The Schoolmaster* Ascham establishes the famous comparison between those who voluntarily choose rhyme for their verse when their talents would permit them to use sophisticated classical metres and those who prefer eating acorns instead of white bread (II. 289), he proclaims precisely a tendency deeply assimilated by Tudor humanists to relate the natural to the barbarous and rustic, that is, with a medieval past that marred the reputation of the nation's cultural identity by erasing its links with ancient Greece and Rome, for rhyme was the poetic invention of the Goths, as well as the device preferred by 'popish' writers in the Middle Ages. If England aspired to emulate the purity and prestige of the Greek and Latin civilizations, then its national poetic idiom had to be

---

[67] See note 84 in the main text.

founded on a more artificial prosody (the poetic equivalent to the refined 'white bread') which only literary elites could create and also understand; hence the efforts of the quantitative reformers to make the Latin hexameter the sign of English poetic identity. The appropriation of classical metres required a painstaking elaboration and so the presence in English verse of quantitative prosodic patterns was most likely intended to be appreciated (either visually or aurally) only by the cultural elite.[68] Harvey adopts this point of view in his second letter to Spenser (*Variorum* X, 'Letter' V: 463), in which he praises the valuable contribution of Sidney and Dyer to their 'new famous enterprise' aimed at 'the Exchanging of Barbarous and Balductum Rymes with Artificial Verses'; he equates the device of rhyme to 'base ylfauored Copper', whereas 'Artificial' poetry is like 'pure and fine Goulde'. Webbe understands this contrast in similar terms, and urges the noble poets of England to 'labour to adorn their country and advance their style with the highest and most learnedest top of true poetry' (p. 62).

4.3 Historical Overview of the Elizabethan Quantitative Movement: First Experiments, First Impediments

The quantitative movement in England was initiated in the 1540s by a generation of Cambridge scholars which included, most prominently, Roger Ascham, John Cheke and Thomas Watson, and had therefore been a tradition in St John's for three decades before Harvey and Spenser concerned themselves with the writing of English verse in classical metre in the late 1570s. Although Ascham, Cheke and Watson established the ideological and theoretical bases for this movement and encouraged their students to experiment, they were not actually confronted with the practical obstacles that the adoption of Latin prosody posed for the English language. Neither Ascham nor Checke were poets, and no hexameters from them have survived that might demonstrate how they contributed to this experimentation; only two lines attributed to Watson by Ascham remain, which he hailed as an example of the perfect use of Latin prosody. Webbe borrows these lines from *The Schoolmaster* to show his recognition of the senior Johnians' authority, although in his confusion of blank verse with quantity (also inherited from Ascham), he ascribes to Surrey the merit of being the first to attempt to develop the form.[69] It was not until the 1560s that Thomas Drant, a student and Fellow at St John's, first formulated some rules for the appropriate incorporation of Latin prosody unto English verse, but no record of these rules survives, and

---

[68] On the humanist implications of quantitative verse see Derek Attridge, *Well-Weighed Syllables: Elizabethan verse in classical metres* (Cambridge: Cambridge University Press, 1974), pp. 105–08; and note 155 in the main text.
[69] On Watson see note 229 in the main text.

we cannot figure them out from Drant's own poetic examples since only four couplets are extant in his posthumous *Three godly and learned Sermons*, composed around 1578 (May: 33). However, Spenser's and Harvey's comments in their correspondence, as well as Philip Sidney's first extant list of prosodic rules appended to the St John's manuscript of the *Old Arcadia* (Ringler, 1950), reveal that Drant proposed a rigorous transposition of Latin prosodic rules into English. Sidney was next to defend and experiment with quantitative metres, along with his friend and colleague Edward Dyer, and both are supposed to have been the founders of the legendary 'Areopagus' group formed with this purpose. Sidney's rules were therefore based on Drant's, although when it came to applying them in the quantitative poems of the *Arcadia*, the result was a more natural poetry than that the other quantitative reformers could ever achieve. It is difficult to understand the reason why Webbe does not mention either Sidney — as a poet or as one of the leaders of the movement — or Dyer in his commendations of English contemporary poets. His only allusion to Sidney is as the dedicatee of Spenser's *Calendar*; but even if he had not heard about his poems, he would have likely known about his efforts in quantitative verse and about his revision of the Drantian rules of prosody through the Spenser-Harvey correspondence, as Spenser mentioned these in his second letter to Harvey of April 1580 (*Variorum* X, 'Letter' II: 16), in which he observed that he had received from Sidney himself his comments on Drant's rules. We might assume either that Webbe's geographical isolation prevented him from having heard about Sidney's poetic career (Sidney may have started to write his quantitative verses for the *Arcadia* in the late 1570s, when Webbe's whereabouts are unknown) or that Webbe had a clear and realistic mind so as to whom he should demonstrate his skills and interest in poetry in order to be accepted in literary circles actually within his reach. His modest discourse throughout the treatise reveals a Webbe perfectly conscious of his own limitations; therefore, he is unlikely to have aspired to higher literary spheres than those derived from the persistence of Cambridge collegiality. In other words, it seems that his ambition did not stretch towards courtly spheres, but focused on the academic coteries under the influence of Harvey's leadership, or we could also consider as an alternative the idea that his treatise aimed specifically at gaining popularity within an Inn of Court.

Spenser and Harvey's interest in hexameters seems to have been at its greatest point of intensity in the mid 1570s before the publication of the *Calendar* in 1579. When Spenser left for London as Young's secretary in 1578, and the two scholars separated from each other, it began to lose steam. Although they were the two most enthusiastic promoters of the reformation of verse, hardly any poems that attest to their experiments have survived. Spenser included his 'Iambicum Trimetrum' in his first letter to Harvey, dated on 1579 (*Variorum* X, 'Letter' I: 7–8), and Harvey's 'Speculum Tuscanismi', a poem ridiculing the Earl of Oxford's Italianate manners, is one of the few extant pieces of evidence (all are found in his letters to Spenser) of his alleged experiments (*Variorum* X, 'Letter' V: 467). Webbe is aware of Harvey's labour in this regard and wants publicly to recognise his efforts 'to beautify' English verse 'with brave devices' (p. 84). He appears certain that Harvey may have composed other significant examples circulated in private among his friends, which would be essential to animate, or, more properly, to revive the reformation that he and Spenser had taken up so wholeheartedly during their Cambridge period. Webbe's allusion to the 'hateful obscurity' in which these texts remain may be interpreted as a complimentary reproach from someone who desires to extol the mastery of his most admired icons while urging them to get their texts into print. Hadfield (109) affirms that the Spenser-Harvey correspondence already denotes disillusionment with the enterprise, whereas A.C. Hamilton (347) considers it the full expression of their enthusiasm. All in all, I would add that their letters — particularly those sent by Harvey — undoubtedly display their awakening realisation that they might be dealing with an unfeasible project, unless contemporary poets could achieve a consensus regarding how Latin rules of prosody were to be applied, as I will discuss shortly. Harvey refers to the reformation as 'our new famous enterprise' (*Variorum* X, 'Letter' V: 463), thus implying his wish to keep on searching for a solution, but it is also true that his tone is that of someone who does not envisage an easy and successful outcome.[70] Webbe may have perceived this despondent attitude when he read the letters, as he shows himself quite anxious in his attempt to renew in both poets the enthusiasm for the project and their awareness of the responsibility they have to their nation.

Revisiting the evolution of interest in quantitative metre and the adaptation of Latin prosodic rules to English linguistic traits, I should mention another notable absence in Webbe's account of contemporary poets and quantifiers: Richard Stanyhurst, who in 1582 published his translation of the *First Foure Bookes of Virgil his Aeneis* which included his experiments in Latin versification. As Attridge (195) has observed, Stanyhurst is a rigorous follower of Latin prosodic rules as traditionally inculcated by grammar school training, and he made 'very few concessions to the native tradition of English verse'. Despite his dogmatism, he was one of the few reformers, along with Sidney, Webbe, and Campion, who seriously attempted to provide English versions of the Latin rules. But Webbe does not seem to have had access to his *Aeneid*, as he does not include him in his account of translators either.

---

[70] Harvey utters: 'I am of Opinion, there is no one more regular and iustifiable direction, eyther for the assured, and infallible Certaintie of our English Artificiall Prosodye particularly, or generally to bring our Language into Arte, and to frame a Grammer of Rhetorike thereof: than first of all vniuersally to agree vpon one and the same Ortographie, in all pointes conformable and proportionate to our Common Natural Prosodye' (ibid.: 464). A few lines below I will develop the connotations that this consensus on the rules implied.

But the one alleged to be the most prolific and successful in his experiments in English hexameter by contemporary critics is Abraham Fraunce (Attridge: 192–94), who published his first quantitative metres in *Lamentations of Amyntas* (1587), a translation of Thomas Watson's Latin poem *Amyntas* (1585). As I have already mentioned, Webbe seems to have read and approved of Fraunce before his poems came to public light, judging by his compliments and his allusion to the works being circulated among the poet's friends; and this again offers Webbe the opportunity implicitly to request the publication of works that he considers key pieces in the consolidation of the English canon or in the development of prosodic reformation (pp. 82–83). As Sidney's protégé, Fraunce follows his master's approach to Latin metres, prone to apply Latin conventions strictly, although unlike any of his predecessors he manages to make his verse sound relatively natural by skilfully combining the demands of quantitative verse with a profusion of repetitive rhetorical figures which, by adding rhythm, prevent his poems from sounding too alien to the natural stresses of traditional accentual poetry (Attridge: 193). Fraunce seems to have been one of the most persuasive and enduring advocates of quantitative metres, especially during the second half of the 1580s, the period in which Spenser and Harvey's interest for this metrical reformation has been argued to have lost momentum. Fraunce left St John's when he was formally admitted to Gray's Inn in June 1583, but there is evidence of his ongoing association with Cambridge colleagues for at least another five years, when he published *Arcadian Rhetorike* (1588) and was called to the Bar. May (38–40) ascribes to Fraunce's direct encouragement the interest that the next generation of Cambridge students like James Reshoulde and Robert Mill (who obtained their B.A. and M.A. respectively from St John's in 1587) took in keeping the experimentation with quantitative metres alive until the '90s, and suggests that Fraunce was the principal promoter of a community of Cantabrigian writers which produced several manuscripts of quantitative and Latin verse, which included, among others, his fellow students Robert Greene and Brian Melbancke (registered in St John's in 1575, B.A in 1580) and the younger Reshould and Mill.[71]

Due to his rural isolation, Webbe might actually have been unaware of the remaining activism around the reformation of verse that was still alive in the mid 80s, for the younger members of St John's, if not for Spenser and Harvey, but I tend to conclude that, besides his probable lack of information, he intentionally aims his demands principally towards those two figures because he considered that, on the one hand, the creation of a common platform of prosody he urges in his preface as the only means of animating the successful consolidation of quantitative metres should be centralised in the poetic examples of the two

---

[71] See Stephen W. May, 'Marlowe, Spenser, Sidney and — Abraham Fraunce?', pp. 34–35.

Cambridge leaders; and on the other, it seems obvious that Webbe sought their attention for some kind of patronage. In this context, Webbe resorts to the debate contained in the Spenser-Harvey correspondence not only to show his public compromise with the controversial use of Latin rules, but also as an attempt to reconcile the apparently conflicted positions of the only two poets able to lead this enterprise towards success.

The principal inconvenience posed by incorporating Latin rules of prosody was commonly noticed by all verse reformers from Drant to Thomas Campion, the last of the Elizabethan poets to contribute to the debate by elaborating his own proposal of prosodic rules in *Observations in the Art of English Poesy* (1602). Like the rest of the reformers, Webbe is aware that Latin rules of prosody — such as position, penultimate syllable, vowel after vowel, or diphthong — would frequently alter the natural accentual pattern of English words, forcing traditional pronunciation to be modified. But the main handicap was caused by the natural structure of English morphology, as the profusion of monosyllables and consonant clusters significantly limited the occurrence of long syllables. Let us remember, for instance, that the Latin rule of position — which the English poets usually considered pre-eminently important above the rest — established that a vowel was long when it preceded two consonants, a double consonant or the letters *I* and *J* followed by a vowel in the same word.[72] However, as Sharon Schuman explains (1977: 339), the length of English vowels is not intrinsically determined by their position within a word, but tends to depend on the type of consonants that surround them.[73] To the incongruities that Latin rules imposed on English verse, we may also add the uncertainty that the Elizabethans demonstrate about the actual nature of syllabic quantity: in Latin, a long syllable requires twice the time of a short one to be pronounced; however, Tudor scholars seem to refer to quantity from a relative disparity of perspectives dependent on whether quantity was considered to be an aural or a visual characteristic. This introduction does not offer the space for a detailed analysis of the diverse approaches to quantity proposed by Tudor quantitative reformers, which Derek Attridge's study (1974) exhaustively accomplishes, in any case; however, to understand Webbe's contribution to the debate, I need briefly to refer to how

---

[72] For a complete account of the Latin rules of prosody see John Carey, *The Latin Prosody Made Easy* (London: Longman, Hurst, Rees and Orme, 1808); and Attridge, chapter 10: 136–62.

[73] Sharon Schuman observes that the *e* in 'bed' is longer than the *e* in 'bet'; she explains that a vowel will be longer or shorter depending on the lightly stressed syllables following it. For instance, the *e* in 'The scéne was beautiful' will be longer than the *e* in 'The scénery was beautiful'. She concludes that: 'Although in Latin syllabic length depends only on vowel quality and postvocalic consonantal combinations, in English the duration of a given syllable changes with its syntactic position: "her" in "I gave her a book" is shorter than the same word in "I couldn't hear her"'. In 'Sixteenth-Century English Quantitative Verse: Its Ends, Means, and Products', *Modern Philology*, 74.4 (May, 1977), 335–49, p. 339.

these uncertainties are in evidence in the Spenser-Harvey correspondence, which is most likely the text that encourages our author's wish to take part in it, not only with the intention of displaying his own interest in the subject, but also in the hope that it would enliven the debate they had initiated but did not conclude.

On the question of whether quantity was a trait to be pronounced or just observed in a verse by Tudor poets, the ambiguity of Spenser's words in his second letter to Harvey proves the confusion around this issue: 'For, why a Gods name may not we, as else the Greekes, haue the kingdome of oure owne Language, and measure the Accentes, by the sounde, reseruing the quantity to the Verse?' (*Variorum* X, 'Letter' III: 16). Spenser utters this despairing self-justification as an answer to Harvey's severe objections ('Letter' II: 442) to some of the lines of his 'Iambicum Trimetrum', arising from the forced pronunciation that Spenser's strict observation of Sidney's rules (derived from Drant's) provokes in these specific cases. Is Spenser therefore urging that quantity should only concern the visual appearance of the lines, which would consequently not affect their original accentual structure when pronounced? Or does he mean, in accordance with the humanist conception of poetry as an elitist activity, that verse should require a different pronunciation from that of common speech?[74]

The main preoccupation in Harvey and Spenser's discussion was how fidelity to Latin prosodic rules should be given precedence over the structural accentual features of the English tongue. Within this context, some scholars, such as Gladys Willcock (1934: 5–6), classified the versifiers into two groups:[75] those who were moderate in their application of Latin rules, like Harvey, and gave pre-eminence to natural stress over imposed quantity; and those who followed Drant (including Sidney and Spenser) whose priority was the strict adoption of the rule of position, thus allowing odd pronunciations for verse. Harvey, on the contrary, expresses in his letters to Spenser his blatant opposition to the violation of the natural accents of English words. Willcock's categorical division implies an assumption that Elizabethan poets took quantity to be an aural feature. By contrast, though, G. L. Hendrickson (1949: 246)[76] argues that English poets conceived quantity to be a visual device and that therefore Spenser was not proposing an anomalous pronunciation, but a distinction between written verse and read verse, and that Latin prosody was a visual convention with the result, in Schuman's words, that 'we are to reserve one kind of pronunciation for speech and another for verse' (342). But Schuman concludes that this categorical division between a visual and an aural conception of quantity does not seem to represent the actual concerns of the poets striving to find a way of adapting the original Latin rules as

---

[74] See Schuman, pp. 341–42.
[75] Gladys Willcock, 'Passing Pitefull Hexameters', *Modern Language Review*, 29.1 (1934), 1–19.
[76] G. L. Hendrickson, 'Elizabethan Quantitative Hexameters', *Philological Quaterly*, 28.2 (1949), 237–60.

appropriately as possible to their language. She argues that they rather adopted both approaches as criteria for elaborating specific English rules, positing therefore both the rule of position (visual version) and the accentual requirements (aural approach) in combination. And it is in this point that the arbitrariness of their efforts is demonstrated. The foremost obstacle of the hexametrists was that if they did not agree on the conventions to be followed to apply Latin rules, the reformation would became impossible or even absurd, because only upon a consensus would they be able to found an elite prosodic system to be appreciated by learned poets and readers (Attridge: 138). Spenser asks Harvey to pass on to him the rules he is using for his own hexameters or, otherwise, to dedicate some time to examining the rules that he (Spenser) is following according to Sidney's commentaries on Drant ('Letter' III: 16); he is obviously eager to find a consensus so that both could work in the same direction. Spenser reproaches Harvey for having departed from Drant's rules whereas Harvey makes a great fuss at the idea of being subjected to rules that imply a violation of natural pronunciation. In his first letter Spenser advocates the distortion of the natural stress arguing that custom would turn this phenomenon into a common feature of English quantitative verse: 'But it is to be wonne with Custome, and rough words must be subdued with Vse' ('Letter' III: 16); although, as mentioned above, reacting to his mentor's rejection of this difference in stress, he claims to want to work in tandem to find a solution.

Webbe's position in this debate is to urge poets to find an intermediate solution to the conflict. He fully trusts the resilience of the English language and the capacity of national poets to adapt by means of practice and labour quantitative metres to their own linguistic scenery. To encourage poets with the prospect of success, he insists on equating the process of metrical refinement that Latin poetry underwent through imitation of Greek metres with the current situation of English prosody:

> For why may I not think so of our English, seeing that among the Romans a long time, yea even till the days of Tully, they esteemed not the Latin poetry almost worth anything in respect of the Greek, as appeareth in the oration *Pro Archia Poeta*, yet afterwards it increased in credit more and more, and that in short space, so that in Virgil's time wherein were they not comparable with the Greeks? (p. 117)

In his preface as well as in the section dedicated to quantitative metres, Webbe insists on one of the main conclusions at which Spenser and Harvey arrive in their letters: that without a consensus about how quantity should be applied, the project cannot work. But whereas Spenser seems to demand Harvey either to follow Drant's rules or the ones Harvey was putting into practice in his own experiments, Harvey is reluctant to subject himself to constrictive rules (either Drant's or his own) and argues that he will have to reflect more in the company of his pillow before daring to consider them prescriptive. Likewise, Harvey insists on his respect for Sidney and Dyer, but does not show much interest in their rules. Webbe seems to take Harvey's position in this regard; his own theoretical approach does not advocate Latin rules as the referent for the verse reformation but is more in tune with Harvey's emphasis on allowing only those devices which do not interfere with the natural accent of words, and so Webbe insists that a true reformation of poetry should involve the elaboration of 'some perfect platform or *prosodia* of versifying ... either in imitation of Greeks and Latins, or, where it would scant abide the touch of their rules, the like observations selected and established by the natural affectation of the speech' ('Preface', p. 63). He is very much concerned to avoid distorting the natural accent, as if he wanted to demonstrate his support of Harvey's firm rejection of any subrogation to foreign rules to the detriment of their vernacular language. He therefore advocates the moderate use of ancient rules according to the natural requirements of English and insists that only poets can create this platform of prosody, because it should not be the product of prescription but of experimentation and practice, with decorum as its sole condition, that is, 'fitting the measures according to the matter' (p. 118). Webbe defends the idea that the first Latin poets did not need rules to follow because their works and experiments were enough to establish a path for the next generations of poets to transform their usages into custom, thus consolidating their national prosody, and once again his arguments recall Harvey's:

> we *Beginners* haue the start, and aduauntage of our Followers, who are to frame and conforme both their examples, and Precepts, according to that President which they haue of vs: as no doubt *Homer* or some other *Greeke*, and *Ennius*, or I know not who else in *Latine*, did preiudice, and ouerrule those, that followed them, as well for the quantities of syllables, as number of feete, and the like: their onely Examples going for current payment, and standing in steade of Lawes, and Rules with the posteritie. ('Letter' V: 464)

So far Webbe does not seem to support, at least in theory, Spenser's view on the extent to which Drant's rules were to be followed; on several occasions, he shows his concern for the preservation of the traditional accentual structure of English words, thus giving the impression at first that quantity is for him a visual feature which should not interfere with proper pronunciation. However, Webbe's practice is not consistent with his theory because the strategies he claims to have followed in his experiments are clearly subjected to the rule of position. In his account of his own experiments, he proposes modifying the spelling of some words to make them fit this rule; and profiting from the flexibility of early modern English orthography, he advocates making natural accent coincide with the requirements of position by modifying the spelling of, for instance, adverbs composed with 'full' ('mournfuly' instead of 'mournfully'), thereby avoiding having to consider the penultimate syllable as long by the rule of position which would result in distortion of natural stress. In addition, Webbe admits that sometimes he felt he could not use the best words because they did not fit the metre, or was unable to avoid middle syllables becoming 'a little wrested' (p. 121). It seems that, as Schuman (345–46) and Attridge (158–59) proposed, for Webbe, as for the other reformers, quantity was an aural property, but was conveniently complemented by visual elements, as in the case of the adverbs just cited. That said, in practice he does not follow his own rule of trying not to create strange pronunciations, and his hexameters result in forced verse. The rules he suggests are reduced to the enumeration of words which present him with a series of problems difficult to solve when it comes to how best to apply Latin rules to syllabic structures exclusive to the English language and which are consequently not encompassed by Latin prescriptive guidelines, as, for instance, in the case of the final *e* in 'able' or 'noble'. In the cases of unwieldy solutions his position is closer to Spenser's, who in the presentation of 'Iambicum Trimetrum' explains that his priority was to achieve lines 'precisely perfect for the feete' and which 'varie not one inch from the Rule' ('Letter' I: 7). Similarly, Webbe acknowledges that he 'in truth did rather always omit the best words and such as would naturally become the speech best than I would commit anything which should notoriously impugn the Latin rules'.

Webbe is clearly conscious of his limitations in contributing to that 'perfect platform of prosody' that should result from a selective and reasoned application of the Latin rules, and so he urges the best English poets to labour in that enterprise. He is aware that his suggestions for avoiding the violation of Latin rules are not true solutions, but modest resources 'which herein I had only for my direction' (ibid.). And when he introduces his translation of Virgil's eclogues he insists on the idea that his approach is only provisional while he awaits 'some more special direction which might lead to a less troublesome manner of writing' (p. 123). And, like Harvey, he thinks that this 'special direction' cannot be achieved by subjugating English verse to the constraints of Latin rules, but from a sort of idealised combination of classical prosody with new vernacular rules that would replace their Latin equivalents in those situations in which natural pronunciation was at stake. This would be a convenient manner of using classical prosody to refine English poetic idiom, and simultaneously of safeguarding the idiosyncrasy of their language: 'But cannot we then, as well as the Latins did, alter the canon of the rule according to the quality of our word, and where our words and theirs will agree, there to jump with them, where they will not agree, there to establish a rule of our own to be directed by?' (p. 118). But Webbe does not seem to have noticed that he was demanding a utopian and unfeasible solution.

5. The Present Edition

This modern-spelling edition of Webbe's *A Discourse of English Poetry* collates its copy text, the 1586 quarto (Q), with the old-spelling editions by Arber, Haslewood and Smith. I have used the EEBO digitalized text of the quarto preserved at the Huntington Library. I have consulted and contrasted the two extant copies at the Huntington Library and at the Bodleian Library, Oxford. No variants between the two copies have been found.

This edition of William Webbe's *A Discourse of English Poetry* is the result of collating the text of its only original edition with those by Arber, Haslewood and Smith. It has been regularized according to present-day standards. Archaic printing conventions like i/j and u/v have been regularized to modern standards. Punctuation and paragraphing are mostly editorial, although these have not been included in the textual notes. Capitalization and italization have been regularized too: therefore, proper names do not appear in italics, except for titles, and I have only kept the capital letters for those nouns that stand for personifications like 'Lady Learning'. Abbreviations, macrons and the ampersand have been expanded and numerals have been turned into letters. Likewise, I have dissolved æ and œ. Obsolete or archaic words like 'spake' have not been modernized.

Present-day 'wrote' appears as 'wrote', 'writt', 'wryt', 'wrytte', 'writ': while the first has been kept, the others have been regularized to 'writ', which, according to *OED*, is the most stable historical form from Middle English to the eighteenth century.

In order to regularize the indistinct usage of 'trauell' and 'trauayl' I have adopted 'travel', as it is the most frequent form. The names of metrical feet are given in the Latin version in their first occurrence in the text, and have been modernized and regularized in the subsequent usages.

Greek and Latin names have been regularized when given in Anglicized form ('Virgill' and 'Virgyl' become 'Virgil'; 'Terens', 'Terence' and 'Plinie', 'Pliny'); they have also been expanded when given in abbreviated form in the original ('Sex. Propert.' appears now as 'Sextus Propertius'). However, when the Latinized forms are given, they have been kept so, like 'Hesiodus', 'Lucretius', 'Statius', etc. A similar procedure has been followed with the titles of ancient works. When Webbe's version seems to be an attempt to Anglicize, I have regularized them ('*Tusculane* questions' becomes '*Tusculan Questions*'). However, when titles are provided in their early modern Latin versions, I have regularized them, but kept them as they are given ('*de arte Poetica*' is kept as '*De Arte Poetica*', '*De fastis*' as '*De Fastis*' and '*Tristibus*' stands for '*Tristia*'). In the case of Homer's *Iliad*, which appears in two different Latinized forms (twice as '*Iliads*' and once as '*Iliades*'), I have adopted '*Iliads*' as it is the most frequent form. The Latinized forms *Odissea* as well as *Aeneidos* have been kept too.

The abbreviations of the names of English authors have always been expanded, except when the initials stand for unknown or uncertain identities and in the particular case of 'Sp.', for the obvious reason of maintaining the coherence with the alleged anonymity of the *Calendar*.

Errors in the Latin texts were generally not corrected by the previous editors. I have silently amended them in all cases following the versions given in the Loeb Classical Library, only bringing to the textual notes those which I have considered to be Webbe's own errors or the specific case of 'habeo', which is originated in E.K's gloss to 'May', quoted by Webbe. Greek and Latin citations and quotes do also follow Loeb's texts and translations.

I have adopted *The Shepherds' Calendar* for the original *The Shepheardes Calender* as I consider that the plural form has greater coherence with the almanac of eclogues uttered by several shepherds in diverse moods and stanzas than *The Shepherd's Calendar*; the example of the only modern-spelling edition by Brooks-Davies has helped me to confirm my decision. As regards Spenser's texts, they have been collated with the editions of 1579, 1581 and 1586. In several occasions, Webbe (or the printer) alters the readings of Spenser's quartos, although archaisms are faithfully reproduced. In those cases, I have always amended Webbe in accordance with Q_1. Variants from other re-editions are registered in the textual notes. Unlike with Elyot's or Phaer's quotes, for which I have sometimes considered appropriate to keep Webbe's choices, with Spenser my decision of amending all variants obeys the fact that the *Calendar* has a present canonical reading authorized by modern editions, which is not the case of Elyot's or Phaer's texts. In order to be coherent with Webbe's intention to present the *Calendar* as a model for poets, I have found it fundamental to offer the versions of the original edition. Modernization also affects Spenser's texts in punctuation and spelling; for this task I have found very useful examples in Brooks-Davies' modern-spelling edition; however, I have not followed him in all his choices, as for instance the usage of the hyphen. Quotes from the *Calendar* and references to lines or pages used in the introduction or in the footnotes follow Brooks-Davies' text. Likewise, in these two aforementioned contexts quotations from Sidney's *Defence* and Puttenham's *The Art* — the main texts used for contrast with Webbe's — follow Gavin Alexander's and Frank Whigham and Wayne E. Rebhorn's modern-spelling editions respectively in accordance with my will to provide a text available for a wide range of readers. For the rest of the Tudor works for which there are no modernized editions, I have generally used either the most recent and authorized texts or, in specific cases, the first editions. In the particular case of Elyot's *The Governour*, I have directly quoted from Stephen Croft's text, and for *The Schoolmaster* from William Aldis Wright's, both original-spelling editions. The five letters between Harvey and Spenser are quoted from the tenth volume of the *Variorum* edition, where Harvey's letters appear as an appendix; for other works by Harvey I have used the complete works edited by Grosart.

Elyot's translations of the classical poets or the passages from Phaer's *Aeneid* have been collated with their early editions previous to the publication of *A Discourse*. In the case of *The Governour*, the texts of 1531 and 1580; for Phaer, those of 1573 and 1584. The editing of these quotes has posed one of the most problematic points, as Webbe's text includes frequent emendations or printing errors. I have decided to revert Q's readings to their originals in those cases when I have considered them likely to be printing errors, using for that purpose the first quartos of both works. In contrast, in the few occasions in which I have interpreted these variants as purposeful emendations by the author, aimed at improving the style or the accuracy of the translations, I have kept Q's versions. The collation of the quartos appears in the textual notes, or I give an extended explanation of my choice in a footnote when needed. The same procedure has been followed for occasional quotes from Arthur Golding's *Metamorphoses*, Barnaby Googe's *The Zodiake of Life* or *The Paradise of Dainty Devices*.

Webbe's translation into quantitative verse of Virgil's eclogues and his Sapphic version of Spenser's song to Elisa have also been modernized, although I have maintained archaisms like 'belovde', 'evne' or 'araisde', and abbreviations like 'cor'nation' so as to avoid modifying what seems to be Webbe's purposeful modification of spelling in order to stick to the Latin rules of prosody.

Glossary entries for obsolete, archaic and uncommon words have been provided at the end of the text after the textual notes and have been indicated in the text with superscript circles.

A Discourse of English Poetry

[A1ʳ] # A DISCOURSE OF ENGLISH POETRY

Together with the Author's judgement touching the reformation of our English verse.

By William Webbe, Graduate. Imprinted at London, by John Charlewood for Robert Walley. 1586.

[A2ʳ] *To the right, worshipful, learned, and most gentle gentleman, my very good master, Master[i] Edward Sulyard, Esquire, William Webbe wisheth his heart's desire.*

May it please you, sir, this once more to bear with my rudeness in presenting unto your view another slender conceit[1] of my simple capacity, wherein, although I am not able to bring you anything which is meet° to detain you from your more[ii] serious matters, yet upon my knowledge of your former courtesy and your favourable countenance° towards all enterprises of learning, I dare make bold to crave your accustomed patience in turning over some of these few leaves, which I shall account a greater recompense than the writing thereof may deserve.

The firm hope of your wonted gentleness, not any good liking of my own labour, made me thus presumptuously to crave your worship's patronage for my poor book. A pretty [A2ᵛ] answer is reported by some[2] to be made by Apelles to King Alexander, who in disport,° taking up one of his pencils to draw a line, and asking the painter's judgement of his draught:° "it is done" quoth Apelles, "like a king," meaning indeed it was drawn as he pleased but was nothing less than good workmanship. Myself in like sort, taking upon me to make a draught of English poetry, and requesting your worship's censure° of the same, you will perhaps give me this verdict: "it was done like a scholar", meaning "as I could", but indeed more like to a learner than one through° grounded in poetical workmanship.

Alexander, in drawing his line, leaned sometimes too hard, otherwhile° too soft, as never having been apprentice to the art. I, in drawing this poetical discourse, make it somewhere too straight, leaving out the chief colours and ornaments of poetry, in another place too wide, stuffing in pieces little pertinent to true poetry, as one never acquainted with the learned Muses. What then? As

---

[1] another slender conceit] Webbe had previously presented to Sulyard a translation of Virgil's *Georgics* composed 'two or three years' before the present text, as we learn from his several allusions to it. The date of composition oscillates between 1584 and 1585: 'I bestowed some time in it two or three years since' (pp. 104–05 below). No manuscript of his *Georgics* has been preserved and there exists no other allusion to this work by contemporary scholars. Thomas Warton includes Webbe in his list of English translators of classical poetry, mentioning his *Georgics* and his two *Bucolics*, the latter included in *A Discourse* (Warton, *The History of English Poetry*, pp. 400–04).

[2] reported by some] Alexander's artistic incompetence was a literary topos. Although many anecdotes had been provided by Latin historians, the one Webbe mentions here has not been located as such in any of the possible sources. See Pliny, *Natural History*, 35.36, 85–87 and Aelian, *Historical Miscellany*, 2.3. Aelian was translated by Abraham Fleming: *A Registre of Hystories* (London: for Thomas Woodcocke, 1576).

he, being a king, might meddle in what science him listed,° though therein he had no skill, so I, being a learner, will try my cunning in some parts of learning, though never so simple.

Now, as for my saucy pressing upon your expected favour in craving your judgement, I beseech you let me make this excuse: that whereas true gentility did never withdraw her loving affection from lovely[iii] Lady Learning,[3] so I am persuaded that your worship cannot choose but continue your wonted favourable benignity towards all the endeavourers to learning, of which corporation I do indeed profess myself one silly° member.

For, sith° the writers of all ages have sought as an undoubted bulwark° and steadfast safeguard the patronage of nobility (a shield as sure as can be to learning) wherein to shroud [A3ʳ] and safely place their several inventions, why should not I seek some harbour for my poor travel° to rest and stay upon, being of itself unable to shift the carping cavils° and biting scorns of lewd° controllers?

And in truth, where might I rather choose a sure defence and ready refuge for the same than where I see perfect gentility and nobleness of mind to be fast linked with excellency of learning and affable courtesy? Moreover, add this to the end of mine excuse: that I send it into your sight not as any witty piece of work that may delight you, but being a sleight somewhat compiled for recreation in the intermissions of my daily business (even this summer evenings)[iv] as a token of that earnest and unquenchable desire I have to show myself dutiful and well-willing towards you. Whereunto I am continually inflamed more and more when I consider either your favourable friendship used towards myself, or your gentle countenance° showed to my simple travels.° The one I have tried in that homely translation[4] I presented unto you; the other I find true in your courteous putting to my trust and doing me so great honesty and credit with the charge of these toward° young gentlemen your sons.[5]

To which pregnant imps of right excellent hope[6] I would I were able, or you might have occasion, to make trial of my loving mind, who should well perceive myself to remain unto them a faithful and trusty Achates,[7] even so far as my

---

[3] Lady Learning] The fondness of noblemen for literature is a commonplace in Tudor defences of poetry. See also pp. 68–69 below; Sidney, *Defence*, pp. 40–42; Puttenham, *The Art*, 1.16. In his account of English poets, Webbe argues that learning had been traditionally esteemed in England since the times of William of Normandy; he mentions Henry I as its earlier favourer; see p. 78 below.

[4] homely translation] his translation of Virgil's *Georgics*; see note 1 above.

[5] your sons] Webbe was the tutor — probably in classical literature — of Sulyard's two sons, Edward and Thomas, from 1583 or 1584 (he mentions having presented to Sulyard his translation of the *Georgics* 'two or three years since' on p. 105 below) until at least the summer of 1586, when *A Discourse* was written.

[6] pregnant imps ... hope] their skills anticipate brilliant careers as adults.

[7] Achates] Aeneas' faithful friend, referred by Virgil as 'fidus Achates'; see *Aeneid*, 1.188; 1.312; 1.469; 3.523; 4.34; 8.466.

wealth, my woe, my power or peril, my pen or wit, my health or life may serve to search mine ability.

Huge heaps of words I might pile together to trouble you withal, either of myself or of my doings (as some do), or of your worship's commendable virtues (as the most do); but I purposely choose rather to let pass the spreading [A3ᵛ] of that worthy fame which you have ever deserved than to run in suspicion of fawning flattery, which I ever abhorred.

Therefore, once again craving your gentle pardon and patience in your overlooking this rude epistle, and wishing more happiness than my pen can express to you and your whole retinue, I rest

Your worship's faithful servant,
William Webbe.ᵛ

[A4r] # A PREFACE TO THE NOBLE POETS OF ENGLAND

Among the innumerable sorts of English books and infinite fardels° of printed pamphlets wherewith this country is pestered,° all shops stuffed,[8] and every study furnished, the greatest part I think in any one kind are such as are either mere poetical or which tend in some respect (as either in matter or form) to poetry. Of such books, therefore, sith° I have been one that have had a desire to read not the fewest, and because it is an argument which men of great learning have no leisure to handle, or at the least,[i] having to do with more serious matters, do least regard, if I write something concerning what I think of our English poets, or adventure to set down my simple judgement of English poetry, I trust the learned poets will give me leave and vouchsafe my book passage, as being for the rudeness thereof no prejudice to their noble studies, but even, as my intent is, an *instar cotis*[9] to stir up some other of meet° ability to bestow travel° in this matter; whereby I think we may not only get the means which we yet want to discern between good writers and bad, but perhaps also challenge from the rude multitude of rustical rhymers,[10] who will be called poets, the right practice and orderly course of true poetry.[ii]

It is to be wondered at of all, and is lamented of many, that whereas all kind of good learning have aspired to royal dignity and stately grace in our English tongue, being not only founded, defended, maintained, and enlarged, but also purged from faults, weeded of errors, and polished from barbarousness by men of great authority [A4v] and judgement, only poetry hath found fewest friends

---

[8] all shops stuffed] Ascham, *Schoolmaster*, p. 290 (Aldis, 1904): 'And shoppes in London should not be so full of lewd and rude rymes, as commolie they are'.

[9] *instar cotis*] 'instar' (adv. Lat.): like, in the manner of; 'cotis' (n. gen. Lat.): 'cos, cotis', sharpening stone. Webbe means that his words should act as a sharpening stone so as to incite the poets to work hard in the reformation of poetry. In Alexander Neckam's *De Naturis Rerum* (12th century) we find an example of this usage: 'Multi sunt qui instar cotis alios exacuunt, sed ipsi non efficiuntur acuti', chapter 9 (There are many men who incite others like a sharpening stone, but they themselves are not sharpened enough [*my translation*]).

[10] rustical rhymers] Webbe assimilates Ascham's conception of rhyme as a rustic and barbarous device. Ascham, *Schoolmaster*, pp. 289, 290, 292: 'our rude beggerly ryming', 'lewd and rude rymes', 'rude barbariousnesse in ryming'. Spenser-Harvey, 'Letter' I: 'balde rhymers' (*The Works of Edmund Spenser: A Variorum Edition. The Prose Works*, ed. by Edwin Greenlaw and others, 11 vols. Baltimore: The Johns Hopkins University Press, 1949, X, p. 6); Spenser, *SC*, 'Dedicatory epistle', 119: 'rakehelly rout of our ragged rhymers' (Brooks-Davies, p. 22); see also Puttenham, *The Art*, 1.6.

to amend it: those that can, reserving their skill to themselves; those that cannot, running headlong upon it, thinking to garnish it with their devices,[11] but more corrupting it with fantastical errors. What should be the cause that our English speech in some of the wisest men's judgements hath never attained to any sufficient ripeness, nay not fully avoided the reproach of barbarousness in poetry? The rudeness of the country or baseness of wits? Or the coarse dialect of the speech?[12] Experience utterly disproveth it to be any of these. What then? Surely the cankered enmity of curious custom which, as it never was great friend to any good learning, so in this hath it grounded in the most such a negligent persuasion of an impossibility in matching the best, that the finest wits and most divine heads have contented themselves with a base kind of fingering, rather debasing their faculties in setting forth their skill in the coarsest manner than, for breaking custom, they would labour to adorn their country and advance their style with the highest and most learnedest top of true poetry.[13] The rudeness or unaptness of our country to be either none or no hindrance, if reformation were made accordingly, the exquisite excellency in all kinds of good learning now flourishing among us, inferior to none other nation, may sufficiently declare.

That there be as sharp and quick wits in England as ever were among the peerless Grecians or renowned[iii] Romans, it were a note of no wit at all in me to deny. And is our speech so coarse, or our phrase so harsh, that poetry cannot therein find a vein whereby it may appear like itself? Why should we think so basely of this, rather than of her sister, I mean, rhetorical elocution? [B1ʳ] Which, as they were by birth twins, by kind the same, by original° of one descent,[14] so

---

[11] devices] Sir Egerton Brydges (1810) interprets this as an allusion to *The Paradise of Dainty Devices* (1576) in S. E. Brydges, ed., *The Paradise of Dainty Devices*, (London: Robert Triphook and William Sancho, 1810), 'Preface', pp. xxiii–xiv.

[12] What should be [...] speech?] This was a generalized concern among the Elizabethan scholars, who agreed that English poetic eloquence had not yet reached the ripeness of the Italian or French, but remained stalled in medieval rudeness. Spenser, *SC*, 'Dedicatory Epistle', 82–85: 'that our mother tongue (which truly of itself is both full enough for prose and stately enough for verse) hath long time been counted most bare and barren of both' (Brooks-Davies, p. 21). Sidney, *Defence*, p. 4: 'poor Poetry, which from almost the highest estimation of learning is fallen to be the laughing-stoke of children'; and 7: 'poetrie, which is among us thrown down to so ridiculous an estimation'.

[13] finest wits [...] true poetry] Like Ascham, Webbe ascribes the rudeness of English poetry to the use of simple poetic devices like rhyme ('base kind of fingering') in contrast to the refined quantitative metres of classical poetry ('the highest and most learned top of true poetry'). Ascham, *Schoolmaster*, p. 289: 'if soch good wittes, and forward diligence, had bene directed to follow the best examples, and not have bene caryed by tyme and custome, to content themselues with that barbarous and rude Ryming'. For further information about the cultural implications of the debate on rhyme and quantitative verse see Derek Attridge, *Well-Weighed Syllables*, pp. 89–124 and chapters 7 and 8.

[14] her sister [...] one descent] Elocution was one of the five parts of classical rhetoric (invention, disposition, elocution, memory, pronunciation) according to Cicero (*De Oratore*) and

no doubt, as eloquence hath found such favourers in the English tongue[15] as she frequenteth not any more gladly, so would poetry, if there were the like welcome and entertainment given her by our English poets, without question aspire to wonderful perfection and appear far more gorgeous and delectable among us. Thus much I am bold to say in behalf of poetry; not that I mean to call in question the reverend and learned works of poetry written in our tongue by men of rare judgement and most excellent poets, but even as it were by way of supplication to the famous and learned laureate masters of England, that they would but consult one half hour with their heavenly muse what credit they might win to their native speech, what enormities they might wipe out of English poetry, what a fit vein they might frequent, wherein to show forth their worthy faculties if English poetry were truly reformed, and some perfect platform or *prosodia* of versifying were by them ratified and set down, either in imitation of Greeks and Latins, or, where it would scant° abide the touch of their rules, the like observations selected and established by the natural affectation of the speech.[16] Thus much I say, not to persuade you that are the favourers of English poetry, but to move it to you, being not the first that have thought upon this matter,[17] but one that by consent of others have taken upon me to lay it once again in your ways, if perhaps you may stumble upon it and chance to look so low from your divine cogitations,° when your muse mounteth to the stars and ransacketh° the spheres of heaven, whereby perhaps you may take compassion of noble poetry, pitifully mangled and defaced [B1ᵛ] by rude smatterers and barbarous imitators of your worthy studies. If the motion be worthy your regard, it is enough to move it. If not, my words would simply prevail in persuading you, and therefore I rest upon this only request: that of your courtesies you will grant passage, under your favourable corrections, for

---

Quintilian (*Institutio Oratoria*); it was originally considered the main ground of coincidence between rhetoric and poetry. Aristotle and Cicero observed that the only difference between poetic and rhetoric style was metre, whereas rhythm and metaphor — although being more essential in poetry — were also relevant devices in oratory. See Donald Lemen Clark, *Rhetoric and Poetry in the Renaissance: A Study of Rhetorical Terms in English Renaissance Literary Criticism* (New York: Columbia University Press, 1922), pp. 35–37 and 73.

[15] eloquence [...] English tongue] Likely referring to John Lyly, whose *Euphues* (1578) Webbe praises below. See pp. 95–96 and note 115 below.

[16] perfect platform [...] speech] Prosody was one of the traditional four parts of grammar; the study of the rules of prosody, which determined the quantity of Latin syllables, was a primary discipline in Elizabethan education. The extent to which Latin rules of quantity had to be followed in the composition of quantitative English metres was a common subject of debate among the Elizabethan reformers of verse. On this debate see Spenser-Harvey, *Letters* (1580); see also Attridge, *Well-Weighed Syllables*, pp. 138–42, 152–58.

[17] being not [...] matter: Webbe's main sources on this matter are Ascham's *Schoolmaster* (1570), Gascoigne's *Certain Notes of Instruction* (1575) and Spenser and Harvey's *Letters* (1580).

this my simple censure° of English poetry wherein, if you please to run it over, you shall know briefly mine opinion of the most part of our[iv] accustomed poets, and, particularly in his place, the little somewhat which I have sifted out of my weak brain concerning this reformed versifying.

William Webbe[v]

[B2ʳ] A DISCOURSE OF ENGLISH POETRY

Intending to write some discourse of English poetry, I think it not amiss° if I speak something generally of poetry, as what it is, whence it had the beginning, and of what estimation it hath always been and ought to be among all sorts of people. Poetry, called in Greek ποετρια, being derived from the verb ποίεω, which signifieth in Latin *facere*, in English 'to make', may properly be defined the art of making.¹⁸ Which word, as it hath always been especially used of the best of our English poets to express the very faculty of speaking or writing poetically, so doth it indeed contain most fitly the whole grace and property of the same, the more fully and effectually than any other English verb. That poetry is an art (or rather a more excellent thing than can be contained within the compass of art), though I need not stand long to prove, both the witness of Horace, who wrote *De Arte Poetica*,ⁱ and of Terence, who calleth it *artem musicam*,¹⁹ and the very natural property thereof may sufficiently declare. The beginning of it, as appeareth by Plato, was of a virtuous and most devout purpose, who witnesseth that, by occasion of meeting of a great company of young men to solemnize the feasts which were called *Panegyrica*,ⁱⁱ and were wont to be celebrated every fifth year there, they that were most pregnant in wit, [B2ᵛ] and indued° with great gifts of wisdom and knowledge in music above the rest, did use commonly to make

---

¹⁸ ποετρια] Webbe gives an erroneous etymology for 'poetry' (in Greek ποίησις, *poiesis*); it is a Greek letter version of the Latin word *poetria* ('poetess', derived from ποιήτρία); this Latin word had been coined by Geoffrey de Vinsauf in *Nova Poetria*, c. 1200. See G. Gregory Smith, ed., *Elizabethan Critical Essays*, 2 vols, I (London: Oxford University Press, 1904), p. 408, note 230.6. In several occasions Webbe acknowledges to be better instructed in Latin than in Greek studies.

¹⁹ *artem musicam*] Terence, *Phormio*, 'Prologue' 16–17: 'in medio omnibus/palmam esse possitam qui artem tractant musicam' ('competition for the prize is open to all followers of dramatic art'). In Spenser, *SC*, gloss to 'December' ('music'): 'that is, poetry, as Terence saith: *Qui artem tractant musicam* (speaking of poets)'. Puttenham, *The Art*, 2.11: 'This proportion consisteth in placing of every verse in a staff or ditty by such reasonable distances as may best serve the ear for delight, and also show the poet's art and variety of music'. The association of poetry to music was a commonplace among the Elizabethans and was linked to the search for proportion and symmetry in all things as analogies of the cosmic harmony created by God. Quantitative metre, subject to exact proportions and patterns, provided a fit ground to attain perfect harmony. In *Observations in the Arte of English Poesie* (1602) Thomas Campion explains the relevance of observing quantity in verse: 'The world is made by Simmetry and proportion, and is in that respect compared to Musick, and Musick to Poetry: for Terence saith, speaking of Poets, *artem qui tractant musica*, confounding Musick and Poesy together. What musick can there be where there is no proportion observed?' (Smith II, p. 329). See Attridge, *Well-Weighed Syllables*, pp. 115–16.

goodly verses, measured according to the sweetest notes of music, containing the praise of some noble virtue, or of immortality, or of some such thing of greatest estimation, which unto them seemed so heavenly and joyous a thing that, thinking such men to be inspired with some divine instinct from heaven, they called them *vates*. So when other among them of the finest wits and aptest capacities began in imitation of these to frame ditties of lighter matters and tuning them to the stroke° of some of the pleasantest kind of music, then began there to grow a distinction and great diversity between makers and makers. Whereby (I take it) began this difference: that they which handled in the audience of the people grave and necessary matters were called wise men or eloquent men, which they meant by *vates*, and the rest which sang of love matters or other lighter devices alluring unto pleasure and delight were called *poetae*, or makers.[20] Thus it appeareth both eloquence and poetry to have had their beginning and original° from these exercises, being framed in such sweet measure of sentences and pleasant harmony called *'ρυθμός*,[iii][21] which is an apt composition of words or clauses, drawing as it were by force the hearers' ears[iv] even whether soever it listeth,° that Plato affirmeth therein to be contained *γοητεία*,[v] an enchantment, as it were to persuade them anything whether they would or no.[22] And here-hence is said that men were first withdrawn from a wild and savage kind of life to civility and gentleness,[23] and the right knowledge of humanity by the force of this measurable or tuneable speaking.

---

[20] The beginning of it [...] makers] From Spenser, *SC*, gloss to 'October' ('to restrain'); E.K. erroneously cites Plato's *Laws* 1 as a source, although the story is rather made up from diverse commonplaces (Brooks-Davies, pp. 166–67). Webbe's distinction between '*vates*' and '*poetae* or makers' on the grounds of the gravity of matter is due to his particular interpretation of E.K.'s account and has no precedent. For E.K. '*vatem*' evolved into '*poets or makers*' once their verses incorporated lighter subjects and melodies. Webbe links *vates* to Cicero's philosophical concept of the orator ('wise men or eloquent men'). On *vates* for 'poet' see Thomas Elyot, *Governour*, 1.13 (Croft I, 1883); Sidney, *Defence*, pp. 6 and 11; *videntes* in Puttenham, *The Art*, 1.3. On the origin of poetry see also Aristotle, *Poetics*, 4.
[21] *'ρυθμός*] On the evolution of the Greek term *rithmos* into 'rhyme' and 'rhythm' with the meanings of 'rhyming line-ends' and either 'quantitative proportion' or 'accentual regularity' respectively, see Attridge, *Well-Weighed Syllables*, pp. 94–95. See also Puttenham, *The Art*, 2.3, 2.6 and Webbe p. 106 below. For them the common use of the word *rhyme* is abusive, as its original meaning is related to proportion of words and syllables. Attridge observes that neither of them seems to be certain about the nature of this proportion that they associate to *rithmos*, although it certainly implies absence of rhyme.
[22] Plato [...] or no] *The Republic*, 10.4. According to Neil Rhodes 'witchcraft' is the usual translation for *goēteia*; he quotes Webbe as one of the few Elizabethans who cites Plato regarding the magical coerciveness of poetry and rhetoric and observes that this conception is at odds with their links to philosophy. Neil Rhodes, *The Power of Eloquence and English Renaissance Literature* (New York: St Martin's Press, 1992), p. 7.
[23] civility and gentleness] The Elizabethan emphasis on the civilizing power of poetry coexists with the idea of its magical influence on the listeners; this duality is usually grounded on the myth of Orpheus. See Rhodes, ibid. chapter 1.

This opinion shall you find confirmed throughout the whole works of Plato and Aristotle. And that such was the estimation of this poetry at those times, that they supposed all wisdom and knowledge to be included mystically in that divine instinction,° wherewith they thought their *vates* to be inspired. Whereupon, throughout the noble works of those most excellent philosophers before named, are the authorities of poets very often alleged. And Cicero in his *Tusculan Questions*[vi][24] [B3ʳ] is of that mind that a poet cannot express verses abundantly, sufficiently and fully, neither his eloquence can flow pleasantly, or his words sound well and plenteously without celestial instinction,°[25] which poets themselves do very often and gladly witness of themselves, as namely Ovid in sixth *Fasto:*

Est deus in nobis; agitante calescimus[vii] *illo,* etc.[26]

Whereunto I doubt not equally to adjoin the authority of our late famous English poet, who wrote *The Shepherds' Calendar,* where lamenting the decay of poetry at these days, saith most sweetly to the same:[27]

---

[24] *Tusculan Questions*] *Tusculan Disputations,* 1.26: 'ut ego aut poëtam grave plenumque carmen sine caelesti aliquo mentis instinctu' ('or suffer me to think that the poet pours out his solemn, swelling strain without some heavenly inspiration'); and in *Pro Archia Poeta,* 8.18: 'quasi divino quodam spiritu inflari' ('infused with a strange supernatural inspiration').
[25] celestial instinction] Webbe paraphrases Elyot, *Governour,* 1.13: 'as it shall be manifest to them that shall be so fortunate to rede the noble warkes of Plato and Aristotle, wherin he shall fynde the autoritie of poetes frequently alleged; ye and that more is, in poetes was supposed to be science misticall and inspired, and therfore in latine they were called *Vates,* which worde signifyeth as moche as prophetes. And therfore Tulli in his Tusculane questyons supposeth that a poete can nat abundantly expresse verses sufficient and complete, or that his eloquence may flowe without labour wordes wel sounyng and plentuouse, without celestiall instinction'. The divine origin of the poet's inspiration is a commonplace among the Elizabethans. On this topic Sidney quotes Plato, *Ion,* 534 (*Defence,* p. 40). See also Spenser, *SC,* 'Argument' to 'October'; Sidney, *Defence,* pp. 9–10; Puttenham, *The Art,* 1.1; and Thomas Lodge, *Defence of Poetry* (1579), ll. 7–10 (Smith II).
[26] Fasto [...] etc.] *Fasti,* 6.5. From Spenser, *SC,* emblem to 'October' (Brooks-Davies, p. 166); E.K.'s gloss to this emblem: 'Hereby is meant, as also in the whole course of this egloque, that poetry is a divine instinct and unnatural rage passing the reach of common reason' (ibid., p. 171).
[27] Whereunto [...] the same] Webbe avoids mentioning Spenser's name throughout the whole treatise in order to preserve his anonymity as the author of *SC;* although his identity was known in academic circles, there is no evidence of its public circulation until Fraunce's casual allusion in *The Arcadian Rhetorike* (1588). See Kathrine Koller, "Abraham Fraunce and Edmund Spenser", *ELH,* 7.2 (1940), 108–20. Webbe's reference to Cicero, Ovid and Spenser is reproduced *verbatim* by Francis Meres in *Palladis Tamia* (1598), p. 313 (Smith II); but Meres adds an explicit mention of Spenser's authorship, which was already a public fact when he wrote this treatise.

> Then make thee wings of thine aspiring wit,
> And, whence thou camest, fly back to heaven apace, etc.[28]

Whose fine poetical wit, and most exquisite learning, as he showed abundantly in that piece of work, in my judgement inferior to the works neither of Theocritus in Greek, nor Virgil in Latin, whom he narrowly imitateth; so I nothing doubt, but if his other works were common abroad, which are as I think in the close custody of certain his friends, we should have of our own poets whom we might match in all respects with the best. And among all other his works whatsoever, I would wish to have the sight of his *English Poet*,[29] which his friend E.K. did once promise to publish, which, whether he performed or not, I know not. If he did, my hap° hath not been so good as yet to see it.[30]

But, to return to the estimation of poetry, besides[viii] the great and profitable fruits contained in poetry for the instruction of manners and precepts of good life (for that was chiefly respected in the first age of poetry),[31] this is also added to the eternal commendations° of that noble faculty: that kings and princes, great and famous men, did ever encourage, maintain, and reward poets in all ages, because they were thought only to have the whole power in their hands of making men either immortally famous for their valiant exploits and virtuous exercises, or perpetually infamous for their vicious lives. Whereupon it is said of Achilles that this only vantage [B3ᵛ] he had of Hector: that it was his fortune to be extolled and renowned[ix] by the heavenly verse of Homer. And, as Tully recordeth to be written of Alexander, that with natural tears he wept over Achilles' tomb in joy

---

[28] Then [...] etc.] Spenser, *SC*, 'October', 79–84: 'O peerless Poesy, where is then the place?/If nor in prince's palace thou do sit/ (And yet is prince's palace the most fit),/ Ne breast of baser birth doth thee embrace,/ Then make thee wings of thine aspiring wit/ And, whence thou camest, fly back to heaven apace' (Brooks-Davies, pp. 163–64).

[29] *English Poet*] Spenser, *SC*, 'Argument' to 'October': 'as the author hereof elsewhere at large discourseth in his book called *The English Poet* — which book, being lately come to my hands, I mind also by God's grace upon further advisement to publish' (Brooks-Davies, p. 159). For further references see also Smith I, p. 408, note 232.21. Webbe mentions it again below, along with other not extant works by Spenser like *Dreams, Legends, Court of Cupid*; see note 81 below.

[30] Whose fine [...] see it] Laurie Magnus and Andrew Hadfield point out that this passage seems to be a direct answer to Sidney's objection to the 'rustic language' of *SC*, but there is no evidence in *A Discourse* of Webbe having had access to the manuscript of *The Defence of Poesy*, which was circulating among literary circles before its publication in 1595. Laurie Magnus, *Documents Illustrating Elizabethan Poetry* (London: George Routledge and Sons Ltd.; New York: E. P. Dutton and Co., 1906), p. 201, note 3. Andrew Hadfield, *Edmund Spenser: A Life*, 2012, p. 129. Sidney, *Defence*, p. 44: '*The Shepheardes Calender* hath much poetry in his eclogues, indeed worthy the reading, if I be not deceived. That same framing of his style to an old rustic language I dare not allow, since neither Theocritus in Greek, Virgil in Latin, nor Sannazaro in Italian did affect it'.

[31] the great [...] poetry] Ascham's Ciceronian view of the arts of *oratio* as an instrument to improve courtliness and humanity. On the Elizabethan conception of Ciceronian *humanitas* see Mike Pincombe, *Elizabethan Humanism* (Harlow: Longman, 2001), chapter 2, pp. 15–37.

that he conceived at the consideration how it was his hap° to be honoured with so divine a work as Homer's was. Aristotle, a most prudent and learned philosopher, being appointed schoolmaster to the young Prince Alexander, thought no work so meet° to be read unto a king as the work of Homer, wherein the young Prince being by him instructed thoroughly, found such wonderful delight in the same when he came to maturity, that he would not only have it with him in all his journeys, but in his bed also under his pillow to delight him and teach him both nights and days. The same is reported of noble Scipio, who, finding the two books of Homer in the spoil of King Darius, esteemed them as wonderful precious jewels, making one of them his companion for the night, the other for the day. And not only was he thus affected to that one piece or part of poetry, but so generally he loved the professors thereof, that in his most serious affairs and hottest wars against Numantia and Carthage he could no whit° be without that old poet Ennius in his company. But to speak of all those noble and wise princes who bare° special favour and countenance° to poets were tedious, and would require a rehearsal° of all such in whose time there grew any to credit and estimation in that faculty. Thus far therefore may suffice for the estimation of poets.[32] Now I think most meet° to speak somewhat concerning what hath been the use of poetry, and wherein it rightly consisted, and whereof consequently it obtained such estimation.

To begin therefore with the first that was first worthily memorable in the excellent gift of poetry, the best writers agree that it was Orpheus, who by the sweet gift of his heavenly poetry, withdrew men from ranging uncertainly and wandering brutishly about, and made them gather together and keep company, make houses, and keep[x] fellowship together, who therefore is reported, as Horace saith, to assuage the [B4ʳ] fierceness of tigers and move the hard flints. After him was Amphion, who was the first that caused cities to be built, and men therein to live decently and orderly according to law and right. Next was Tyrtaeus, who began to practise warlike defences, to keep back enemies and save themselves from invasion of foes. In this place I think were most convenient to rehearse° that ancient poet Pindarus. But of the certain time wherein he flourished I am not very certain. But of the place where he continued most, it should seem to be the city of Thebes, by Pliny, who reporteth that Alexander, in sacking the same

---

[32] Whereupon [...] of poets] From Spenser, *SC*, gloss to 'October' ('For ever'); Webbe misreads E.K. and erroneously ascribes Scipio instead of Alexander the spoil of King Darius. On these anecdotes see Pliny, *Natural History*, 7. 29; Plutarch, *Alexander*, 26.1–4; Elyot, *Governour*, 1.10. Alexander's lament upon Achilles' tomb is accounted by Cicero, *Pro Archia Poeta*, 10.24: 'O fortunate, inquit, adolescens, qui tuae virtutis Homerum praeconem inveneris!' ('Fortunate youth, to have found in Homer an herald on thy valour!'). On Alexander's affection for Homer see Puttenham, *The Art*, 1.8; Sidney, *Defence*, p. 37; Lodge, *Defence of Poetry*, ll. 23–26. Scipio's affection for Ennius is in Cicero, ibid. 9. 22: 'Carus fuit Africano superiori noster Ennius' ('Our great Ennius enjoyed the close affection of the elder Africanus').

city, would not suffer the house wherein he dwelt to be spoiled as all the rest were. After these was Homer, who, as it were in one sum comprehended all knowledge, wisdom, learning, and policy° that was incident to the capacity of man.³³ And who so list° to take view of his two books, one of his *Iliads*,ˣⁱ the other his *Odissea*, shall throughly° perceive what the right use of poetry is, which indeed is to mingle profit with pleasure, and so to delight the reader with pleasantness of his art, as in the meantime his mind may be well instructed with knowledge and wisdom. For so did that worthy poet frame those his two works, that in reading the first, that is, his *Iliads*, by declaring and setting forth so lively the Grecians' assembly against Troy, together with their prowess and fortitude against their foes, a prince shall learn not only courage and valiantness, but discretion also and policy° to encounter with his enemies, yea a perfect form of wise consultations with his captains, and exhortations to the people, with other infinite commodities.°³⁴

Again, in the other part, wherein are described the manifold and dangerous adventures of Ulysses, may a man learn many noble virtues, and also learn to escape and avoid the subtle practices and perilous entrappings° of naughty° persons. And not only this, but in what sort also he may deal to know and perceive the affections of those which be near unto him, and most familiar with him, the better to put them in trust with his matters of weight and importance. Therefore, [B4ᵛ] I may boldly set down this to be the truest, ancientest, and best kind of poetry to direct one's endeavour always to that mark, that with delight they may evermore adjoin commodity° to their readers, which, because I ground upon Homer, the prince of all poets, therefore have I alleged the order of his work as an authority sufficiently proving this assertion.³⁵

Now what other poets which followed him, and been of greatest fame, have done for the most part in their several works, I will briefly, and as my slender ability will serve me, declare. But, by my leave, I must content myself to speak not of all, but of such as myself have seen and been best acquainted withal, and those not all nor the most part of the ancient Grecians, of whom I know not how many there were, but these of the Latinists, which are of greatest fame and most obvious among us.

---

³³ To begin [...] man] Horace's chronology of first poets: Orpheus, Amphion, Tyrtaeus and Homer (*Ars Poetica*, 391–403). Webbe adds Pindar before Homer, a chronological mistake that proves his confusion regarding the timeline of ancient authors. For further catalogues of the first poets see Aristophanes, *The Frogs*, 1030; Sidney, *Defence*, pp. 4–5; Puttenham, *The Art*, 1.3. On the legend of Alexander's preservation of Pindar's house, see Pliny, *Natural History*, 7.29.109; Spenser, *SC*, gloss to 'October' ('For ever'); Lodge, *Defence of Poetry*, ll. 28–29.

³⁴ And who [...] commodities] Webbe grounds his definition of the function of poetry on the Horatian idea of profit and delight: 'Aut prodesse volunt aut delectare poetae/aut simul et iucunda et idonea dicere vitae' (*Ars Poetica*, 333–34). See also Aristotle, *Poetics*, 4; Sidney, *Defence*, pp. 11 and 48.

³⁵ For so did [...] assertion] From Elyot, *Governour*, 1.10.

Thus much I can say, that Aristotle reporteth none to have greatly flourished in Greece, at leastwise° not left behind them any notable memorial, before the time of Homer. And Tully saith as much, that there were none writ worth the reading twice in the Roman tongue before the poet Ennius.³⁶ And surely as the very sum or chiefest essence of poetry did always for the most part consist in delighting the readers or hearers with pleasure, so, as the number of poets increased, they still inclined this way rather than the other, so that most of them had special regard to the pleasantness of their fine conceits, whereby they might draw men's minds into admiration of their inventions more than they had to the profit or commodity° that the readers should reap by their works. And thus as I suppose came it to pass among them, that for the most part of them they would not write one work containing some serious matter, but for the same they would likewise pour forth as much of some wanton or lascivious invention. Yet some of the ancientest sort of Grecians, as it seemeth were not so much disposed to vain delectation,° as Aristotle saith of Empedocles, that in his judgement he was only a natural philosopher, no poet at all, nor that he was like unto Homer in anything but his metre, or number of feet, that is, that he [C1ʳ] wrote in verse.³⁷ After the time of Homer there began the first comedy writers, who compiled their works in a better style which continued not long before it was expelled by penalty, for scoffing° too broad at men's manners, and the privy revengements which the poets used against their ill-willers.° Among these was Eupolis, Cratinus, and Aristophanes, but afterward the order of this writing comedies was reformed and made more plausible: then writ Plato Comicus,ˣⁱⁱ Menander, and I know not who more.³⁸

---

³⁶ Aristotle [...] Ennius] *Poetics*, 4. With this remark Cicero alluded to Livius Andronicus' plays; *Brutus*, 71: 'et Livianae fabulae non satis dignae quae iterum legantur' ('and the plays of Livius are not worth a second reading'). Smith ascribes Webbe's interpretation to the original vagueness of Cicero's passage (Smith I, p. 409, note 235.33).

³⁷ as Aristotle [...] verse] *Poetics*, 1: 'But Homer and Empedocles have nothing in common except the metre, so that it would be proper to call the one a poet and the other not a poet but a scientist'. Aristotle affirms that verse does not make a poet and mentions Empedocles as an example, arguing that his writings do only have metre in common with Homer's. See Sidney, *Defence*, p. 5.

³⁸ After [...] more] On the fall of the Old Comedy, Horace, *Ars Poetica*, 281–83: 'successit vetus his comoedia, non sine multa/laude; sed in vitium libertas excidit et vim dignam lege regi' ('To these succeeded Old Comedy, and won no little credit, but its freedom sank into excess and a violence deserving to be checked out by law'). The chronology of ancient comedy writers is taken from Horace, *Satires*, 1.4.1–2: 'Eupolis atque Cratinus Aristophanesque poetae/atque alii, quorum comoedia prisca virorum est' ('Eupolis and Cratinus and Aristophanes, true poets, and the other good men to whom Old Comedy belongs'). Webbe reproduces the anachronism of Eupolis as senior to Cratinus. The association of Plato Comicus (Middle Comedy) and Menander (New Comedy) comes from Horace, *Satires*, 2.3. 11–12: 'quorsum pertinuit stipare Platona Menandro, /Eupolin, Archilochum, comites educere tantos?' ('What was the use of packing Plato with Menander, and of taking out of town Eupolis and Archilochus, such weighty comrades?'). See Lodge, *Defence of Poetry*, ll. 11–14.

There be many most profitable works of like antiquity, or rather before them, of the tragedy writers, as of Euripides and Sophocles.³⁹ Then was there Phocylides^xiii and Theagenes,^xiv with many other. Which tragedies had their invention by one Thespis, and were polished and amended by Aeschylus.^xv ⁴⁰ The profit or discommodity which ariseth by the use of these comedies and tragedies, which is most, hath been long in controversy, and is sore° urged° among us at these days.⁴¹ What I think of the same perhaps I shall briefly declare anon.°

Now concerning the poets which wrote in homely manner, as they pretended, but indeed with great pith° and learned judgement, such as were the writers of shepherds'^xvi talk and of husbandly precepts, who were among the Grecians that excelled, besides Theocritus and Hesiodus, I know not. Of whom the first, what profitable works he left to posterity, besides his *Idillia*, or contentions° of goatherds, tending most to delight and pretty inventions, I cannot tell. The other, no doubt for his argument he took in hand, dealt very learnedly and profitably,

---

³⁹ Euripides and Sophocles] Euripides (480–406 BC), fifteen years younger than Sophocles, became a distinguished tragic poet of his time; *Orestes* and *Medea* are among his best known tragedies. Sophocles (495–406 BC) is said to be the example of perfection in tragedy and the author of one hundred and thirty plays; among his extant works are *Antigone*, *Electra* and *Oedipus*. Sophocles observed that the difference between him and Euripides was that the latter represented men as they ought to be, whereas he depicted them as they are. See Puttenham, *The Art*, 1.11.
⁴⁰ Then was [...] Aeschylus] Phocylides] Phocylides of Miletus (fl. 540 BC) was a gnomic poet contemporary with the tragic poet Theognis and who is also supposed to be the author of epic poems and elegies; due to the didactic character of his verse, Suidas considered him a philosopher. On Phocylides as example of a Greek moral philosopher see Sidney, *Defence*, pp. 5 and 10. Theagenes] Webbe mistakes Theagenes for the tragic poet Theognis, a contemporary with Aristophanes not to be mistaken for Theognis of Megara (fl. 548 BC or 544 BC); his plays were exhibited in the period between 425 BC and 411 BC. Theagenes was the hero of Heliodorus' romance *Aethiopica*. Sidney, *Defence*, p. 9: 'so true a lover as Theagenes'. Thespis] The first tragic actor who took the role of an individual character separated from the chorus; Aristotle's lost dialogue *On Poets* is traditionally taken as the source for Thespis. See A. Cantor, 'Aristotle and the History of Tragedy', in David Perkins, ed., *Theoretical Issues in Literary History* (Cambridge, Mass.: Harvard University Press, 1991), pp. 60–84. Horace, *Ars Poetica*, 275–77: 'Ignotum tragicae genus invenisse Camenae/dicitur et plaustris vexisse poemata Thespis, quae canerent agerentque peruncti faecibus ora' ('Thespis is said to have discovered the Tragic Muse, a type unknown before, and to have carried his pieces in wagons to be sung and acted by players with faces smeared with wine-lees'). Aelius Donatus, 'De tragoedia et comoedia' (in Thomas Marsh, 1583, sig. A7): 'Thespis tragoedia primus inuentor'. Aeschylus] Born in Attica (525 BC), he is the first of the three principal tragedy authors of ancient Greece together with Sophocles and Euripides; he introduced significant advances regarding the elementary productions of Thespis. Aristotle pointed out that he was pioneer in increasing the number of characters to two, followed by Sophocles, who added a third one (*Poetics*, 4.16). Author of *The Persians*, *Agamemnon* or *Eumenides*.
⁴¹ The profit [...] days] He may be referring to the controversy initiated by Stephen Gosson's *Schoole of Abuse* (1579).

that is, in precepts of husbandry, but yet so as he mixed much wanton stuff among the rest.⁴²

The first writers of poetry among the Latins should seem to be those which excelled in the framing of comedies, and that they continued a long time without any notable memory of other poets. Among whom, the chiefest that we may see or hear tell of were these: Ennius, Caecilius, Naevius, Licinius, Atilius, Turpilius,ˣᵛⁱⁱ Trabea, Lucius,ˣᵛⁱⁱⁱ Plautus, and Terence, of whom these two last named have been ever since their time most famous, and to these days are esteemed as great [C1ᵛ] helps and furtherances to the obtaining of good letters.⁴³ But here cannot I stay to speak of the most famous, renowned,ˣⁱˣ and excellent that ever wrote among the Latin poets: Publius Virgil, who performed the very

---

⁴² Now [...] the rest] Theocritus] (c. 270 BC) known as the creator of Greek bucolic poetry and the model for Virgil's eclogues; he was also the author of a poem entitled *Berenice*, of which only five lines have survived, and a collection of epigrams. Out of the thirty poems contained in his *Idylls* several of them display features closer to the lyric or epic genres rather than pastoral. Hesiodus] Hesiod (fl. 750 BC), Homer's contemporay; author of *Works and Days* and *Theogony*. The former is a long didactic poem written in the form of a shepherds' calendar describing agricultural and farming habits; the latter offers an interpretation of the origin of the cosmos and a genealogy of the ancient Greek gods which has been considered to inform Greek mythology. On Hesiod see Sidney, *Defence*, p. 53; Meres, *Palladis*, p. 323.

⁴³ The first [...] letters] Most of these poets are only known through ancient references. Ennius] Cicero, *De Optimo Genere*, 1.1.2: 'Itaque licet dicere (et) Ennium summum epicum poetam' ('Therefore one may call Ennius supreme in epic'); Horace, *Epistles*, 2.1.50: 'Ennius et sapiens et fortis et alter Homerus' ('Ennius, the wise and valiant, the second Homer'). Caecilius] Caecilius Statius (d. 168 BC), friend of Ennius; he was considered among the ancients of the category of Terence and Plautus. Cicero mentions him as an ideal of perfection together with Ennius and Pacuvius (*De Optimo Genere*, 1.1.2), but he also alludes to him as a poor authority: 'malus enim auctor Latinitatis est' ('as he is a poor authority in Latinity'), *Letters to Atticus*, 7.3. Naevius] (b. 274/264 BC–d. c. 204 BC) He also wrote an epic poem, *Bellum Punicum* and was copied by Ennius and Virgil. Horace, *Epistles*, 2.1.53: 'Naevius in manibus non est et mentibus haeret/paene recens?' ('Is not Naevius in our hands, and clinging to our minds, almost as of yesterday?'). Licinius] For Licinius Imbrex (fl. c. 2 BC), see Francis Meres, *Palladis*, p. 120. Atilius] Marcus Atilius translated Sophocles' *Electra*; Cicero, *De Finibus* 1.2.5: 'cum Sophocles vel optime scripserit Electram, tamen male conversam Atili mihi legendam putem' ('admitting the Electra of Sophocles to be a masterpiece, I yet think Atilius's poor translation of it worth my while to read'); Cicero, *Letters to Atticus*, 14.20: 'Atilius, poëta durissimus' ('Atilius, the most wooden of poets'). Meres mentions him among the Latin tragic poets, although he wrote more comedies than tragedies (*Palladis*, l. 24, p. 319). Turpilius] Sextus Turpilius (d. 101 BC), a friend of Terence; his plays belonged to the *Comoedia Palliata*. Only titles and fragments of his plays have survived. See Meres, *Palladis*, p. 320. Trabea] Quintus Trabea (c. 130 BC); Varro classifies him with Atilius and Caecilius (*On the Latin Language*, 5). No works extant except six lines quoted by Cicero in *Tusculan Disputations*, 4.31 and *De Finibus* 2.4.13. Lucius] Luscius Lavinius, comic poet, contemporary and rival of Terence, mentioned by the latter in the prologues to *Eunuch* and *Phormio*.

For further catalogues of Latin comedy writers see Lodge, *Defence of Poetry*, ll. 24–31. For Ascham Latin Comedy writers like Plautus, Terence, Ennius and Caecilius are inferior to their Greek predecessors as regards 'meter and verse' (*Schoolmaster*, p. 288).

same in that tongue which Homer had done in Greek, or rather better, if better might, as Sextus Propertius in his *Elegies* gallantly recordeth in his praise:

> Nescio quid maius[xx] nascitur Iliade.[44]

Under the person of Aeneas he expresseth the valour of a worthy captain and valiant governor, together with the perilous adventures of war and politic devices at all assays. And as he imitateth Homer in that work, so doth he likewise follow the very steps of Theocritus, in his most pithy° inventions of his eclogues; and likewise Hesiodus, in his georgics, or books of husbandry, but yet more gravely, and in a more decent style. But, notwithstanding his sage gravity and wonderful wisdom, did he not altogether restrain his vein, but that he would have a cast at some wanton and scant° comely° an argument, if indeed such trifles as be fathered upon him were his own.[45] There followed after him very many rare and excellent poets, whereof the most part writ light matters, as epigrams and elegies, with much pleasant dalliance,° among whom may be accounted Propertius, Tibullus, Catullus,[46] with[xxi] diverse whom Ovid speaketh of in diverse places of his works.[47] Then are there two historical poets, no less profitable than delightsome to be read: Silius and Lucan; the one declaring the valiant prowess of two noble captains, one enemy to the other, that is, Scipio and Hannibal; the other, likewise, the fortitude of two expert warriors (yet more lamentably than

---

[44] *Nescio* [...] *Iliade*] Propertius, *Elegies*, 2.34.66: 'Something greater than the Iliad now springs to birth'. Quoted from Webbe by Meres, *Palladis*, p. 316: 'As Sextus Propertius said, Nescio quid magis nascitur Iliade', but applied to Spenser's *Fairie Queene*. Webbe echoes Elyot, *Governour*, 1.10: 'in his warke called *Eneidos*, is most lyke to Homer, and all moste the same Homere in latine'; Elyot considers that studying Homer and Virgil together makes their understanding easier to students and he provides a list of topics from Virgil that render his works appropriate for children.

[45] But [...] his own] Webbe could be referring to the epigrams that Aelius Donatus (fl. 350), Virgil's biographer, attributed to him (*Vitae Vergilianae*, 17.69). See Puttenham, *The Art*, 1.27.

[46] There [...] Catullus] Sextus Propertius (b. 51 BC), Albius Tibullus (59/54 BC–18 BC) and Gaius Valerius Catullus (87–57 BC) are the three most representative of the Roman elegiac poets.

[47] with diverse [...] works] *Tristia*, 4.10.41–54: 'saepe suas volucres legit mihi grandior aevo/ quaeque nocet serpens, quae iuvat herba, Macer./saepe suos solitus recitare Propertius ignes,/iure sodalicii, quo mihi iunctus erat./Ponticus heroo, Bassus quoque clarus iambis/dulcia convictus membra fuere mei./et tenuit nostras numerosus Horatius aures,/dum ferit Ausonia carmina culta lyra./Vergilium vidi tantum: nec avara Tibullo/tempus amicitiae fata dedere meae./ successor fuit hic tibi, Galle, Propertius illi;/quartus ab his serie temporis ipse fui.' ('Ofttimes Macer, already advanced in years, read to me of the birds he loved, of noxious snakes and healing plants. Ofttimes Propertius would declaim his flaming verse by right of the comradeship that joined him to me. Ponticus famed in epic, Bassus also, famed in iambics, were pleasant members of that friendly circle. And Horace of the many rhythms held in thrall our ears while he attuned his fine-wrought songs to the Ausonian lyre. Vergil I only saw, and to Tibullus greedy fate gave no time for frienship with me.Tibullus was thy successor, Gallus, and Propertius his; after them came I, fourth in order of time').

the other because these wars were civil), Pompey and Caesar.⁴⁸ The next in time, but (as most men do account, and so did he himself) the second in dignity, we well adjoin Ovid, a most learned and exquisite poet. The work of greatest profit which he wrote was his book of *Metamorphoses* which, though it consisted of feigned fables for the most part and poetical inventions, yet being moralized according to his meaning, and the truth of every tale being discovered, it is a work of exceeding wisdom and sound judgement. If one list° in like manner to [C2ʳ] have knowledge and perfect intelligence of those rites and ceremonies which were observed after the religion of the heathen, no more profitable work for that purpose than his books *De Fastis*. The rest of his doings, though they tend to the vain delights of love and dalliance° (except his *Tristibus*, wherein he bewaileth° his exile), yet surely are mixed with much good counsel and profitable lessons, if they be wisely and narrowly read.⁴⁹ After his time I know no work of any great fame till the time of Horace,⁵⁰ a poet not of the smoothest style, but in sharpness of wit inferior to none, and one to whom all the rest, both before his time and since, are very much beholding.° About the same time were Juvenal and Persius, then Martial, Seneca, a most excellent writer of tragedies, Boethius, Lucretius, Statius, Valerius Flaccus, Manilius, Ausonius, Claudian, and many other, whose just times and several works to speak of in this place were neither much needful nor altogether tolerable, because I purposed another argument.⁵¹ Only I will add

---

⁴⁸ Then are [...] Caesar] Elyot, *Governour*, 1.10: 'The two noble poetis Silius and Lucane, be very expedient to be lerned: for the one setteth out the emulation in qualities and prowess of the two noble and valiant capitaynes, one, enemy to the other, that is to say, Silius writeth of Scipio the Romane, and Haniball duke of Cartaginensis: Lucane declareth a semblable mater, but moche lamentable: for as moche as the warres were ciuile, and, as it were, in the bowelles of the Romanes, that is to say, under the standerdes of Julius Cesar and Pompei'. Silius and Lucan are here chronologically misplaced as they were born after Ovid had died. They rather belong to the group of poets after Horace. C. Silius Italicus (born *c*. 25 AD) was the author of the heroic poem *Punica*, a narration in seventeen books of the second Punic War, influenced by Virgil's *Aeneid*; mentioned in Martial, *Epigrams*, 8.66. Unknown in the Middle Ages, he was rediscovered by Poggio in 1417 and introduced into England by Italian humanism. M. Annaeus Lucanus (39–65 AD) wrote *Pharsalia*, a poem in ten books on the civil war between Caesar and Pompey. See Meres, *Palladis*, p. 315.
⁴⁹ The rest [...] read] Webbe differs from Elyot regarding the didactic profits of Ovid's *Metamorphoses* and *Fasti*: 'But by cause there is litell other lernyng in them, concerning either virtuous maners or policie, I suppose it were better that as fables and ceremonies happen to come in a lesson, it were declared abundantly by the maister than that in the saide two bokes, a longe tyme shulde be spente and almost lost: which mought be better employed on suche autors that do minister both eloquence, ciuile policie, and exhortation to vertue' (*Governour*, 1.10).
⁵⁰ Horace] Horatius Flaccus (65–8 BC); Webbe errs in locating Horace chronologically after Ovid (43 BC–17/18 AD) as the former was Virgil's (70–19 BC) contemporary and therefore Ovid's senior.
⁵¹ About the [...] argument] Boethius and Lucretius are wrongly positioned in the chronology of Latin poets. Ernst Curtius quotes Webbe's list to illustrate that 'the Elizabethans appear to

two of later times, yet not far inferior to the most of them aforesaid: Palingenius,[xxii][52] and Baptista Mantuanus.[53] And for a singular gift in a sweet heroical verse, match with them Christopher Ocland,[54] the author of our *Anglorum Praelia*. But now, lest I stray too far from my purpose, I will come to our English poets, to whom I would I were able to yield their deserved commendations,° and afford them that censure° which I know many would, which can better, if they were now to write in my stead.°

I know no memorable work written by any poet in our English speech until twenty years past, where, although learning was not generally decayed at any time, especially since the conquest of King William Duke of Normandy, as it may appear by many famous works and learned books (though not of this kind)

---

have had rather confused ideas about antique poetry' (*European Literature and the Latin Middles Ages*, 1953, p. 263). Juvenal] Decimus Junius Juvenali, a satirist, likely Martial's contemporary. Persius] Aulus Persius Flaccus: Roman satirist, younger than Horace and older than Juvenal; he was contemporary with Lucan and the lyric poet Caesius Bassus and Seneca. Martial] M. Valerius Martialis (43–104 AD), an epigrammatist. Seneca] L. Annaeus Seneca (4 BC–65 AD), a philosopher, native of Corduba, Spain, author of tragedies like *Phaedra* or *Thyestes*. Boethius] Manlus Severinus Boethius (b. 470–475 AD), known for his translations of Greek philosophers and for his *Consolatio Philosophiae*. Lucretius] Titus Lucretius Carus (c. 95–c. 55 BC), author of *De Rerum Natura*, a philosophical didactic poem in heroic hexameters; misplaced here, as he is an Augustan poet and a great influence for Virgil and Horace. Statius] P. Papinius Statius (c. 61–c. 96 AD), author of *Silvarum Libri V*, a collection of thirty-two occasional poems written mostly in heroic hexameters. Valerius Flaccus] (d. c. 88 AD) Author of *The Argonautica*, a heroic poem in eight books following Apollonius Rhodius. Manilius] Marcus Manilius (first century): author of the astrological poem *Astronomica*. Ausonius] Decimus Magnus Ausonius (fourth century), author of 150 epigrams (*Epigrammatum Liber*), short poems addressed to friends (*Parentalia*) or poems connected with the calendar (*Eclogarium*). Claudian] Claudius Claudianus (fourth-fifth centuries), the last of the classical Latin poets, author of panegyrics and nuptial poems.
[52] Palingenius] Palingenius Stellatus (fl. 1510–1540), author of the moral poem *Zodiacus Vitae* (1537) arranged in twelve books each representing a sign of the zodiac. It belongs to the tradition of the literary calendar that influenced Spenser's *SC*; translated by Barnaby Googe (1574).
[53] Baptista Mantuanus] Baptista Spagnuoli, or Mantuanus (1448–1516): Italian Latin poet, author of a collection of ten eclogues imitating Virgil's used in grammar schools in England (*Eclogues*, 1498). Spenser's *SC* is widely influenced by them; see 'Dedicatory Epistle', 148–51 (Brooks-Davies, p. 23). Meres mentions Mantuan and Palingenius among the Latin Neoterics (*poetae novi*), an innovative poetic movement initiated in the first century B.C. and represented by Catullus (*Palladis*, p. 315).
[54] Christopher Ocland] (d. 1590) English Latin poet, appointed master in several grammar schools of royal foundation. His *Anglorum Praelia* (1580, 1582), a historical poem in hexameters, was dedicated to Queen Elizabeth, who appointed it as a text book in every grammar school in England. I agree with Laurie Magnus when she affirms that his forced inclusion in a list of Latin poets starting with Ennius evinces that Webbe is seeking favourable consideration among the upper literary spheres of his time (*Documents Illustrating Elizabethan Poetry*, p. 210, note 9).

written by bishops and others. Yet surely that poetry was in small price among them it is very manifest and no great marvel, for even that light of Greek and Latin poets which they had they much contemned,° as appeareth by their rude versifying, which of long time was used (a barbarous use it was) wherein they converted the natural property [C2ᵛ] of the sweet Latin verse to be a bald° kind of rhyming, thinking nothing to be learnedly written in verse, which fell not out in rhyme, that is, in words whereof the middle word of each verse should sound alike with the last, or of two verses, the end of both should fall in the like letters, as thus:

> *O male viventes versus audite sequentes.*[55]

And thus likewise:

> *Propter haec et alia dogmata doctorum,*
> *Reor esse melius et magis decorum:*
> *Quisque suam habeat, et non proximorum.*[56]

This brutish poetry, though it had not the beginning in this country, yet so hath it been affected here that the infection thereof would never (nor I think ever will) be rooted up again: I mean this tinkerly° verse which we call rhyme. Master Ascham saith that it first began to be followed and maintained among the Huns and Gothians, and other barbarous nations who, with the decay of all good learning, brought it into Italy. From thence it came into France, and so to Germany, at last conveyed into England by men indeed of great wisdom and

---

[55] *O [...] sequentes*] John Foxe, *Actes and Monuments* 4, p. 192, sig. Q5ᵛ (ed. 1583, vol. I): 'Upon this ruffeling of Anselme with maried priestes, were runing verses made to helpe the matter withall, when reason coulde not serue. Which verses for the folly therof, I thought here to annexe. O malè viuentes versus audite sequentes,/Vxores vestras, quas odit summa potestas:/Linquite propter eum, tenuit qui morte trophaeum,/Quod si non facitis, inferna claustra petetis:/Christi sponsa iubet, ne praesbyter ille ministret:/Qui tenet vxorem, domini quia perdit amorem./Contradicentem fore dicimus insipientem,/Non ex rancore loquor haec, potius sed amore.'

[56] *Propter [...] Proximorum*] John Foxe, *Actes and Monuments* 4, p. 253, sig. Y1ʳ (ed. 1583, vol. I): 'Moreouer, in the said Councel was stablished and ratified the wretched and impious act, compelling Priestes to abiure lawful Matrimonie. Whereupon these meeters or verses were made the same time against hym, whych here folow vnder wrytten. Non est Innocentius, imo nocens vere,/Qui quod facto docuit, verbo vult delere./Et quod olim iuuenis voluit habere,/Modo vetus pontifex studet prohibere./ Zacharias habuit prolem et vxorem,/Per virum quem genuit adeptus honorem,/Baptizauit etenim mundi saluatorem:/Pereat qui teneat nouum hunc errorem./Paulus coelos rapitur ad superiores,/Vbi multas didicit res secretiores./Ad nos tandem rediens instruensque mores,/Suas inquit habeant quilibet vxores./Propter haec et alia dogmata doctorum,/Reor esse melius et magis decorum,/Quisque suam habeat et non proximorum,/Ne incurrat odium vel iram eorum./Proximorum feminas, filias, et neptes/ Violare nefas est, quare nil deceptes,/Vere tuam habeas, et in hac delectes/Diem vt sic vltimum tutius expectes.'

learning, but not considerate nor circumspect in that behalf.⁵⁷ But of this I must entreat more hereafter.

Henry, the first king of that name in England, is wonderfully extolled in all ancient records of memory for his singular good learning in all kind of noble studies, in so much as he was named by his surname *Beauclerk*, as much to say as *Fairclerk* (whereof perhaps came the name of *Fairclough*).ˣˣⁱⁱⁱ ⁵⁸ What knowledge he attained in the skill of poetry I am not able to say. I report his name for proof that learning in this country was not little esteemed of at that rude time, and that like it is, among other studies, a king would not neglect the faculty of poetry. The first of our English poets that I have heard of was John Gower, about the time of King [C3ʳ] Richard the Second, as it should seem by certain conjectures both a knight,⁵⁹ and questionless a singular well learned man, whose works I could wish they were all whole and perfect among us, for no doubt they contained very much deep knowledge and delight, which may be gathered by his friend Chaucer, who speaketh of him oftentimes in diverseˣˣⁱᵛ places of his works.⁶⁰ Chaucer, who for that excellent fame which he obtained in his poetry was always accounted the 'god of English poets' (such a title for honour's sake hath been given him), was next after, if not equal in time to Gower, and hath left many works both for delight and profitable knowledge, far exceeding any other that as yet ever since his time directed their studies that way. Though the manner of his style may seem blunt° and coarse to many fine English ears at these days, yet in truth, if it be equally pondered, and with good judgement advised and confirmed with the time wherein he wrote, a man shall perceive thereby even a true picture or perfect shape of a

---

⁵⁷ Master Ascham [...] behalf] *Schoolmaster*, p. 289: 'They [*Cheke and Watson*] wished as *Virgil* and *Horace* were not wedded to follow the faultes of former fathers (a shrewd marriage in greater matters) but by right *Imitation* of the perfit Grecians, had brought Poetrie to perfitnesse also in the Latin tong, that we Englishmen likewise would acknowledge and vnderstand rightfully our rude beggarly ryming, brought first into Italie by *Gothes* and *Hunnes*, whan all good verses and all good learning to, were destroyd by them: and after caryed into France and Germanie: and at last receyued into England by men of excellent wit in deede, but of small learning, and lesse iudgement in that behalf'. Notice that Webbe departs from Ascham when he ascribes the consolidation of rhyme to the English poets' heedlessness instead of to deficient learning, a view in tune with his tendency to avoid undervaluing national users of rhyme, especially Spenser. This is the main argument used to persuade Harvey and his brothers to take up the reformation of verse (see p. 85 and note 80 below).
⁵⁸ Henry [...] Fairclough] Elyot, *Governour*, 1.12: 'that kynge Henry the first, sonne of willyam conquerour, and one of the moste noble princes that euer reigned in this realme, was openly called Henry beau clerke, whiche is in englysshe, fayre clerke, and is yet at this day so named'.
⁵⁹ John Gower [...] knight] Puttenham, *The Art*, 1.31: 'And those of the first age were Chaucer and Gower, both of them, as I suppose, knights'. There are no hints about the conjectures that made Webbe and Puttenham think that he was a knight unless his regular relations with the courtly society had led to this misconception.
⁶⁰ His friend [...] works] *Troilus and Criseyde*, book 5, l. 1.856: 'O moral Gower'; no other direct references are known.

right poet.⁶¹ He by his delightsome vein so gulled the ears of men with his devices that, although corruption bare° such sway° in most matters that learning and truth might scant° be admitted to show itself, yet without controlment might he gird° at the vices and abuses of all states, and gall° with very sharp and eager inventions, which he did so learnedly and pleasantly that none therefore would call him into question. For such was his bold spirit, that what enormities he saw in any he would not spare to pay them home, either in plain words or else in some pretty and pleasant covert that the simplest might espy him.

Near in time unto him was Lydgate, a poet surely for good proportion of his verse and meetly° current° style, as the time afforded, comparable with Chaucer, yet more occupied in superstitious and odd matters than was requisite in so good a wit, which, though he handled them commendably, yet the matters themselves being not so commendable, his estimation hath been the less.⁶² The next of our ancient poets that I can tell of I suppose to be *Piers Plowman*,ˣˣᵛ who in his doings is somewhat harsh and obscure, but indeed a [C3ᵛ] very pithy° writer, and (to his commendation° I speak it) was the first that I have seen that observed the quantity of our verse without the curiosity° of rhyme.⁶³

---

⁶¹ Chaucer [...] right poet] On Chaucer as 'god of English poets' see Spenser, *SC*, 'June', l. 81 and gloss to 'June' ('Tityrus'); Meres, *Palladis*, p. 124 (Webbe's words *verbatim*). The Elizabethan emphasis on Chaucer's authority derives from what is one of Webbe's main concerns in his treatise, to consolidate English poetic tradition on the grounds of the suitability of their language as a literary vehicle. See Neil Rhodes, *Shakespeare and the Origins of English* (Oxford: Oxford University Press, 2004), p. 124. On Chaucer's relevance see Puttenham, *The Art*, 1.31. On moralizing Chaucer see p. 90 below.
⁶² Near [...] the less] John Lydgate (1370?–1451?), a monk in the Benedictine monastery of Bury, was the author of the narrative poem *The Falls of Princes* (1430–1438), but Webbe is likely referring to his devotional poems (on the Virgin Mary or on the virtues of the Mass) and hagiographical writings, to which he refuses to ascribe didactic value, evincing the Protestant connotations of his criticism. On Lydgate see Puttenham, *The Art*, 1.31 and Spenser, *SC*, 'Dedicatory Epistle', 9–10.
⁶³ The next [...] rhyme] *Piers Plowman* was frequently considered eponymous, although John Bale had revealed Langland as its author in *Scriptorum Illustrium Maioris Brytanniae, quam nunc Angliam et Scotiam uocant: Catalogus* (Basel: Johannes Oporinus, 1557–1559), p. 474; Puttenham ignores his identity, but he distinguishes between title and author (*The Art*, 1.11). See Meres, *Palladis*, p. 314 (Webbe's words *verbatim*). For a contextualized account of this fact and for an interpretation of Webbe's criticism on Langland see Barbara A. Johnson, *Reading Piers Plowman and The Pilgrim's Progress: Reception and the Protestant Reader* (Carbondale: Southern Illinois University Press, 1992), pp. 135–37. Puttenham, *The Art*, 1.31: 'his verse is but loose meter and his terms hard and obscure'. Quantity of our verse] Webbe may mean that Langland disregards rhyme and concentrates on accent; his use of the word 'quantity' is generally ambiguous, referring to natural stress in contexts dealing with English metre ('to place the words in such sort as none of them be wrested contrary to the natural inclination or affectation of the same, or more truly the true quantity thereof', p. 107 below) and to syllable length in references to classical versification ('it seemeth not current for an English verse to run upon true quantity', p. 118 below). See Attridge, *Well-Weighed Syllables*, p. 110.

Since these I know none other till the time of Skelton, who writ in the time of King Henry the Eighth,[xxvi] who as indeed he obtained the Laurel Garland, so may I with good right yield him the title of a poet. He was doubtless a pleasant conceited fellow, and of a very sharp wit, exceeding bold, and would nip to the very quick where he once set hold.[64] Next him I think I may place Master George Gascoigne,[65] as painful° a soldier in the affairs of his prince and country as he was a witty poet in his writing, whose commendations,° because I found in one of better judgement than myself, I will set down his words and suppress mine own. Of him thus writeth E.K. upon the eleventh[xxvii] *Eclogue* of the new poet:

> Master George Gascoigne, a witty gentleman and the very chief of our late rhymers who, and if some parts of learning wanted not (albeit[xxviii] is well known he altogether wanted not learning), no doubt would have attained to the excellency of those famous poets; for gifts of wit and natural promptness appear in him abundantly.[66]

I might next speak of the diverse works of the old Earl of Surrey, of the Lord Vaux, of Norton of Bristol,[xxix] Edwards, Tusser, Churchyard, William Hunnis, Heywood,[xxx] Sand., Hill, S.Y., M.D., and many others.[67] But to speak of their

---

[64] Since [...] set hold] Despite Skelton's (1460?-1529) discredit among the Elizabethans, Webbe incorporates him to his canon of English poets adducing his title of poet laureate, which was a merely academic honour granted to him by the Universities of Oxford and Cambridge seemingly on no other grounds than to be skilful in rhetoric and poetry. The fact that he does not allude to his particular use of language or verse — his most outstanding and, at the same time, controversial features — denotes Webbe's will to avoid the debate about a poet who was apparently one of the main influences for Spenser's *SC*. Puttenham was one of Skelton's harshest detractors (*The Art*, 1.31 and 2.10) and Meres differs from Webbe in this regard (*Palladis*, p. 314).

[65] Master George Gascoigne] (1525?-1577) Poet and soldier, to whom Harvey dedicated an elegy now lost, he had been a student at Trinity College, Cambridge. His *Certain Notes of Instruction Concerning the Making of Verse or Rhyme in English* — originally published within *The Posies* (1575) — inspires Webbe's prescriptions for the improvement of English rhyme. See also Puttenham, *The Art*, 1.31.

[66] Master [...] abundantly] Spenser, *SC*, gloss to 'November', 'Philomel' (Brooks-Davies, p. 185).

[67] I might [...] others] Webbe seems to ignore the identity of most of them; except for Surrey, Norton and Tusser they are all contributors to *The Paradise of Dainty Devices* (1576). Surrey] Henry Howard, Earl of Surrey (1517?-1547); his poems were first published in *Tottel's Miscellany* (1557) together with those of Thomas Wyatt and other poets mentioned in this list, like Churchyard, Vaux and Heywood. He was praised by Ascham for his translations of Virgil in English verse avoiding 'the fault of Ryming' (*Schoolmaster*, p. 291). There is no mention of *Tottel's Miscellany* in *A Discourse*. L. Vaux] Lord Thomas Vaux (1510-1556), probably educated in Cambridge, belonged to the literary circles of the courts of Henry VIII and Edward VI. One of the principal contributors to *Paradise* with twelve poems, two of his best known sonnets were published in *Tottel's*. See Puttenham, *The Art*, 1.31. Of Norton of Bristol] In Q: 'of Norton, of Bristow'; from Ascham, *Schoolmaster*, p. 289: 'Chauser, Th. Norton, of Bristow, my L. of Surrey, M. Wiat, Th. Phaer'. Ascham refers to Thomas Norton of Bristol (fl. 1477), author of a

several gifts and abundant skill showed forth by them in many pretty and learned works would make my discourse much more tedious.

I may not omit the deserved commendations° of many honourable and noble lords and gentlemen in her Majesty's Court, which in the rare devices of poetry have been and yet are most excellent skilful, among whom the right honourable Earl of Oxford[68] may challenge to himself the title of the most excellent among the rest. I can no longer forget those learned gentlemen which took such profitable pains in translating the Latin poets into our English tongue, whose deserts° in that behalf are more than I can utter. Among these I ever esteemed,

---

chemical tract in verse; Webbe may have copied the name ignoring the identity or he may have thought that Ascham meant Thomas Norton (1532-1584), a Cambridge graduate known for his collaboration with Sackville in *Gordobuc*, and author of some poems in *Tottel's*. Edwards] Richard Edwards (1523?-1566), educated at Corpus Christi, Oxford. Appointed gentleman of the Chapel Royal and Master of the Children in 1561, his plays were represented in the Queen's presence. In the front page of *Paradise*: 'aptly furnished, with sundry pithie and learned inuentions: deuised and written for the most part, by M. Edwards, sometimes of her Maiesties Chappel' (1576, sig. A1ʳ). Tusser] Thomas Tusser (1524?-1580); author of *Fiue Hundreth Good Pointes of Husbandrie* (1557), a formally varied collection of instructional poems including some in calendar frame, which became one of the most popular books of poetry in the Elizabethan period. He matriculated as servant of Trinity Hall at Cambridge during the London plague in 1573-1574. Churchyard] Thomas Churchyard (1520?-1604), Surrey's page in 1543, had Sidney and Raleigh among his literary patrons. He contributed to *Tottel's Miscellany* and *Paradise*. He published *The Firste Parte of Churcheyeards Chippes, containing twelve severall Labours* (1575), a varied collection of prose and verse writings. William Hunnis] (d. 1597) He succeeded his fellow poet Richard Edwards as a Master of the Children of the Chapel in 1566; he contributed with fourteen poems to *Paradise*, one to *A Handful of Pleasant Delights* (1584) and two to *Englands Helicon* (1600). Author of *Certayne Psalmes chosen out of the Psalter of David and drawn furth into English meter* (1550). Heywood] Jasper Heywood (1535-1598), son of John Heywood the epigrammatist; author of eight poems in *Paradise* and translator of Seneca's *Troas* (1559) and *Thyestes* (1560). Sand.] According to Rollins, who cites Webbe's reference, this name corresponds to the 'D.S.', 'D. Sand' or 'D. Sande' in *Paradise*, author of four poems in this collection. In H. E. Rollins, ed., *The Paradise of Dainty Devices* (Cambridge: Harvard University Press, 1927), p. lxi. Due to his uncertain identity I have not expanded the abbreviation here. Hill] Richard Hill; although his authorship in *Paradise* is undisputed (seven poems are signed by 'Richard Hill' or 'R.H.'), there are no other hints of his identity. S.Y.] For Rollins, Webbe is probably referring to the 'Master Yloop' of the *Paradise*, whose identity remains obscure (*Paradise*, p. lxv). Brydges associates 'Yloop' with the Pooley (read backwards) who appears in *The Castell of Courtesie* (1582), a miscellany published by James Yates (Brydges, xvii). M.D.] Rollins observes that Webbe 'was obviously writing with his eye on *Paradise* and probably did not know the identity of M.D' (*Paradise*, p. xlvi); although he observes these initials could correspond to 'Master Dyer' (Edward Dyer), he is more inclined to consider them a variation from the unidentified 'R.D.'.

[68] Earl of Oxford] Edward de Vere, seventh Earl of Oxford (1550-1604), studied at St John's, Cambridge; a patron to men of letters, he was an honorific member of Gray's Inn. John Lyly's *Euphues and his England* (1580) is dedicated to him. Ascribed seven poems in *Paradise*, Webbe's special mention is in tune with his interest in gaining the grace of influential men of letters.

and while I live in my conceit I shall account, Master [C4ʳ] Thomas Phaer,ˣˣˣⁱ without doubt the best, who, as indeed he had the best piece of poetry whereon to set a most gallant verse, so performed he it accordingly, and in such sort as in my conscience I think would scarcely be done again, if it were to do again. Notwithstanding, I speak it but as mine own fancy, not prejudicial to those that list° to think otherwise. His work whereof I speak is the Englishing of *Aeneidos* of Virgil, so far forth as it pleased God to spare him life, which was to the half part of the tenth book, the rest being since with no less commendations° finished by that worthy scholar and famous physician Master Thomas Twyne.⁶⁹

Equally with him may I well adjoin Master Arthur Golding⁷⁰ for his labour in Englishing Ovid's *Metamorphoses*, for which gentleman surely our country hath for many respectsˣˣˣⁱⁱ greatly to give God thanks, as for him which hath taken infinite pains without ceasing, travelleth° as yet indefatigably, and is addicted without society° by his continual labour to profit this nation and speech in all kind of good learning. The next very well deserveth Master Barnaby Googe⁷¹ to be placed, as a painful° furtherer of learning: his help to poetry, besides his own devices, as the translating of Palingenius' *Zodiac*.ˣˣˣⁱⁱⁱ Abraham Fleming, as in many pretty poesies of his own, so in translating hath done to his commendations.⁷² To whom I would here adjoin one of his name, whom I know to have excelled as well in all kind of learning as in poetry most especially, and

---

⁶⁹ I can no [...] Twyne] Webbe's interest for Latin translation as a method for improving English poetic idiom derives on a great extent from his reading of Ascham's *Schoolmaster* (see pp. 268–72); see also Elyot, *Governour*, 1.26. Master Thomas Phaer] (1510–1560) Phaer translated Virgil's *Aeneid* into rhyming fourteeners (1558). Thomas Twyne] (1543–1613) He finished Phaer's translation in 1573. Although Surrey's translation of two books of the *Aeneid* appeared in 1557, Phaer's was the first attempt of a complete translation. In 1582 Richard Stanyhurst (1547–1618) translated the first four books of *Aeneid* (1582) into quantitative metre in an attempt to demonstrate that it fitted English verse; there is no mention to Stanyhurst in *A Discourse*, likely due to the bad reputation he had among his contemporaries; see Puttenham, *The Art*, 2.13.

⁷⁰ Master Arthur Golding] (1535/36–1606) Educated at Queen's College, Cambridge, he translated some of Caesar's works and Calvin's sermons. His translation of Ovid's *Metamorphoses* (1567) in fourteeners was a relevant influence for Shakespeare. Webbe mentions him again in association with Phaer to prove the potential of English eloquence for matching Latin sources; see p. 101 below. See Puttenham 1.31; Meres, *Palladis*, p. 322.

⁷¹ Barnaby Googe] (1540–1594) Poet and translator; educated at Christ's College, Cambridge, and at New College, Oxford. He translated Marcellus Palingenius' *Zodiacus Vitae* as *The Zodiake of Life* (1565). In his rendering of Heresbach's *Foure Bookes of Husbandry* (1577) he included his translation of some passages of Virgil's *Georgics*. Among his 'own devices', the collection of *Eclogs, Epytaphs and Sonettes* (1563) dedicated to William Lovelace; the pastoral poems it contained are known to have influenced Spenser's eclogues. Webbe mentions Googe in the section dedicated to the georgics, p. 104 below.

⁷² Abraham Fleming [...] commendations] Abraham Fleming (1552?–1607) translated Virgil's *Eclogues* (1575) and *Georgics* (1589); see note 151 below. Webbe refers here to his diverse Latin and English verses prefixed or subjoined to other writers' works, like Googe's *Zodiake of Life* (1576) and Whetstone's *The Rocke of Regard* (1576).

would appear so if the dainty morsels and fine poetical inventions of his were as common abroad as I know they be among some of his friends.⁷³ I will crave leave of the laudable authors of Seneca in English, of the other parts of Ovid, of Horace, of Mantuan, and diverse other, because I would hasten to end this rehearsal,° perhaps offensive to some, whom either by forgetfulness or want of knowledge I must needs overpass.⁷⁴

And once again I am humbly to desire pardon of the learned company of gentlemen scholars and students of the Universities and Inns of Court if I omit their several commendations° in this place, which I know a great number [C4ᵛ] of them have worthily deserved in many rare devices and singular inventions of poetry, for neither hath it been my good hap° to have seen all which I have heard of, neither is my abiding° in such place where I can with facility get knowledge of their works.

One gentleman notwithstanding among them may I not overslip, so far reacheth his fame and so worthy is he, if he have not already, to wear the laurel wreath: Master George Whetstone,⁷⁵ a man singularly well skilled in this faculty of poetry. To him I will join Anthony Munday, an earnest traveller in this art, and in whose name I have seen very excellent works, among which surely the most exquisite vein of a witty poetical head is showed in the sweet sobs of shepherds and nymphs, a work well worthy to be viewed and to be esteemed as very rare poetry.⁷⁶ With

---

⁷³ To whom [...] friends] Referring to Abraham Fraunce (1558–1592), a committed promoter of classical quantitative verse; like Webbe, he translated Virgil's 'Eglogue II' into hexameters and took Spenser's *SC* as a model. He was entered in St John's in 1575, two or three years after Webbe's B.A. Although Fraunce's first hexameters, *The Lamentations of Amyntas*, were not published until 1587, Webbe could have had access to his manuscripts. On the relations of Fraunce with Cambridge and Webbe, see Steven W. May, 'Marlowe, Spenser, Sidney and — Abraham Fraunce?', 2010.

⁷⁴ I will [...] overpass] For Seneca, Jasper Heywood (*Troas*, 1559; *Thyestes*, 1560) and John Studley (*Agammenon*, 1566). Ovid's *Heroides* (1567) were translated by Turberville — along with Mantuan's *Eglogues* (1567) — and *Tristia* by Churchyard (1572). Horace's *Ars Poetica* was first rendered into English by Thomas Drant (1567).

⁷⁵ George Whetstone] (1544?–1587) English dramatist, author of the play *Promos and Cassandra* (1578) and of a collection of tales in prose and verse adapted from the Italian entitled *The Rocke of Regard* (1576); he was acclaimed for his elegy on Gascoigne — who died in 1577 while a guest of Whetstone's family, a fragment from which appears in *Paradise*. Webbe's interest in magnifying his merits as a poet was probably due to Whetstone's privileged position within the Elizabethan literary circles. Puttenham does not mention him and Meres includes him as an elegiac poet (*Palladis*, p. 321).

⁷⁶ To him [...] poetry] Anthony Munday (1553–1633) was a poet and dramatist who worked in association with Dekker, Middleton, Drayton and Webster; author of the lyric collection *The Mirror of Mutability* (1579). Webbe is likely referring to his *Sweete Sobbes and Amorous Complaintes of Sheppardes and Nymphs in a Fancy*, not extant. The metaphoric reference 'traveller of this art' alludes to Munday's frequent and well known trips overseas (playing with 'traveller' as 'labourer' and also 'one who travels') whereas by 'earnest' Webbe seems to defend him from past accusations of having deceived his master John Allde (1581).

these I may place John Grange, Knight, Wilmot, Darrell, F.C., F.K., G.B., and many other whose names come not now to my remembrance.⁷⁷

This place have I purposely reserved for one who, if not only, yet in my judgement principally deserveth the title of the rightest English poet that ever I read, that is, the author of *The Shepherds' Calendar*, intituled° to the worthy gentleman Master Philip Sidney. Whether it was Master Sp.⁷⁸ or what rare scholar in Pembroke Hall soever, because himself and his friends, for what respect I know not, would not reveal it, I force not greatly to set down. Sorry I am that I cannot find none other with whom I might couple him in this catalogue in his rare gift of poetry, although one there is, though now long since seriously occupied in graver studies (Master Gabriel Harvey), yet as he was once his most special friend and fellow poet, so because he hath taken such pains, not only in his Latin poetry (for which he enjoyed great commendations° of the best both in judgement and dignity in this realm), but also to reform our English verse and to beautify the same with brave devices, of which I think the chief lie hid in hateful obscurity.⁷⁹

---

⁷⁷ With these [...] remembrance] John Grange] (fl.1577) Author of *The Golden Aphroditis* (1577), a prose love tale including poems of diverse subjects and metres. His style is unnaturally charged with mythological allusions, but his experiments with verse form match Webbe's interest for poetic innovation; quoted below in *A Discourse* as an example of rare rhyming devices (see p. 116). Knight] Probably Edward Knight, the poet who signed as 'Ed. Knight' a fourteen-line poem recommending Munday's *The Mirror of Mutability* (1579); although presented as 'E.K. Gentleman in commendation of the Author', he is unlikely the glosser of Spenser's *SC*. There are no records of his identity. Wilmot] Robert Wilmot (fl. 1568-1608) was a dramatist, author of *The Tragedy of Tancred and Gismond* (1591), represented before Queen Elizabeth at Inner Temple in 1567. The quarto included two complimentary poems addressed to the Queen's maids of honour and a prefatory letter written by William Webbe, signed the eighth of August, which is the only extant text by our author appart from this treatise; see 'Introduction'. Darrel] There are no extant records or hints of his identity. F.C.] These initials could be a mispelling for F.G., who signs one poem in *Paradise*; no evidence links this author with Fulke Greville. F.K.] In *Paradise* the initials F.K. or M.K. correspond to Francis Kindlemarsh or Kinwelmarsh, author of nine of its poems. In 1557 he entered as a fellow student of Gray's Inn, where he met Gascoigne; they colaborated in the translation of Euripides' *Jocasta* in blank verse (1566). G.B.] Likely the M.B. or Master Bewe of the *Paradise*, of unknown identity and author of two poems. If it were so, that means that Webbe was adding the initial for his first name (George?), thus proving that he might have heard of him in other contexts too.

⁷⁸ Master Sp.] Edmund Spenser (1552-1599) entered Pembroke Hall in 1569 and obtained his M.A. on June 1576. He may have been serving Gabriel Harvey as a sizar. Although Webbe avoids mentioning Spenser's name, his uncertainty about Spenser's authorship seems to be feigned, motivated by the poet's will to remain anonymous. See 'Introduction'.

⁷⁹ Sorry I [...] obscurity] Spenser's friend and fellow poet Gabriel Harvey (1545?-1639) was entered at Christ's College in 1566 and obtained his B.A. in 1569-70; this year he was elected fellow at Pembroke Hall. He is the author of the collection of Latin elegies on Sir Thomas Smith *Musarum lachrymae* (1578) and of Latin poems dedicated to Elizabeth with the title of *Gratulationum Valdinensium* (1578); for further references to his Latin works see Spenser, *SC*, gloss to 'September' ('Colin Clout'). Harvey's experiments on English hexameters were not published. See 'Introduction'.

Therefore will I adventure to set them together as two of the rarest wits and learnedest masters [D1ʳ] of poetry in England, whose worthy and notable skill[xxxiv] in this faculty I would wish, if their high dignities and serious businesses would permit, they would still grant to be a furtherance to that reformed kind of poetry, which Master Harvey did once begin to ratify. And surely in mine opinion, if he had chosen some graver matter and handled but with half that skill which I know he could have done, and not poured it forth at a venture as a thing between jest and earnest, it had taken greater effect than it did.[80]

As for the other gentleman, if it would please him or his friends to let those excellent poems, whereof I know he hath plenty, come abroad, as his *Dreams*, his *Legends*, his *Court of Cupid*, his *English Poet*,[81] with other, he should not only stay the rude pens of myself and others, but also satisfy the thirsty desires of many which desire nothing more than to see more of his rare inventions. If I join to Master Harvey his two brethren, I am assured, though they be both busied with great and weighty callings° (the one a godly and learned divine, the other a famous and skilful physician), yet if they listed° to set to their helping hands to poetry, they would as much beautify and adorn it as any others.[82]

If I let pass the uncountable rabble of rhyming ballet makers and compilers of senseless sonnets, who be most busy to stuff every stall full of gross devices and unlearned pamphlets, I trust I shall with the best sort be held excused. For[xxxv] though many such can frame an alehouse song of five or[xxxvi] six score verses, hobbling upon some tune of a northern jig,[xxxvii] or Robin Hood, or La lubber,

---

[80] Therefore [...] it did] In the time Webbe is writing, Spenser was bishop John Young's secretary (from 1578) and Harvey had recently been elected Doctor of Laws in Trinity Hall, London; the enthusiasm for classical metres they had shown in their correspondance (*Letters*, 1580) had by then cooled down. Webbe reproaches Harvey not having done all his best in order to disseminate his English hexameters, which would have served as models for other poets. Webbe's familiar tone regarding Harvey denotes a relative intimacy between them, or at least personal acquaintance.

[81] As for [...] *Poet*] Spenser, *SC*, 'Dedicatory epistle', 176-79: 'hoping that this will the rather occasion him to put forth divers other excellent works of his which sleep in silence, as his *Dreams*, his *Legends*, his *Court of Cupid*, and sundry others' (Brooks-Davies, p. 24). Spenser-Harvey, *Letters* III: 'Nowe, my *Dreames*, and *dying Pellicane*, being fully finished (as I parteIye signified in my laste Letters) and presentlye to bee imprinted' (*Variorum* X, p. 17); on *The English Poet* see note 29 above.

[82] If I join [...] others] John (1563?-1592) and Richard Harvey (baptized 1560-1623?); John was an astrologer; pensioner in Queens' College since June 1578, got his B.A. in 1580 and M.A. in 1584. In 1583 he published an astrological supplement annexed to one of Gabriel's discourses, together with a version of Hermes Trismegistus' *Iatromathematica* on the study of astrology for practical use in medicine. Richard matriculated as a pensioner of Pembroke Hall in June 1575, had his B.A. in 1577-78 and M.A. in 1581, when he was elected fellow. A prestigious judicial astrologer, he wrote *An Astrological Discourse upon the great and notable Conjunction of two Superiour Planets, Saturne and Jupiter, which shall happen on the 28 day of April 1583* (1583), which was dedicated to John Aylmer, bishop of London.

etc., and perhaps observe just number of syllables, eight in one line, six in another, and therewithal an A to make a jerk in the end.[83] Yet if these might be accounted poets (as it is said some of them make means to be promoted to the laurel), surely we shall shortly have whole swarms of poets, and every one that can frame a book in rhyme, though for want of matter, it be but in commendations° of copper noses or bottle ale, will catch at the garland due to poets, whose pottical° (poetical, I should say) heads, I would wish, at their worshipful commencements might, [D1ᵛ] instead of laurel, be gorgeously garnished with fair green barley, in token of their good affection to our English malt.[84] One speaketh thus homely of them, with whose words I will content myself for this time, because I would not be too broad with them in mine own speech:

'In regard whereof'[xxxviii] (he meaneth of the learned framing the new poet's works which writ *The Shepherds' Calendar*) 'I scorn and spew out the rakehelly° rout of our ragged rhymers (for so themselves use to hunt the letter) which without learning boast, without judgement jangle, without reason rage and foam,[xxxix] as if some instinct of poetical spirit had newly ravished them above the meanness of common capacity and, being in the middest[xl] of all their bravery, suddenly either[xli] for want of matter, or of rhyme, or having forgotten their former conceit, they seem to be so pained and travelled° in their remembrance, as it were a woman in childbirth, or as that same Pythia when the trance came upon her: *Os rabidum, fera corda domans*, etc.'[85]

---

[83] For though [...] end] In tune with the aim he expressed in his 'Preface' to provide the means to 'discern between good writers and bad', Webbe excludes the artificers of the easy rhymes of popular ballads from his canon. Robin Hood] Different episodes of the life of this popular personage had been the subject of popular ballads from the twelve century; they used to be associated to several specific tunes for dancing. See Joseph Ritson, *Robin Hood. A Collection of all the Ancient Poems, Songs and Ballads, now extant, Relative to that Celebrated English Outlaw* (London: for T. Egerton, Whitehall, and J. Johnson, 1795). La lubber] Another popular tune likely associated with a social dance.

[84] and every one [...] malt] An allusion to William Elderton (d. 1592), a popular writer of ballads with the reputation of a drunkard; Harvey alludes to 'Eldertons ale-crammed nose' (*Foure Letters* 1592, Grosart, p. 201). His first registered ballad, "The Pangs of Love", is dated in 1552. He was a frequent visitor of London taverns, where he improvised burlesque songs and dances, and was the target of numerous gibes. Webbe's reference is based on Elderton's "New Merry News" (1576): 'Be it therefore enacted and made,/That such as doe vse the vintners trade,/And shall hereafter see anyone passe,/Hard by his doore with copper or brasse,/In any part of his nose or his face,/He shall fill a quart, and hie him apace,/Strait for to greet him,/As soon as they meete him,/ with a cup of good wine,/ to keepe his colour fine,/Vpon paine for to lose,/The custome of a copper nose'. This song originated its author's nicknames regarding his 'red nose'; see Hyder E. Rollins, 'William Elderton: Elizabethan Actor and Ballad-Writer', *Studies in Philology*, 17.2 (1920), 199-245, p. 120.

[85] In regard [...] etc.] Spenser, *SC*, 'Dedicatory epistle', 118-28 (Brooks-Davies, p. 22). *Os rabidum* [...] etc.] *Aeneid*, 4.79-80: 'tanto magis ille fatigat/os rabidum, fera corda domans, fingitque premendo' ('so much the more he tires her raving mouth, tames her wild heart, and moulds her by constraint').

Thus far forth have I adventured to set down part of my simple judgement concerning those poets with whom for the most part I have been acquainted through mine own reading, which, though it may seem something impertinent to the title of my book, yet I trust the courteous readers will pardon me, considering that poetry is not of that ground and antiquity in our English tongue, but that speaking thereof only as it is English would seem like unto the drawing of one's picture without a head.

Now therefore by your gentle patience will I with like brevity make trial what I can say concerning our English poetry, first in the matter thereof, then in the form, that is, the manner of our verse, yet so as I must evermore° have recourse to those times and writers whereon the English poetry taketh, as it were, the descent and propriety.[86]

[D2r] English poetry therefore, being considered according to common custom and ancient use, is where any work is learnedly compiled in measurable speech and framed in words, containing number or proportion of just syllables, delighting the readers or hearers as well by the apt and decent framing of words in equal resemblance of quantity, commonly called verse, as by the skilful handling of the matter whereof it is entreated. I spake somewhat of the beginning of this measuring of words in just number, taken out of Plato:[87] and indeed the regard of true quantity in letters and syllables seemeth not to have been much urged before the time of Homer in Greece, as Aristotle witnesseth.[88]

The matters whereof verses were first made were either exhortations to virtue, dehortations from vices,[xlii] or the praises of some laudable thing. From thence they began to use them in exercises of imitating some virtuous and wise man at their feasts, whereas someone should be appointed to represent another man's

---

[86] Now therefore [...] propriety] Webbe's analysis of English poetry is articulated attending to the two premises that determine Ascham's humanist conception of poetry: imitation and the Ciceronian ideal of cohesion between matter and form, which is based on the consideration of words as living expression of moral virtue. On humanist ideas of form and matter see Rhodes 2004, *Shakespeare and the Origins of English*, chapter 1. On the one hand, Webbe searches to legitimize his canon on the grounds of direct cultural and mimetic links with Greek and Roman antecedents; thus his insistence in systematically providing classical precursors for English poetic achievements. On the other hand, his exposition of poetic genres (matter) and modes of versification (form) — the two next sections of the treatise — are interwoven by an underlying concern to demonstrate that the national poetic idiom has attained the maturity provided by a perfect integration of matter and form as proclaimed by Ascham: 'we finde alwayes, wisdome and eloquence, good matter and good vtterance, neuer or seldom a sonder. For all soch Authors, as be fullest of good matter and right iudgement in doctrine, be likewise alwayes, most proper in wordes, most apte in sentence, most plaine and pure in vttering the same' (*Schoolmaster*, p. 265).
[87] I spake [...] Plato] See p. 66 above: 'Thus it appeareth both eloquence and poetry to have had their beginning and original ... would or no'.
[88] And indeed [...] witnesseth] Aristotle, *Poetics* 4; Meres, *Palladis*, p. 314: 'As Homer was the first that adorned the Greek tongue with true quantity'.

person of high estimation, and he sang fine ditties and witty sentences tuneably to their music notes. Of this sprang the first kind of comedies, when they began to bring into these exercises more persons than one, whose speeches were devised dialoguewise in answering one another. And of such like exercises, or, as some will needs have it, long before the other, began the first tragedies, and were so called of τράγος, because the actor, when he began to play his part, slew and offered a goat to their goddess: but comedies took their name of κωμάζειν καὶ ἄδειν, *comessatum ire*, to go a feasting, because they used to go in procession with their sport about the cities and villages, mingling much pleasant mirth with their grave religion, and feasting cheerfully together with as great joy as might be devised. But not long after (as one delight draweth another) they began to invent new persons and new matters for their comedies, such as the devisers thought meetest° to please the people's[xliii] vein. And from these they began to present in shapes of men the natures of virtues and vices, and affections and qualities incident to men, as justice, temperance, poverty, wrath, vengeance, sloth, valiantness, [D2ᵛ] and such like as may appear by the ancient works of Aristophanes.[89] There grew at last to be a greater diversity between tragedy writers and comedy writers, the one expressing only sorrowful and lamentable histories, bringing in the persons of gods and goddesses, kings and queens, and great states, whose parts were chiefly to express most miserable calamities and dreadful chances, which increased worse and worse, till they came to the most woeful plight that might be devised.

The comedies, on the other side, were directed to a contrary end which, beginning doubtfully, drew to some trouble or turmoil, and by some lucky chance always ended to the joy and appeasement of all parties. This distinction grew, as some hold opinion, by imitation of the works of Homer, for out of his *Iliads* the tragedy writers found dreadful events whereon to frame their matters, and the other out of his *Odissea* took arguments of delight and pleasant ending after

---

[89] From thence [...] Aristophanes] Aelius Donatus, 'De Tragoedia et Comoedia', in Marsh 1583, sigs. A7ʳ–A7ᵛ: 'Initium tragoediae et comoediae àrebus diuinis est inchoatum: quibus pro fructibus vota soluentes, operabantur antiqui. Nam incensis iam altaribus, et admoto hirco, id genus carminis, quod sacer chorus reddebat Libero patri, Tragoedia dicebatur: vel ἀπό τοῦ τράγου, hoc est ab hirco hoste vinearum, et àcantiiena. (eius ipsuis [*ipsius*] rei apud Virgilium plena fit mentio) vel quod hirco donabatur eius carminis poëta: vel quòd uter eius musti plenus solenne praemium cantoribus fuerat: vel quòd ora sua faecibus perlinebant scenici, ante usum personarum ab Aeschylo repertum: faeces enim dicuntur Graecè τρύγες. Et his quidem causis tragoediae nomen est inuentum. At verò nondum coactis in urbem Atheniensibus, cum Apollini Nomio, id est, pastorum vicinorúmque praesidis deo, constructis aris, in honore diuinaerei, circum Atticae vicos, villas, pagos, and compita, festum carmen solenniter cantarent, orta est comoediae ἀπό τοῦ κομάζειν καὶ ἄδειν, quod est comessatum ire cantantes, quod à poetis solenni die, vel amatorie lasciuientibus choris comicis non absurdum est'. On Renaissance sources for the origin of tragedy and comedy see D.S. Wilson-Okamura, *Spenser's International Style*, (Cambridge: Cambridge University Press, 2013), p. 207.

dangerous and troublesome doubts.⁹⁰ So that, though there be many sorts of poetical writings, and poetry is not debarred° from any matter which may be expressed by pen or speech, yet for the better understanding and briefer method of this discourse, I may comprehend the same in three sorts, which are: comical, tragical, historical.^xliv Under the first may be contained all such epigrams, elegies, and delectable ditties which poets have devised respecting only the delight thereof. In the second, all doleful° complaints, lamentable chances, and whatsoever is poetically expressed in sorrow and heaviness. In the third we may comprise the rest of all such matters which, as^xlv indifferent° between the other two, do^xlvi commonly occupy the pens of poets: such are the poetical compiling of chronicles, the friendly greetings between friends, and very many sorts besides, which for the better distinction may be referred to one of these three kinds of poetry.⁹¹ But once again, lest my discourse run too far awry, will I buckle myself more nearer to English poetry, the use whereof, because it is nothing different from any other, I think best to confirm by the testimony of Horace, a man worthy to bear authority [D3ʳ] in this matter, whose very opinion is this: that the perfect perfection of poetry is this, to mingle delight with profit in such wise that a reader might by his reading be partaker of both, which, though I touched in the beginning, yet I thought good to allege in this place, for more confirmation thereof, some of his own words. In his treatise *De Arte Poetica*, thus he saith:

> *Aut prodesse volunt aut delectare poetae,*
> *Aut simul et iucunda et idonea dicere vitae.*⁹²

---

⁹⁰ This distinction [...] doubts] The idea that Homer's works were the sources of comedy and tragedy is in Donatus: 'Homerus tamen, qui ferè omnis poeticae largissimus fons est, etiam his carminibus exempla praebuit, et velut quadam suorum operum lege praescripsit: qui Iliadem instar tragoediae, Odysseam ad imaginem comoediae fecisse monstratur ('De Tragoedia et Comoedia', in Marsh 1583, sig. A7ᵛ). And in Scaliger, *Poetice Libri Septem*, 1.5: 'Aiunt enim Iliadem priorem Odyssea. Iliadem Tragoediae modulum, Comoediae Odysseam'.

⁹¹ I may comprehend [...] poetry] Although the system of classification of literary genres in the sixteenth century was quite discretional, Webbe's approach to this matter is strikingly simplistic as he defines the traditionally dramatic categories of comedy and tragedy on the grounds of the expression of emotional states such as delight or sorrow, thus including lyric verse under these two genres. The general tendency for Elizabethan scholars followed the Horatian tradition, based on the distinction between dramatic and non-dramatic texts; Horace mentioned as the chief genres epic, elegy, lyric, iambic verse, comedy, tragedy (*Ars Poetica*, 73–98). For Ascham the four *genera dicendi* were *poeticum, historicum, philosophicum* and *oratorium*; and poetry, according to variations of style, subject and metre, resulted into *comicum, tragicum, epicum* and *melicum* or lyric (*Schoolmaster*, pp. 283–84). Sidney divided poetry into heroic, lyric, tragic, comic, satiric, iambic, elegiac, and pastoral (*Defence*, p. 11).

⁹² Aut prodesse [...] vitae] 'Poets aim either to benefit, or to amuse, or to utter words at once both pleasing and helpful to life'; *Ars Poetica*, 333–34.

As much to say: all poets desire either by their works to profit or delight men, or else to join both profitable and pleasant lessons together for the instruction of life. And again:

> Omne tulit punctum qui miscuit utile dulci,
> Lectorem[xlvii] delectando pariterque monendo.[93]

That is, he misseth nothing of his mark which joineth profit with delight, as well delighting his readers as profiting them with counsel. And that whole epistle which he writ of his *Art of Poetry*, among all the parts thereof, runneth chiefly upon this: that, whether the argument which the poet handleth be of things done or feigned inventions, yet that they should bear such an image of truth that as they delight they may likewise profit. For these are his words: *Ficta voluptatis causa sint proxima veris*[94] (let things that are feigned for pleasure's sake have a near resemblance of the truth). This precept may you perceive to be most duly observed of Chaucer. For, who could with more delight prescribe such wholesome counsel and sage advice, where he seemeth only to respect the profit of his lessons and instructions? Or who could with greater wisdom, or more pithy° skill, unfold such pleasant and delightsome matters of mirth as though they respected nothing but the telling of a merry tale?[95] So that this is the very ground of right poetry: to give profitable counsel, yet so as it must be mingled with delight. For among all the ancient [D3ᵛ] works of poetry, though the most of them incline much to that part of delighting men with pleasant matters of small importance, yet even in the vainest trifles among them there is not forgotten some profitable counsel, which a man may learn either by flat precepts which therein are prescribed or by loathing such vile vices, the enormities whereof they largely discover. For surely I am of this opinion, that the wantonest poets of all, in their most lascivious works wherein they busied themselves, sought rather by that means to withdraw men's minds (especially the best natures) from such foul vices than to allure them to embrace such beastly follies as they detected.

Horace, speaking of the general duties of poets, saith: *Os tenerum pueri balbumque poeta figurat*,[xlviii][96] and many more words concerning the profit to be had out of poets, which because I have some of them comprised into an English translation of that learned and famous knight Sir Thomas Elyot, I will set down his words:

---

[93] Omne [...] monendo] 'He has won every vote who has blended profit and pleasure, at once delighting and instructing the reader' (*Ars Poetica* 343–44).
[94] *Ficta* [...] *veris*] *Ars Poetica*, 338–40: 'Ficta voluptatis causa sint proxima veris/Ne quodcumque velit poscat sibi credi/Neu pransae Lamiae vivum puerum extrahat alvo' ('Fictions meant to please should be close to the real, so that your play must not ask for belief in anything it chooses, nor from the Ogress's belly, after dinner, draw forth a living child').
[95] This precept [...] tale] On Webbe's admiration for Chaucer see note 61 above.
[96] *Os* [...] *figurat*] 'The poet fashions the tender, lisping lips of childhood'; *Epistles*, 2.1.126.

The poet fashioneth by some pleasant mean,
The speech of children tender^xlix and unsure,
Pulling^l their ears from words and things^li 97 unclean,
Giving to them precepts that are pure,
Rebuking envy and wrath if it dure.
Things well done he can by example commend,
The^lii needy and sick he doth also his cure
To recomfort, if ought^liii he can amend.⁹⁸

And many other like words are in that place of Horace to like effect. Therefore poetry, as it is of itself without abuse, is not only not unprofitable to the lives and studies of men, but wonderful commendable and of great excellency. For nothing can be more acceptable to men, or rather to be wished, than sweet allurements to virtues and commodious caveats° from vices,^liv of which poetry is exceeding plentiful, pouring into gentle wits, not roughly and tyrannically, but as it were with a loving authority.⁹⁹ Now, if the ill and undecent provocations [D4ʳ] whereof some unbridled wits take occasion by the reading of lascivious poems be objected — such as are Ovid's love books and *Elegies*, Tibullus', Catullus', and Martial's works, with the comedies for the most part of Plautus and Terence — I think it easily answered.¹⁰⁰ For, though it may not justly be denied that these works are indeed very poetry, yet that poetry in them is not the essential or formal matter or cause of the hurt therein might be affirmed. And although that reason should come short, yet this might be sufficient, that the works themselves do not corrupt, but the abuse of the users, who, undamaging their own dispositions by reading the discoveries of vices, resemble foolish folk who, coming into a garden without

---

⁹⁷ words and things unclean] 'words unclean' in *Governour* 1531, 1580. Likely Webbe's purposeful addition in order to recall the Ciceronian pair *verba et res*, on which Ascham's idea of the didactic potential of style (words) as evocative of matter (things) is grounded. *Schoolmaster*, p. 265: 'Ye know not, what hurt ye do to learning, that care not for words, but for matter, and so make a deuorse betwixt the tong and the hart'.
⁹⁸ The poet [...] amend] *Governour*, 1.13. From Horace, *Epistles*, 2.1.126–131: 'Os tenerum pueri balbumque poeta figurat,/Torquet ab obscenis iam nunc sermonibus aurem,/Mox etiam pectus praeceptis format amicis,/Asperitatis et invidiae corrector et irae,/Recte facta refert, orientia tempora notis/Instruit exemplis, inopem solatur et aegrum' ('The poet fashions the tender, lisping lips of childhood; even then he turns the ear from unseemly words; presently, too, he moulds the heart by kindly precepts, correcting roughness and envy and anger. He tells of noble deeds, equips the rising age with famous examples, and to the helpless and sick at heart brings comfort').
⁹⁹ For nothing [...] authority] Ascham, *Schoolmaster*, p. 197: 'that yong children should rather be allured to learning by ientilnes and loue, than compelled to learning, by beating and feare'.
¹⁰⁰ Now [...] answered] From Elyot's train of reflections in defence of poetry; Webbe adds Tibullus and Plautus. *Governour*, 1.13: 'But they whiche be ignoraunt in poetes wyll perchaunce obiecte, as is their maner, agayne these verses, sayeng that in Therence and other that were writers of comedies, also Ouide, Catullus, Martialis, and all that route of lasciuious poetes that wrate epistles and ditties of loue'.

any choice or circumspection, tread down the fairest flowers and wilfully thrust their fingers among the nettles.[101]

And surely, to speak what I verily think, this is mine opinion: that one having sufficient skill to read and understand those works, and yet no stay of himself to avoid inconveniences° which the remembrance of unlawful things may stir up in his mind, he, in my judgement, is wholly to be reputed a lascivious disposed person, whom the recital of sins, whether it be in a good work or a bad, or upon what occasion soever, will not stay him but provoke him further unto them. Contrariwise, what good lessons the wary and skilful readers shall pick out of the very worst of them, if they list° to take any heed and read them not of an intent to be made the worse by them, you may see by these few sentences, which the foresaid° Sir Thomas Elyot gathered as he saith at all adventures, entreating of the like argument. First Plautus, in commendations° of virtue, hath such like words:

> Verily virtue doth all things excel,
> For if liberty, health, living, and[lv] substance,°
> Our country, our parents, and children do well,
> It happeneth by virtue; she doth all advance.
> Virtue hath all things[lvi] under governance:
> And in whom of virtue is found great plenty
> Anything that is good may never be dainty.[102]

[D4ᵛ] Terence, in *Eunucho*, hath a profitable speech in blazing forth the fashions of harlots before the eyes of young men. Thus saith Parmeno:

> In this thing I triumph in mine own conceit,
> That I have found for all young men the way
> How they of harlots shall know the deceit,
> Their wits, their[lvii] manners, that thereby they may
> Them perpetually hate; for so much as they
> Out of their own houses be fresh and delicate,

---

[101] And although [...] nettles] In this context Sidney also ascribes the contempt for poetry to some readers' wickedness: 'and not say that poetry abuseth man's wit, but that man's wit abuseth poetry' (*Defence*, p. 35). Webbe adds irony and acridness to Elyot's original metaphor of the garden; in *Governour*, 1.13: 'No wyse man entreth in to a gardein but he sone espieth good herbes from nettles, and treadeth the nettles under his feete whiles he gadreth good herbes. Wherby he taketh no damage, or if he be stungen he maketh lite of it and shortly forgetteth it. Semblablye if he do rede wanton mater mixte with wisedome, he putteth the warst under foote and sorteth out the best'.

[102] Verily [...] dainty] *Governour*, 1.13. From Plautus, *Amphitryon*, 2.2.648–653: 'Uirtus praemium est optumum;/Uirtus omnibus rebus anteit profecto:/Libertas, salus, uita, res et parentes,/Patria et prognati/Tutantur, seruantur:/Uirtus omnia in sese habet, omnia assunt/ Bona quem penest uirtus' ('Courage does indeed outdo everything: freedom, safety, life, possessions and parents, home and relatives are protected and preserved. Courage has all goods within itself, all goods are with the man who has courage').

Feeding curiously, at home all the[lviii] day
Living beggarly in most wretched estate.[103]

And many more words of the same matter, but which may be gathered by these few.

Ovid, in his most wanton books of love and the remedies thereof, hath very many pithy° and wise sentences which a heedful reader may mark and choose out from the other stuff.[104] This is one:

Time is a medicine[lix][105] if it shall profit,
Wine given out of time may be annoyance.
A[lx] man shall irritate vice if he prohibit,[lxi]
When time is not meet° unto his utterance.
Therefore, if thou yet by counsel are recuperable,
Fly thou from idleness and alway[lxii] be stable.[106]

Martial, a most dissolute writer among all other, yet not without many grave and prudent speeches as this, is one worthy to be marked of these fond youths which entangle their wits in raging love, who stepping once over shoes in their fancies, never rest plunging till they be over head and ears in their folly:[107]

---

[103] In this thing [...] estate] *Governour*, 1.13. From Terence, *The Eunuch*, 5.930: 'Id verost quod ego mihi puto palmarium,/Me repperisse, quo modo adulescentulus/Meretricum ingenia et mores posset noscere,/Mature ut quom cognorit perpetuo oderit./Quae dum foris sunt, nil videtur mundius,/Nec magis compositum quicquam nec magis elegans/Quam cum amatore cenam uom ligurriunt./Harum videre inluviem sordes inopiam,/Quam inhonestae solae sint domi atque avidae cibi,/Quo pacto ex iure hesterno panem atrum vorent,/Nosse omnia haec salutist adulescentulis' ('my veritable masterpiece I consider it, in having found means to let a stripling into the characters and ways of that class so early in life that his acquaintance with them will lead to a lifelong loathing. When they are away from home nothing looks in better taste, nothing more orderly and elegant, than when they lick up a dinner in a lover's company. To see their filth, meanness and poverty, their hideousness and greed for food when they're by themselves at home, the way they gobble the black bread from yesterday's broth, to see all this is salvation to a young man').
[104] Ovid [...] stuff] *Governour*, 1.13: 'Also Ouidius, that semeth to be moste of all poetes lasciuious, in his mooste wanton bokes hath righte commendable and noble sentences'.
[105] is a medicine] in medicine *Governour* 1531; is medicine ibid. 1580. If he prohibit] if be prohite *Governour* 1531; he be prohibite ibid. 1580. An example of Webbe's purposeful editing of Elyot's translation with the intention to improve its style.
[106] Time [...] stable] *Governour*, 1.13. From Ovid, *Remedia Amoris*, 131–36: 'Temporis ars medicina fere est: data tempore prosunt,/Et data non apto tempore vina nocent./Quin etiam accendas vitia inritesque vetando,/Temporibus si non adgrediare suis./Ergo ubi visus eris nostra medicabilis arte,/Fac monitis fugias otia prima meis' ('The art of being timely is almost a medicine: wine timely given helps, untimely, harms. Nay, you would inflame the malady, and by forbidding irritate it, should you attack it at an unfitting time).
[107] Martial [...] folly] *Governour*, 1.13: 'Martialis, whiche, for his dissolute wrytynge'; the idea that Martial's poems are commendable to enamoured youths is Webbe's original addition.

If thou will eschew bitter adventure,
And avoid the gnawing°^lxiii of a pensiful° heart,
[E1ʳ] Set in no one person all wholly^lxiv thy pleasure,
The less mayst thou joy,^lxv but the^lxvi less shall thou smart.[108]

These are but few gathered out by hap,° yet sufficient to show that the wise and circumspect readers may find very many profitable lessons dispersed in these works, neither take any harm by reading such poems, but good, if they will themselves. Nevertheless, I would not be thought to hold opinion that the reading of them is so tolerable as that there need no respect to be had in making choice of readers or hearers. For if they be prohibited from the tender and unconstant wits of children and young minds, I think it not without great reason.[109] Neither am I of that devilish opinion, of which some there are and have been in England, who, having charge of youth to instruct them in learning, have especially made choice of such unchildish stuff to read unto young scholars, as it should seem of some filthy purpose, wilfully to corrupt their tender minds and prepare them the more ready for their loathsome diets.°

For, as it is said of that impudent work of Lucian — a man were better to read none of it than all of it[110] — so think I that these works are rather to be kept altogether from children than they should have free liberty to read them before they be meet,° either of their own discretion or by heedful instruction, to make choice of the good from the bad. As for our English poetry, I know no such perilous pieces (except a few bold ditties made over the beer pots, which are nothing less than poetry) which any man may use and read without damage or danger; which indeed is less to be marvelled at among us than among the old Latins and Greeks, considering that Christianity may be a stay to such illecebrous° works and inventions as among them (for their^lxvii art sake) might obtain passage.

Now will I speak somewhat of that princely part of poetry wherein are displayed the noble acts and valiant exploits of puissant captains, expert soldiers,

---

[108] If thou […] smart] *Governour*, 1.13. From Martial, *Epigrams*, 12.34: 'Si vitare voles acerba quaedam/Et tristis animi cavere morsus,/Nulli te facias nimis sodalem:/Gaudebis minus et minus dolebis' ('If you wish to avoid certain sournesses and guard against painful heart-bites, to no man make yourself too much a friend. Less will be your joy and less your grief').

[109] Nevertheless […] great reason] *Governour*, 1.13: 'So all thoughe I do nat approue the lesson of wanton poetes to be taughte unto all children, yet thynke I conuenient and necessary that, whan the mynde is become constante and courage is asswaged, or that children of their natural disposition be shamfaste and continent, none aunciente poete wolde be excluded from the leesson of suche one as desireth to come to the perfection of wysedome'.

[110] For […] of it] *Governour*, 1.10: 'but thus moche dare I say, that it were better that a childe shuld neuer rede any parte of Luciane than all Luciane'. Lucian's dubious reputation among the Elizabethans is corroborated by Spenser, *SC*, gloss to 'January' ('Hobbinol'): 'but let no man think that herein I stand with Lucian or his devilish disciple Unico Aretino in defence of execrable and horrible sins of forbidden and unlawful fleshliness, whose abominable error is fully confuted of Perionius and others' (Brooks-Davies, p. 36).

wise men, with the famous reports of ancient times, such as are the heroical [E1ᵛ] works of Homer in Greek and the heavenly verse of Virgil's *Aeneidos* in Latin, which works, comprehending as it were the sum and ground of all poetry, are verily and incomparably the best of all other.[111] To these, though we have no English work answerable in respect of the glorious ornaments of gallant handling, yet our ancient chroniclers and reporters of our country affairs come most near them. And no doubt, if such regard of our English speech and curious handling of our verse[112] had been long since thought upon, and from time to time been polished and bettered by men of learning, judgement, and authority, it would ere this have matched them in all respects.[113] A manifest example thereof may be the great good grace and sweet vein which eloquence hath attained in our speech, because it hath had the help of such rare and singular wits as from time to time might still add some amendment to the same.[114] Among whom I think there is none that will gainsay° but Master John Lyly[115] hath deserved most high commendations,° as he which hath stepped one step further therein than any

---

[111] Now will [...] other] Puttenham, *The Art*, 1.11: 'Such therefore as gave themselves to write long histories of the noble gests of kings and great princes, intermeddling the dealings of the gods, half-gods, or heroes of the gentiles, and the great and weighty consequences of peace and war, they called poets heroic, whereof Homer was chief and most ancient among the Greeks, Vergil among the Latins'. Sidney, *Defence*, p. 29: 'But if anything be already said in the defence of sweet poetry, all concurreth to the maintaining the heroical, which is not only a kind, but the best and most accomplished kind of poetry'.

[112] curious handling of our verse] Webbe refers to the use of quantitative metres in English verse instead of rhyme.

[113] And no doubt[...] respects] Webbe insists on the idea that the inferiority of English poetry as regards ancient and other European literatures is not due to the natural rudeness of their language, but to the national poets' negligence, who have failed to strive towards the metrical perfection attained by Greek and Roman writers. Ascham's humanist convictions that the acculturation of the nation had to be attained primarily through the consolidation of a national idiom, and that any language can attain eloquence through the imitation of classical eloquence pervade *A Discourse* and are used as arguments for Webbe's claim for a poetic reformation, which he addresses to contemporary poets in the 'Preface'. Ascham, *Schoolmaster*, p. 265: 'the rudenes of common and mother tonges, is no bar for wise speaking'.

[114] A manifest [...] same] Once again Webbe refers to rhetoric eloquence as closely related to poetry. See note 14 above.

[115] Master John Lyly] (c. 1554-1569) English poet and playwright who gained extraordinary popularity with his two novels *Euphues: the anatomy of wit* (1578) and *Euphues and His England* (1580); his highly rhetorical prose style, profusely marked with Ciceronian schemes and images (*euphuism*), had as many detractors as supporters. Webbe's admiration is moved by Lyly's representativeness of humanist poetics as regards Ascham's view of style as a landmark of national wisdom; in fact, the title of his novel is indebted to Ascham's passage explaining Plato's concept of 'Εὐφυὴς' (*Schoolmaster*, pp. 194-95). Accordingly, Arthur F. Kinney (1986: 133) attributes to Lyly 'an interest in verbal behavior as an index to the disposition of the mind and soul'. In '"Singuler eloquence and braue composition": John Lyly, Euphues, and Its Sequel', *Humanist Poetics: Thought, Rhetoric and Fiction in Sixteenth-century England* (Amherst: The University of Massachusetts Press, 1986), pp. 133-80.

either before, or since he first began the witty discourse of his *Euphues*. Whose works, surely in respect of his singular eloquence and brave composition of apt words and sentences, let the learned examine and make trial thereof through all the parts of rhetoric, in fit phrases, in pithy° sentences, in gallant tropes, in flowing speech, in plain sense, and surely, in my judgement, I think he will yield him that verdict which Quintilian giveth of both the best orators Demosthenes and Tully: that from the one nothing may be taken away, to the other nothing may be added.[116] But a more nearer example to prove my former assertion true (I mean the meetness° of our speech to receive the best form of poetry) may be taken by conference° of that famous translation of Master Thomas Phaer[117] with the copy itself, whosoever please with courteous judgement but a little to compare and mark them both together, and weigh with himself whether the English tongue might by little and little be brought to the very majesty of a right heroical verse.[118] First, you may mark how Virgil always fitteth his matter in hand with words agreeable unto [E2ʳ] the same affection which he expresseth, as in his tragical exclamations, what pathetical°[lxviii] speeches he frameth. In his comfortable consolations, how smoothly his verse runs. In his dreadful battles and dreary bickerments° of wars, how big and boisterous his words sound. And the like notes in all parts of his work may be observed, which excellent grace and comely° kind of choice, if the translator hath not hit very near in our coarse English phrase judge uprightly;° we will confer some of the places not picked out for the purpose, but such as I took turning over the book at random. When the Troyans were so tossed about in tempestuous weather caused by Aeolus at Juno's request, and driven upon the coast of Affrick with a very near escape of their lives, Aeneas, after he had gone a land and killed plenty of victuals° for his company of soldiers, he divided the same among them, and thus lovingly and sweetly he comforted them (*Aeneidos*,[lxix] Liber 1):

---

[116] I think [...] added] *The Institutio Oratoria*, 10.1.106–107: 'In eloquendo est aliqua diversitas; densior ille hic copiosior, ille concludit adstrictius hic latius, pugnat ille acumine semper hic frequenter et pondere, illi nihil detrahi potest huic nihil adiici, curae plus in illo in hoc naturae' ('In their actual style there is some difference. Demosthenes is more concentrated, Cicero more diffuse; Demosthenes makes his periods shorter than Cicero, and his weapon is the rapier, whereas Cicero's periods are longer, and at times he employs the bludgeon as well: nothing can be taken from the former, nor added to the latter'). Demosthenes and Cicero are hailed by Elyot as models for the teaching of eloquence and 'gentyll manners' (*Governour*, 1.11).
[117] Thomas Phaer] D. Phaer in Q; an error of print?
[118] But a more [...] verse] On Phaer see note 69 above. Neither Webbe nor Meres mentions Richard Stanyhurst's translation of the first four books of Virgil's *Aeneid* into English hexameters (1582); both hail Phaer as the canonical translator of Virgil. See Meres, *Palladis*, p. 322. Harvey praised Stanyhurst for his efforts on classical metres: 'I cordially recommend to the deere louers of the Muses: and namely, to the professed Sonnes of the fame; Edmond Spencer, Richard Stanihurst, Abraham France, Thomas Watson, Samuell Daniell, Thomas Nash, and the rest, whom I affectionately thancke for their studious endeuors, commendably employed in enriching, and polishing their natiue tongue, neuer so furnished, or embellished as of late', *Foure Letters* 1592, Grosart, pp. 218–19.

> *et dictis maerentia pectora mulcet:*
> *"O socii (neque enim[lxx] ignari sumus ante malorum)*
> *O passi graviora, dabit deus his quoque finem.*
> *Vos et Scyllaeam rabiem penitusque sonantis,[lxxi]*
> *Accestis scopulos, vos et Cyclopia[lxxii] saxa*
> *Experti; revocate animos maestumque timorem*
> *Mittite; forsan et haec olim meminisse iuvabit.*
> *Per varios casus, per tot discrimina rerum,*
> *Tendimus in Latium, sedes ubi fata quietas*
> *Ostendunt; illic fas regna resurgere Troiae.*
> *Durate, et vosmet rebus servate secundis."*
> *Talia voce refert, curisque ingentibus aeger*
> *Spem vultu simulat, premit altum corde dolorem.*[119]

Translated thus [E2ᵛ]:

> And then to cheer their heavy hearts with these words he him bent:
> 'O Mates (quoth he) that many a woe have bidden and borne, ere this
> Worse have we seen, and this also shall end when God's will is.
> Through Scylla's[lxxiii] rage (ye wot) and through the roaring rocks we past,°
> Though Cyclops' shore was full of fear, yet came we through at last.
> Pluck up your hearts, and drive from thence both fear and care[lxxiv] away
> To think on this may pleasure be perhaps another day.
> With[lxxv] pains and many a danger sore° by sundry chance we wend
> To come to Italy,[lxxvi] where we trust to find our resting end:
> And where the destinies have decreed Troy's kingdom[lxxvii] eft° to rise.
> Be bold and harden now your hearts,[lxxviii] take ease when[lxxix] ease applies.'
> Thus spake he tho,° but in his heart huge cares him had[lxxx] oppressed,
> Dissembling hope with outward eyes, full heavy was his breast.[120]

Again, mark the wounding of *Dido* in love with Aeneas, with how choice words it is pithily° described both by the poet and the translator, in the beginning of the fourth book:

---

[119] *et dictis [...] dolorem*] Ibid., 197–209: 'and speaking thus, calms their sorrowing hearts: "O comrades — for ere this we have not been ignorant of misfortune — you who have suffered worse, this also God will end. You drew near to Scylla's fury and her deep-echoing crags; you have known, too, the rocks of the Cyclopes; recall your courage and banish sad fear. Perhaps even this distress it will some day be a joy to recall. Through varied fortunes, through countless hazards, we journey towards Latium, where fate promises a home of peace. There it is granted that Troy's realm shall rise again; endure, and live for a happier day". Such words he spoke, while sick with deep distress he feigns hope on his face, and deep in his heart stifles his anguish'.
[120] O Mates[...] breast] Phaer 1584, sig. B3ᵛ. I have kept Webbe's variants in these cases as I assume a deliberate will to improve Phaer's text: fear and care] thought and feare Phaer 1573, 1584 (likely an *amplificatio*, in fact closer to 'maestumque timorem' in the Latin text); hearts] selfs Phaer 1573, 1584 (*amplificatio*).

> *At Regina gravi iamdudum saucia cura*
> *Vulnus alit venis et caeco carpitur igni*, etc.[121]

> By this time pierced sat the queen so sore° with love's desire,
> Her wound in every vain she feeds, she fries in secret fire.
> The manhood of the man full oft, full oft his famous line°
> She doth revolve, and from her thought his face cannot untwine.
> His countenance° deep she draws and fixed fast she bears in breast
> His words also; nor to her careful° heart can come no rest.[122]

And in many places of the fourth book is the same matter so gallantly prosecuted in sweet words, as in mine opinion the copy itself goeth no whit° beyond it.

Compare them likewise in the woeful and lamentable cries of the queen for the departure of Aeneas, towards the end of that book [E3ʳ]:

> *Terque quaterque manu pectus percussa decorum*
> *Flaventisque*[lxxxi] *abscissa comas, "pro Iuppiter! ibit*
> *Hic," ait, "et nostris inluserit*[lxxxii] *advena regnis?"* etc.[123]

> Three times her hands she beat, and four[lxxxiii] times strake° her comely° breast,
> Her golden hair she tore and frantically with mood oppressed,
> She cried, "Oh Jupiter, Oh God", quoth she, "and shall a go?
> Indeed? And shall a flout° me thus within my kingdoms[lxxxiv] so?
> Shall not mine armies out, and all my peoples[lxxxv] them pursue?
> Shall they not spoil their ships or[lxxxvi] burn them all[lxxxvii] with vengeance due?

---

[121] *At regina* [...] etc.] Ibid. book 4, 1–5: 'At Regina gravi iamdudum saucia cura/Vulnus alit venis et caeco carpitur igni/Multa viri virtus animo multusque recursat/Gentis honos; haerent infixi pectore vultus/Verbaque, nec placidam membris dat cura quietem' ('But the queen, long since smitten with a grievous love-pang, feeds the wound with her lifeblood, and is wasted with fire unseen. Oft to her mind rushes back the hero's valour, oft his glorious stock; his looks and words cling fast to her bosom, and longing with holds calm rest from her limbs').

[122] By this [...] rest] Phaer 1584, sig. F1ᵛ.

[123] Terque quaterque [...] etc.] Ibid., book 4, 589–91: 'Terque quaterque manu pectus percussa decorum/Flaventisque abscissa comas, "pro Iuppiter! ibit/Hic," ait, "et nostris inluserit advena regnis?/Non arma expedient totaque ex urbe sequentur,/Deripientque rates alii navalibus? Ite,/Ferte citi flammas, date tela, impellite remos!/Quid loquor? Aut ubi sum? Quae mentem insania mutat?/Infelix Dido, nunc te facta impia tangunt?"' ('thrice and for times she struck her comely breast with her hand, and tearing her golden hair, "O God," she cries, "shall he go? Shall the intruder have made of our realm a laughingstock? Will pursuers not fetch arms and give chase from all the city, and some of them speed ships from the docks? Go, haste to bring fire, serve arms, ply oars! What I say? Where am I? What madness turns my brain? Unhappy Dido, do only now your sinful deeds come home to you?"').

> Out people, out upon them, follow fast with fires and flames,
> Set sails aloft, make out with oars, in ships, in boats, in frames.
> What speak I? Or where am I? What furies me do thus enchant?
> Oh Dido, woeful wretch, now destiny's fell° thy head doth haunt."[124]

And a little after preparing to kill her own self:

> But Dido quaking fierce with frantic mood and grisly hue,
> With trembling spotted cheeks, her huge attemptings[lxxxviii] to pursue,
> Besides herself for rage, and towards death with visage wane,
> Her eyes about she rolled, as red as blood they looked then.[lxxxix] [125]

At last ready to fall upon Aeneas' sword:

> "O happy (wellaway!°) and over happy had I been,
> If never Troyan ship[xc] (alas!) my country shore had seen".
> This[xci] said, she wried° her head. "And unrevenged[xcii] must we die?
> But[xciii] let us boldly die", quoth she, "thus, thus to death I ply."[126]

Now likewise for the brave warlike phrase and big sounding kind of thundering speech in the hot skirmishes of battles, you may confer them in any of the last five books. For example's sake, this is one about the ninth book [E3ᵛ]:

> *It clamor totis per propugnacula muris,*
> *Intendunt acris[xciv] arcus, amentaque torquent.*
> *Sternitur omne solum telis, tum scuta[xcv] cavaeque,*
> *Dant sonitum flictu galeae: pugna aspera[xcvi] surgit, etc.*[127]

---

[124] Three times [...] haunt] Phaer 1584, sigs. G2ʳ-G2ᵛ; 1573, sigs. L2ʳ-L2ᵛ.
[125] But Dido [...] then] Ibid. book 4, 642-45: 'At trepida et coeptis immanibus effera Dido,/Sanguineam volvens aciem, maculisque trementis/Interfusa genas, et pallida morte futura.' ('But Dido, trembling and frantic with her dreadful design, rolling bloodshot eyes, her quivering cheeks flecked with burning spots, and pale at the imminence of death'); Phaer 1584, sig. G3ʳ; 1573, sig. L3ʳ.
[126] O happy [...] ply] Ibid. book 4, 657-60: '"felix, heu! Nimium felix, si litora tantum/ Numquam Dardaniae tetigissent nostra carinae!"/Dixit et os impressa toro, "moriemur inultae, /Sed moriamur," ait. "Sic, sic iuvat ire sub umbras"'. ('"happy, too happy, had but the Dardan keels never touched our shores!" She spoke, and burying her face in the couch, "I shall die unavenged," she cries, "but let me die! Thus, thus I go gladly into the dark!" '); Phaer 1584, sig. G3ʳ.
[127] *It clamor* [...] etc.] Ibid. book 9, 664-67: 'It clamor totis per propugnacula muris,/Intendunt acris arcus amentaque torquent/Sternitur omne solum telis, tum scuta cavaeque,/Dant sonitum flictu galeae, pugna aspera surgit,/Quantus ab occasu veniens pluvialibus Haedis/Verberat imber humum, quam multa grandine nimbi/In vada praecipitant, cum Iuppiter horridus Austris/Torquet aquosam hiemem et caelo cava nubila rumpit.' ('The shout runs from tower to tower, all along the walls; they bend their eager bows and whirl their thongs. All the ground is strewn with spears; shields and hollow helms ring as they clash; the fight swells fierce: mighty as the storm that, coming from the west, beneath the rainy Kid-stars lashes the ground; thick as the hail that storm clouds shower on the deep, when Jupiter, grim with southern gales, whirls the watery tempest, and bursts the hollow clouds in heaven').

A clamorous noise up'mounts on fortress tops and bulwarks'° towers;
They strike, they bend their bows, they whirl from strings sharp shooting showers.
All streets with tools are strowed,° then helmets, skulls, with batterings marred,
And shields dishivering crack, upriseth roughness bickering hard.
Look how the tempest storm when winds^{xcvii} outwrestling° blows at south,
Rain rattling beats^{xcviii} the ground, or clouds of hail from Winter's^{xcix} mouth
Down dashing headlong drives, when God from skies with grisly steven°
His watery showers outwrings, and whirlwind clouds down breaks from heaven.[128]

And so forth much more of the like effect.

Only one comparison more will I desire you to mark at your leisures, which may serve for all the rest, that is, the description of Fame, as it is in the fourth book towards the end, of which it followeth thus:

Monstrum horrendum, ingens, cui, quot sunt corpore plumae
Tot vigiles^c oculi, etc.[129]

A^{ci} monster ghastly great, for every plume her carcass bears
Like number leering° eyes she hath, like number harkening° ears.
Like number tongues and mouths she wags,° a wondrous thing to speak,
At midnight forth she flies, and under shade her sound doth squeak.
All night she wakes, nor slumber sweet doth take, nor never sleeps;
By days on houses tops she sits, or gates, or towns^{cii} she keeps.
On watching towers she climbs, and cities great she makes aghast,
Both truth and falshed^{ciii} forth she tells, and lies abroad doth cast.[130]

But what need I to repeat any more places? There is not one book among the twelve which will not yield you most excellent pleasure in conferring the translation with the copy, and marking the gallant grace[131] which our English

---

[128] A clamorous [...] heaven] Phaer 1584, sig. O5^v. Beats] gets Phaer 1573, 1584. Webbe's variant seems an intentional attempt to provide a more accurate translation to 'verberat'.
[129] *Monstrum horrendum* [...] etc.] Ibid. 181–88: 'Monstrum horrendum, ingens, cui, quot sunt corpore plumae/Tot vigiles oculi subter (mirabile dictu),/Tot linguae, totidem ora sonant, tot subrigit auris./Nocte volat caeli medio terraque per umbram,/Stridens, nec dulci declinat lumina somno;/Luce sedet custos aut summi culmine tecti,/Turribus aut altis, et magnas territat urbes,/Tam ficti pravique tenax quam nuntia veri' ('a monster awful and huge, who for the many feathers in her body has as many watchful eyes beneath — wondrous to tell — as many tongues, as many sounding mouths, as many pricked-up ears. By night, midway between heaven and earth, she flies through the gloom, screeching, and droops not her eyes in sweet sleep; by day she sits on guard on high rooftop or lofty turrets, and affrights great cities, clinging to the false and wrong, yet heralding truth').
[130] A monster [...] cast] Phaer 1584, sigs. F4^r–F4^v.
[131] gallant grace] ornate gracefulness.

speech affordeth. And in truth, the like comparisons may you choose out through the whole translations of the *Metamorphoses* by Master Golding,¹³² who (considering both their copies) hath equally deserved commendations° for the beautifying of the English speech. It would be tedious to stay to rehearse° any places out of him now. Let the other suffice to prove that the English tongue lacketh neither variety nor currentness° of phrase for any matter.

[E4ʳ] I will now speak^civ a little of another kind of poetical writing which might notwithstanding, for the variableness of the argument therein usually handled, be comprehended in those kinds before declared,¹³³ that is, the compiling of^cv eclogues, as much to say as goatherds' tales, because they be commonly dialogues or speeches framed or supposed between shepherds, neatherds, goatherds, or such like simple men, in which kind of writing many have obtained as immortal praise and commendation° as in any other.¹³⁴

The chiefest of these is Theocritus in Greek. Next him, and almost the very same, is Virgil in Latin.¹³⁵ After Virgil, in like sort, writ Titus Calpurnius¹³⁶ and Baptista Mantuan,¹³⁷ with many other both in Latin and other languages very learnedly. Although the matter they take in hand seemeth commonly in appearance rude and homely, as the usual talk of simple clowns, yet do they indeed utter in the same much pleasant and profitable delight. For under these persons, as it were in a cloak of simplicity, they would either set forth the praises of their friends without the note of flattery, or inveigh° grievously against abuses without any token of bitterness.¹³⁸

Somewhat like unto these works are many pieces of Chaucer, but yet not altogether so poetical. But now yet at the last hath England hatched up° one poet of this sort, in my conscience comparable with the best in any respect: even Master Sp., author of *The Shepherds' Calendar*, whose travel° in that piece of English poetry I think verily is so commendable, as none of equal judgement can yield him less praise for his excellent skill and skilful excellency showed forth in

---

¹³² Master Golding] On Golding see note 70 above.
¹³³ those kinds before declared] In comedy, tragedy or history.
¹³⁴ the compiling [...] other] See Puttenham 1.18; Spenser, *SC*, 'General Argument', 1–23 (Brooks-Davies, pp. 26–27).
¹³⁵ The chiefest [...] Latin] Spenser, *SC*, 'General Prologue', 9–10 (Brooks-Davies, p. 26): 'Theocritus (in whom is more ground of authority than in Virgil)'.
¹³⁶ Titus Calpurnius] Titus Calpurnius Siculus or Titus Julius Calpurnius (*c.* 290 AD) was thought to be the author of eleven eclogues in Latin verse imitating Virgil's, although it seems to have been sufficiently proved that four of them were actually written by Nemesianus; this distinction was first made by Angelus Ugoletus' edition at Parma around 1500.
¹³⁷ Baptista Mantuan] See note 53 above.
¹³⁸ For under [...] bitterness] Puttenham, *The Art*, 1.18: 'but under the veil of homely persons and in rude speeches to insinuate and glance at greater matters, and such as perchance had not been safe to have been disclosed in any other sort'.

the same than they would to either Theocritus or Virgil, whom in mine opinion, if the coarseness of our speech (I mean the course of custom which he would not infringe°) had been no [E4ᵛ] more let° unto him than their pure native tongues were unto them, he would have (if it might be) surpassed them.¹³⁹ What one thing is there in them so worthy admiration, whereunto we may not adjoin something of his of equal desert?° Take Virgil and make some little comparison between them, and judge as you shall see cause.¹⁴⁰

Virgil hath a gallant report of Augustus covertly comprised in the First Eclogue; the like is in him of her Majesty, under the name of Elisa.¹⁴¹ Virgil maketh a brave coloured complaint of unsteadfast° friendship in the person of Corydon;¹⁴² the like is him in his Fifth Eclogue. Again behold the pretty pastoral contentions° of Virgil in the Third Eclogue; of him the Eighth^cvi Eclogue. Finally, either in comparison with them or respect of his own great learning, he may well wear the garland and step before the best of all English poets that I have seen or heard, for I think no less 'deserveth' (thus saith E.K.^cvii in his commendations°) 'his wittiness in devising, his pithiness° in uttering, his complaints of love so lovely, his discourses of pleasure so pleasantly, his pastoral rudeness, his moral wiseness, his due observing of *decorum* everywhere, in personages, in seasons,^cviii in matter, in speech, and generally in all seemly simplicity of handling his matter and framing his words'.¹⁴³ The occasion of his work is a warning to other young men, who being entangled in love and youthful vanities, may learn to look to themselves in time and to avoid inconveniences° which may breed if they be not in time prevented. Many good moral lessons are therein contained, as the reverence which young men owe to the aged in the Second Eclogue, the caveat° or warning to beware a subtle professor of friendship in the Fifth Eclogue, the commendation° of good pastors and shame and dispraise of idle and ambitious goatherds in the seventh, the loose and reckless living of popish prelates in the ninth, the learned and sweet complaint of the contempt of learning under the

---

¹³⁹ either Theocritus [...] them] See Webbe p. 68 above. In his allusions to Spenser Webbe hails him as a direct heir of Theocritus and Virgil, insisting on the fact that his elegies are the result of skilful imitation of the ancient masters; thus, he aims at legitimizing Spenser's incorporation to the classical canon of letters while evincing that the English tongue is not devoid of the literary potential of the tongues of the Greeks or Romans.
¹⁴⁰ Take Virgil [...] cause] Webbe inherits from Ascham the idea that imitation and translation are the most efficient methods when it comes to learning rhetoric techniques and developing literary creativity; with the following comparison he seems to be answering Ascham's demands for the compilation of catalogues that shed light on the motifs and methods employed by the Latin poets in their imitations of the Greek models with the aim of providing students with didactic examples. See Ascham, *Schoolmaster*, pp. 267–68.
¹⁴¹ Virgil [...] Elisa] Spenser, *SC*, 'April' 37–153 (Brooks-Davies, pp. 67–72).
¹⁴² Virgil [...] Corydon] *Eclogue* 2.
¹⁴³ 'deserveth' [...] his words'] Spenser, *SC*, 'Dedicatory epistle', 22–28 (Brooks-Davies p. 19).

name of poetry in the tenth.¹⁴⁴ There is also much matter uttered somewhat covertly, especially the abuses of some whom he would not be too plain withal, in which, though it be not apparent to everyone what his special meaning [F1ʳ] was, yet so skilfully is it handled, as any man may take much delight at his learned conveyance, and pick out much good sense in the most obscurest of it. His notable praise deserved in every parcel of that work, because I cannot express as I would and as it should, I will cease to speak any more of, the rather because I never heard as yet any that hath read it which hath not with much admiration commended it. One only thing therein have I heard some curious heads call in question, *viz*: the motion of some unsavoury love, such as in the Sixth Eclogue he seemeth to deal withal, which (say they) is scant° allowable to English ears, and might well have been left for the Italian defenders of loathsome beastliness,¹⁴⁵ of whom perhaps he learned it. To this objection I have often answered (and I think truly) that their nice° opinion overshooteth the poet's meaning, who though he in that, as in other things, imitateth the ancient poets, yet doth not mean, no more did they before him, any disordered love or the filthy lust of the devilish *pederastice* taken in the worse sense, but rather to show how the dissolute life of young men entangled in love of women do neglect the friendship and league with their old friends and familiars.¹⁴⁶ Why (say they) yet he should give no occasion of suspicion, nor offer to the view of Christians any token of such filthiness, how

---

¹⁴⁴ Many good [...] tenth] These interpretations of the moral lessons in SC are inspired on the previous 'Argument' to each eclogue; in 'July' and 'September' Webbe copies *verbatim*. Spenser, SC, 'July': 'This eglogue is made in the honour and commendation of good shepherds, and to the same and dispraise of proud and ambitious pastors, such as Morrell is here imagined to be' (Brook-Davies, p. 113). 'September': 'Herein Diggon Davy is devised to be a shepherd that, in hope of more gain, drove his sheep into a far country, the abuses whereof, and loose living of popish prelates, by occasion of Hobbinol's demand, he discourseth at large' (Brook-Davies, p. 141).
¹⁴⁵ Italian defenders of loathsome beastliness] It was an extended assumption among the Elizabethan humanists that Popish Italy was too tolerant with corrupted forms of literature, among which they counted romance books or Bocaccio's tales. Ascham dedicates a long section in *The Schoolmaster* ('Book 1') to denounce the lewdness of Italian books and to discourage their translation into English; he likewise describes the harmful effects that cultural stays in Italy ('Circes Court', p. 226) might have on the moral and religious integrity of young English students; see pp. 225–37.
¹⁴⁶ devilish *pederastice* [...] familiars] Spenser, SC, gloss to 'January' ('Hobbinol'): 'In this place seemeth to be some savour of disorderly love, which the learned call *paederastikē*: but it is gathered beside his meaning. For who that hath read Plato his dialogue called *Alcibiades*, Xenophon and Maximus Tyrius of Socrates' opinions may easily perceive that such love is much to be allowed and liked of, specially so meant as Socrates used it — who sayeth that indeed he loved Alcibiades extremely, yet not Alcibiades' person but his soul, which is Alcibiades' own self' (Brook-Davies, p. 36). Webbe provides a moralizing interpretation that derives in a vehement defence of the instructive nature of poetry and of the poets' creative freedom that anticipates Sidney's; see *Defence*, pp. 35–36.

good soever his meaning were? Whereunto I oppose the simple conceit they have of matters which concern learning or wit, willing them to give poets leave to use their vein as they see good: it is their foolish construction, not his writing, that is blameable. We must prescribe to no writers (much less to poets) in what sort they should utter their conceits. But this will be better discussed by some, I hope, of better ability.

One other sort of poetical writers remaineth yet to be remembered, that is, the precepts of husbandry, learnedly compiled in heroical verse. Such were the works of Hesiodus[147] in Greek and Virgil's *Georgics* in Latin. What memorable work hath been handled in imitation of these by any English poet I know not (save only one work of Master Tusser, a piece surely of great wit and experience, and withal [F1ᵛ] very prettily handled).[148] And I think the cause why our poets have not travelled° in that behalf is, especially, for that there have been always plenty of other writers that have handled the same argument very largely.[149] Among whom Master Barnaby Googe,[150] in translating and enlarging the most profitable work of Heresbachius, hath deserved much commendation,° as well for his faithful compiling and learned increasing the noble work as for his witty translation of a good part of the *Georgics* of Virgil into English verse.

Among all the translations which hath been my fortune to see, I could never yet find that work of the *Georgics* wholly performed. I remember once Abraham Fleming, in his conversion of the *Eclogues*, promised to translate and publish it: whether he did or not, I know not, but as yet I heard not of it.[151] I myself wot well

---

[147] Hesiodus] On Hesiod see note 42 above.

[148] (save only [...] handled)] Tusser's *A Hundreth Good Pointes of Husbandrie* (London, 1557). On Tusser see note 67 above and Meres, *Palladis*, p. 323.

[149] And I [...] largely] Alastair Fowler quotes Webbe's explanation for the scarcity of English original georgics in the sixteenth century; for Fowler, by 'other writers' Webbe might be referring to abundant English prose writings on gardening or husbandry, or to other European authorities in the matter such as Gallo, Estienne and Liebault, and de Serres. Alastair Fowler, 'The Beginnings of English Georgic', in B. K. Lewalski, ed., *Renaissance Genres: Essays on Theory, History and Interpretation* (Cambridge: Harvard University Press, 1986) 105–25, p. 116).

[150] Master Barnaby Googe] See note 71 above.

[151] I remember [...] it] Abraham Fleming (c. 1552–1607) matriculated in Cambridge as a sizar in 1570, but he did not obtain his B.A. until 1581–82; during this time he could have coincided with Webbe. While being a student, Fleming published a literal rhymed translation of Virgil's *Bucolics* in 1575, with notes and a dedicatory to Peter Osborne; it was printed in London by John Charlewood, who also printed Webbe's tract in 1586. In his dedicatory: 'I intend to preserve them until such time as I have translated Virgil's *Georgics* into English (which I mean to do, by God's assistance, at my convenient leisure when I have cleared my hands of other exercises and as I feel my mind discharged of clogging cares)'; in Neil Rhodes, G. Kendal and L. Wilson, eds, *English Renaissance Translation Theory* (London: Modern Humanities Research Association, 2013), p. 429. In 1589 a new version of the *Bucolics* in regular alexandrine unrhymed verse was published together with the new translation of the *Georgics*, both dedicated

I bestowed some time in it two or three years since, turning it to that same English verse which other such works were in, though it were rudely.¹⁵² Howbeit, I did it only for mine own use, and upon certain respects towards a gentleman mine special friend, to whom I was desirous to show some token of dutiful good will, and not minding it should go far abroad, considering how slenderly° I ran it over. Yet, since then, hath one got it in keeping who, as it is told me, either hath or will unadvisedly publish it, which injury, though he means to do me in mirth, yet I hope he will make me some sufficient recompense, or else I shall go near to watch him the like or a worse turn.

But concerning the matter of our English writers let this suffice. Now shall you hear my simple skill in what I am able to say concerning the form and manner of our English verse.

The most usual and frequented kind of our English poetry hath always run upon and to this day is observed in such equal number of syllables and likeness of words that in all places one verse, either immediately or by mutual interposition, may be answerable to another, both in proportion of length and ending of lines in the same letters.¹⁵³ Which rude kind of verse, though (as I touched before) it rather discrediteth [F2ʳ] our speech, as borrowed from the Barbarians, than furnisheth the same with any comely° ornament.¹⁵⁴ Yet, being

---

to archbishop Whitgift, former master of Pembroke College in Cambridge. See Warton, *The History of English Poetry* 1824, vol. 4, pp. 227–28. This commentary proves that Webbe had read Fleming, and shows his interest for keeping the track of English poetic novelties.
¹⁵² I myself [...] rudely] See note 1 above.
¹⁵³ The most usual [...] letters] Webbe's definition of English metre is based on the number of syllables and the rhyming ends of lines, apparently ignoring the role of accent. On p. 86 above: 'just number of syllables, eight in one line, six in another, and therewithal an A to make a jerk in the end'. Likewise, Ascham ignores that rhymed verse is also subject to accentual regulations: 'ignorant heads, which now can easely recken vp fourten sillables, and easelie stumble on euery Ryme' (*Schoolmaster*, p. 290). Consequently, he identifies blank verse with failed attempts to compose quantitative verse, like in Surrey's and Perez's translations of Virgil and Homer; see ibid., p. 291. Notwithstanding, the analysis of rhymed verse offered by Webbe in this section denotes that he was fully aware of the relevance of accent as, among the three conditions to be observed in order to improve English rhyme, he recommends to have a special regard of the natural stress of words: 'to place the words in such sort as none of them be wrested contrary to the natural inclination or affectation of the same, or more truly the true quantity thereof' (p. 107 below); see Attridge, *Well-Weighed Syllables*, p. 110. Sidney's definition is more accurate in this regard: 'observing only number, with some regard of the accent, the chief life of it standeth in that like sounding of the words which we call rhyme' (*Defence*, p. 52). Sidney even uses the term 'rhyme' to refer to the accentual metrical system: 'Now, for the rhyme, though we do not observe quantity, yet we observe the accent very precisely' (ibid.); see Gavin Alexander, *Sidney's 'The Defence of Poesy'*, p. 52, note to 'the rhyme'.
¹⁵⁴ Which rude [...] ornament] On the consideration of accentual metre as a rustical device see note 13 above.

so engraft° by custom and frequented by the most part, I may not utterly disallow it, lest I should seem to call in question the judgement of all our famous writers which have won eternal praise by their memorable works compiled in that verse.

For my part, therefore, I can be content to esteem it as a thing the perfection whereof is very commendable, yet so as with others I could wish it were by men of learning and ability bettered and made more artificial, according to the worthiness of our speech.[155]

The falling out of verses together in one like sound is commonly called in English 'rhyme', taken from the Greek word ῥυθμός, which surely in my judgement is very abusively applied to such a sense. And by this the unworthiness of the thing may well appear in that, wanting a proper name whereby to be called, it borroweth a word far exceeding the dignity of it and not appropriate to so rude and base a thing. For rhyme is properly the just proportion of a clause or sentence, whether it be in prose or metre, aptly comprised together, whereof there is both a natural and an artificial composition in any manner or kind of speech, either French, Italian, Spanish, or English, and is proper not only to poets, but also to readers, orators, pleaders, or any which are to pronounce or speak anything in public audience.[156]

The first beginning of rhyme (as we now term it), though it be somewhat ancient, yet nothing famous. In Greece (they say) one Simias Rhodius, because he would be singular in something, writ poetically of the fable containing how Jupiter, being in shape of a swan, begot the egg on Leda, whereof came Castor, Pollux, and Helena: whereof every verse ended in this rhyme, and was called therefore ᾠόν. But this foolish attempt was so contemned° and despised that the people would neither admit the author nor book any place in memory of learning.

---

[155] I could [...] speech] The Elizabethan admiration for artificiality derives from their assumption that it was a product of learning and erudition, in contrast to innate and natural potential or — regarding the composition of rhymed verse, according to Ascham and Webbe — to other 'vices' such as custom and the poets' insufficient creative effort. Ascham's emphasis on the relevance of learning and labour in the attainment of true knowledge corresponds with his association of quantitative metres to erudition on the one hand, and rhyme to rudeness on the other; see *Schoolmaster*, pp. 289–90. We may therefore infer that ancient quantitative metre owed its prestige among English humanists mainly to its requirements of sophisticated elaboration and proportion. See Attridge, *Well-Weighed Syllables*, pp. 105–08. Puttenham, *The Art*, 2.5: 'our manner of vulgar poesy is more ancient than the artificial of the Greeks and Latins, ours coming by instinct of nature'; Spenser-Harvey, 'Letter' V: 'our new famous enterprise for the Exchanging of Barbarous and Balductum Rymes with Artificial Verses' (*Variorum* X, p. 463).

[156] The falling [...] audience] On the origin of the Elizabethan confusion regarding the words 'rhyme' and 'rhythm' see Attridge, *Well-Weighed Syllables*, pp. 94–95. Puttenham also considers that the Elizabethans used the word 'rhyme' 'by manner of abusion' and provides an account of the etymology of this confusion (*The Art*, 2.6); see also Puttenham, 2.3. Gascoigne uses both terms 'rhymes' and 'rhythms' to refer to English accentual verses, implying that only classical and quantitative metre are to be called 'verses' (*Certain Notes* 4, p. 240).

Since that, it was not heard of till the time the Huns and Gothians renewed it again and brought it into Italy.[157] But [F2ᵛ] howsoever or wheresoever it began, certain it is that in our English tongue it beareth as good grace, or rather better, than in any other. And is a faculty whereby many may and do deserve great praise and commendation,° though our speech be capable of a far more learned manner of versifying, as I will partly declare hereafter.

There be three special notes necessary to be observed in the framing of our accustomed English rhyme.[158] The first is that one metre or verse be answerable to another in equal number of feet or syllables, or proportionable to the tune whereby it is to be read or measured. The second, to place the words in such sort as none of them be wrested contrary to the natural inclination or affectation of the same, or more truly the true quantity thereof.[159] The third, to make them fall together mutually in rhyme, that is, in words of like sound, but so as the words be not disordered for the rhyme's[cix] sake, nor the sense hindered. These be the most principal observations which I think requisite in an English verse. For, as for the other ornaments which belong thereto, they be more properly belonging to the several gifts of skilful poets than common notes to be prescribed by me. But somewhat perhaps I shall have occasion to speak hereafter.

Of the kinds of English verses which differ in number of syllables there are almost infinite, which every way alter according to his fancy, or to the measure of that metre wherein it pleaseth him to frame his ditty. Of the best and most frequented I will rehearse° some. The longest verse in length which I have seen used in English consisteth of sixteen syllables, each two verses rhyming together thus:[160]

---

[157] Since that [...] Italy] From Ascham, *Schoolmaster*, p. 291; see note 57 above.

[158] There be [...] rhyme] Inspired on Gascoigne's *Certain Notes* (1575). The first of Webbe's notes seems to echo Gascoigne's third note: 'remember to hold the measure wherewith you begin'; the second, Gascoigne's fourth note: 'remember to place every word in his natural emphasis or sound'; and the third one corresponds to the latter's sixth note: 'beware of rhyme without reason', pp. 49–52.

[159] true quantity thereof] Notice the misleading use given in this section to 'quantity'; 'true quantity' is here a reference to 'accent', as on p. 112 below: 'right quantity'. Notwithstanding, Webbe does also employ it alluding to the ancient metrical device of syllabic duration, which he analyses below: 'Now, as for the quantity of our words' (p. 119); or when he erroneously assumes that Surrey attempted to translate Virgil into hexameters: 'the Earl of Surrey, who translated some part of Virgil into verse indeed, but without regard of true quantity of syllables' (p. 122). On the ambiguous use of 'quantity' see Attridge, *Well-Weighed Syllables*, p. 110.

[160] The longest [...] thus] Gascoigne offers a catalogue of stanzas and lines in which twelve- and fourteen-syllable lines are conceived as the commonest and longest measures; when used alternatelly they constitute one of the most popular stanzas among the Elizabethans, named by Gascoigne 'poulter's measure' because it consists in giving 'twelve for one dozen and fourteen for another' (*Certain Notes* 14, pp. 54–56). Puttenham also dedicates a section to describe line measures and mentions fourteen-syllable lines as the longest ones, although he considers that those exceeding twelve syllables 'pass the bounds of good proportion' (*The Art*, 2.4). Neither of them includes lines of sixteen syllables in their catalogues.

> Where virtue wants and vice abounds, there wealth is but a baited hook,
> To make men swallow down their bane,° before on danger deep they look.[161]

This kind is not very much used at length thus, but is commonly divided, each verse into two, whereof each shall contain eight syllables and rhyme crosswise, the first to the third, and the second to the fourth, in this manner [F3ʳ]:

> Great wealth is but a baited hook
> Where virtue wants, and vice abounds:
> Which men devour before they look,
> So them in dangers deep it drowns.

Another kind next in length to this is where each verse hath fourteen syllables, which is the most accustomed of all other, and especially used of all the translators of the Latin poets, for the most part thus:[162]

> My mind with fury fierce inflamed of late, I know not how,
> Doth burn Parnassus hill^{cx} to see, adorned with laurel bough.[163]

Which may likewise, and so it often is, divided, each verse into two, the^{cxi} first having eight syllables, the second six, whereof the two sixes shall always rhyme, and sometimes the eights, sometimes not, according to the will of the maker:

---

[161] Where virtue [...] look] A iambic octameter of unknown source. Webbe seems to be aware of the two trends mentioned by J. C. Andersen concerning the role of long rhyming lines in the process towards the consolidation of stanzas; one was inclined towards ballad verse, dropping the last unit of lines after the caesura forming cross-rhyme stanzas of four lines (abxb) — as showed in the next example with Googe's lines, and the other tended towards 'full Romance verse', retaining the last unit and falling into rhyming couplets which, in the case of sixteen-syllable lines, Webbe considers less frequent. J. C. Andersen, *The Laws of Verse* (Cambridge: Cambridge University Press, 2014. 1st edn 1928), pp. 128–29. The extreme of the couplet-agglutination tendency occurred in metrical romances like Gower's *Confessio Amantis*. Gavin Alexander observes that the fact that Webbe recognises the possibility of joining lines of six and eight syllables to make long lines is not without importance, as it connects him with a trend in modern prosody that considered four-stress lines as basic units in the formation of all line-lengths, except the pentameter (*Sidney's 'The Defence of Poesy'*, p. 415, note 4). Although from a more superficial approach, Puttenham also mentions the connection of cross-rhyme lines with long-length couplets and discourages the break of alexandrines into two shorter lines, attributing this practice to 'common rhymers' or occasionally to printers' convenience (*The Art*, 2.4).

[162] Another kind [...] thus] Like Phaer's translation of Virgil's *Aeneid* or Golding's of Ovid's *Metamorphoses*, both quoted in *A Discourse*. The Tudor poets considered this line to be closer than any other metres to classical hexameters; see Alexander, *Sidney's 'The Defence of Poesy'*, p. 256, note 5.

[163] My mind [...] bough] From Barnaby Googe's *The Zodiake of Life* in its edition of 1576, sig. A1ʳ; see notes 52 and 71 above.

> My mind with fury fierce inflamed
> Of late, I know not how:
> Doth burn Parnassus hill^{cxii} to see,
> Adorned with laurel bough.¹⁶⁴

There are now within this compass as many sorts of verses¹⁶⁵ as may be devised differences of numbers:¹⁶⁶ whereof some consist of equal proportions, some of long and short together, some of many rhymes in one staff (as they call it),¹⁶⁷ some of cross rhyme, some of counter rhyme,¹⁶⁸ some rhyming with one word far distant from another, some rhyming every third or fourth word, and so likewise all manner of ditties appliable to every tune that may be sung or said, distinct from prose or continued speech. To avoid therefore tediousness and confusion, I will repeat only the different sorts of verses out of *The Shepherds' Calendar*, which may well serve to bear authority in this matter.¹⁶⁹

There are in that work twelve or thirteen sundry sorts of verses [F3^v] which differ either in length or rhyme, of distinction of the staves, but of them which differ in length or number of syllables not past six or seven. The first of them is of ten syllables, or rather five feet in one verse, thus:

> A shepherd's boy (no better do him call),
> When Winter's wasteful° spite was almost spent.¹⁷⁰

---

¹⁶⁴ My mind [...] bough] Googe, ibid. from 1561 and 1565 editions, sign. A1^r. Alexander observes that, by simply dividing the lines into two, Webbe shows that the scheme used in hymns and ballads corresponds to the fourteeners couplet (*Sidney's 'The Defence of Poesy'*, p. 256, note 7).
¹⁶⁵ sort of verses] Verse forms.
¹⁶⁶ differences of numbers] He refers to the number of syllables in lines, number of lines in stanzas with different rhyme links or concords, and to all their possible alternations and distributions.
¹⁶⁷ staff] Stanza; pl. 'staves'. Webbe gives a definition in p. 112 below. Like Webbe, Puttenham seems not to be certain of the etymology of the word: 'Staff in our vulgar poesy I know not why it should be so called' (*The Art*, 2.2). Gascoigne, *Certain Notes* 14, p. 244: 'seven such verses make a staff'.
¹⁶⁸ counter rhyme] Webbe coins the term 'counter rhyme' to refer to the rhyme scheme *abba*. Gascoigne can not think of a name for it, and observes that it is not commonly used in English (*Certain Notes*, p. 245); Puttenham calls this scheme 'plain compass', in contrast to the 'entangled' *abab* (*The Art*, 2.11).
¹⁶⁹ There are now [...] matter] Webbe hastily hints the notions of 'distance' and 'situation' in the arrangement of rhyme that Puttenham describes so meticulously using diagrams (*The Art*, 2.11). Although Webbe does not disregard the potential of rhyme for verse sophistication, he is not as condescendant as Puttenham in acknowledging its virtues. Rhyme is for Puttenham 'no less curious than their [*Greeks' and Romans'*] rhythm or numerosity' (*The Art*, 2.6); on p. 114 below Webbe insists that rhyme 'is of least importance' for poetic eloquence.
¹⁷⁰ A shepherd's [...] spent] 'January', 1–2 (Brooks-Davies, p. 30); iambic pentameters form six-line stanzas rhyming *ababcc*. This eclogue contains a love complaint pronounced in a soliloquy uttered by Colin.

This verse he useth commonly in his sweet complaints and mournful ditties, as very agreeable to such affections.[171]

The second sort hath naturally but nine syllables, and is a more rough or clownish manner of verse, used most commonly of him if you[cxiii] mark him in his satirical reprehensions and his shepherds' homeliest talk, such as the Second Eclogue is:

> Ah, for pitty! Will rank° Winter's rage
> These bitter blasts never 'gin to assuage?[172]

The number of nine syllables in this verse is very often altered, and so it may without any disgrace to the same, especially where the speech should be most clownish and simple, which is much observed of him.

The third kind is a pretty round verse,[173] running currently° together commonly seven syllables or sometime eight in one verse, as many in the next, both rhyming together, every two having one the like verse after them, but of rounder words,[174] and two of them likewise rhyming mutually. That verse expresseth notably light and youthful talk, such as is the Third Eclogue between two shepherd's[cxiv] boys concerning love:

> Thomalin, why sitten we so
> As weren overwent with woe
> Upon so fair a morrow?
> The joyous time now nigheth[cxv] fast
> That shall alegge[cxvi] this bitter blast
> And slake the Winter's[cxvii] sorrow.[175]

[F4ʳ] The fourth sort containeth in each staff many unequal verses, but most sweetly falling together, which the poet calleth the tune of 'the water's fall'.[176] Therein is his song in praise of Elisa:

---

[171] This verse [...] affections] While offering a sample of different types of lines according to their number of feet or syllables, Webbe aims at demonstrating that Spenser has attained that Ciceronian perfection that the cohesion between verse form and matter conveys to poetry; see note 86 above. The same stanza pattern is reproduced in 'December' to frame a similar complaint by Colin, on this occasion about the ephemeral ages of man.

[172] Ah [...] to assuage?] 'February' 1–2 (Brooks-Davies, p. 39); this combination of iambs and anapaests in nine-syllable lines, framed in eight-line stanzas distributed in rhyming couplets, results in a more rustic and tougher verse than the iambic pentameters of the first eclogue. This eclogue deals with a generational debate which encloses a satirical approach to ecclesiastical and political corruption. It is metrically similar to 'May', 'July' and 'September'.

[173] round verse] Symmetrical or cyclical verse.

[174] rounder words] More sonorous or full-sounding.

[175] Thomalin [...] sorrow] 'March' 1–2 (Brooks-Davies, p. 55); it consists of stanzas of six lines distributed in two sets of two tetrameters (eight syllables) plus one trimeter (seven syllables).

[176] 'the water's fall'] Hobbinol introduces Colin's ode to Elisa naming with this term the complex structure of its nine-line stanzas (iambic pentameter, dimeter and tetrameter lines) in 'April' 33–36: 'Contented I. Then will I sing his lay/Of fair Elisa, queen of shepherds all,/Which once he made as by a spring he lay/And tuned it unto the water's fall' (Brooks-Davies, p. 67).

Ye dainty nymphs, that[cxviii] in this blessed brook
Do bathe your breast,
Forsake your watery bowers,° and hither look
At my request;
And eke you virgins that on Parnass' dwell
(Whence floweth Helicon, the learned well)
Help me to blaze
Her worthy praise
Which[cxix] in her sex doth all excel, etc.[177]

 The fifth is a divided verse of fourteen[cxx] syllables into two verses, whereof I spoke before, and seemeth most meet° for the handling of a moral matter, such as is the praise of good pastors and the disprase of ill, in the Seventh Eclogue.[178]

 The sixth kind is called a 'round',[179] being mutually sung between two: one singeth one verse, the other the next, each rhymeth with himself:

Perigot. It fell upon a holy eve
Willy. (hey ho holiday)
Perigot. When holy fathers wont to shrive
Willy. (now[cxxi] 'ginneth this[cxxii] roundelay), etc.[180]

 The seventh sort is a very tragical mournful measure, wherein he bewaileth° the death of some friend under the person of Dido [F4ᵛ]:

Up, then, *Melpomene*, thou[cxxiii] mournfullest Muse of nine:
such cause of mourning never hadst afore!
Up, grisly ghosts, and up, my rueful[cxxiv] rhyme!
Matter of mirth now shalt thou[cxxv] have no more,
For dead she is that mirth thee made of yore°[181]
Dido my dear, alas, is dead,
Dead, and lieth wrapped in lead:
O heavy hearse,°
Let streaming tears be poured out in store:
O careful° verse![182]

---

[177] Ye dainty [...] etc.] From Colin's ode to Elizabeth as queen of shepherds and love in 'April' 37–45 (Brooks-Davies, p. 67); it occurs integrated in a conversation between the two shepherds about Colin's love frustrations (repeating the iambic pentameter lines of 'January', except for their distribution in quatrains instead of six-line stanzas).
[178] The fifth [...] Eclogue] 'July' consists of fourteeners divided into two lines of 8 and 6 syllables. This type of verse has already been introduced through examples from Googe's *Zodiake of Life*; see p. 108 above. Webbe skips 'May' and 'June' because the former repeats the nine-syllable pattern of 'February' (tetrameters in couplets), and the latter shares with 'January' the iambic pentameter lines (but with the rhyme scheme *ababbaba*).
[179] round] Webbe gives an English term for the French 'roundelay', originally a brief song with a refrain. Gascoigne calls it 'rondelet' (*Certain Notes* 14, p. 245).
[180] Perigot. [...] etc.] 'August' 53–56 (Brooks-Davies, p. 132); this eclogue is a seventy-two-line roundelay uttered by two shepherds.
[181] For dead [...] yore:] Missing in Q, sigs. F4ʳ–F4ᵛ.
[182] Up, then [...] verse!] 'November' 53–62 (Brooks-Davies, p. 176); a traditional pastoral

These sorts of verses for brevity's sake have I chosen forth of him, whereby I shall avoid the tedious rehearsal° of all the kinds which are used, which I think would have been unpossible, seeing they may be altered to as many forms as the poets please. Neither is there any tune or stroke° which may be sung or played on instruments, which hath not some poetical ditties framed according to the numbers[183] thereof: some to 'Rogero', some to 'Trenchmore', to 'Downright Squire', to galliards, to pavans, to jigs, to brawls, to all manner of tunes, which every fiddler knows better than myself, and therefore I will let them pass.[184]

Again, the diversities of the staves (which are the number of verses contained with the divisions or partitions of a ditty) do oftentimes make great differences in these verses, as when one staff containeth but two verses, or (if they be divided) four: the first or the first couple having twelve syllables, the other fourteen, which versifiers call poulter's measure,[185] because so they tally their wares by dozens. Also, when one staff hath many verses, whereof each one rhymeth to the next, or mutually cross, or distant by three or by four, or ended contrary to the beginning, and a hundred sorts, whereof to show several examples would be too troublesome.[186] Now for the second point.

The natural course of most English verses seemeth to run upon the old iambic stroke,° and I may well think by all likelihood it had the beginning thereof. For if you mark the right quantity of our usual verses, you shall perceive them to contain in sound the very property of iambic feet, as thus:

⏑ − ⏑ − ⏑ − ⏑ − ⏑ − ⏑ −
I that my slender oaten pipe in verse was wont to sound[187]

---

eclogue that includes a metrically complex elegy consisting of ten-line stanzas structured in an opening alexandrine line (six-foot iambic), four iambic pentameters, two iambic tetrameters, a dimeter, another pentameter, and a closing dimeter. 'September' is not included as a metrical sample because its structure in tetrameter couplets is similar to those of 'February' and 'May'; as for 'October' and 'December', they contain six-line stanzas in pentameters similar to those of 'January'.

[183] numbers] Rhythmic or metrical pattern.

[184] some to [...] pass] 'Rogero' and 'Downright Squire' were popular tunes commonly associated with ballads; the others refer to popular dances. Webbe is probably thinking in the popular poems of *A Handful of Pleasant Delights* (1584), mostly linked to these and other similar tunes. See Alexander, *Sidney's 'The Defence of Poesy'*, p. 256, note 9.

[185] poulter's measure] Coined by Gascoigne; see note 160 above.

[186] Also, when [...] troublesome] For a developed description of the types of stanzas according to rhyme distribution see Puttenham, *The Art*, 2.11. Gascoigne limits his exposition to the ones he considers the most frequented verse forms, like the rhyme royal, ballad, rondelet, sonnets, virelays and poulter's rhymes (*Certain Notes* 14, pp. 244–46).

[187] I that [...] sound] Phaer, *Aeneid*, 1; the first line of an experimental opening by Virgil, but traditionally rejected by his ancient publishers who took the famous 'Arma virumque cano' as the actual initial words of the poem. Virgil, *Aeneid*, 1: 'Ille ego, qui quondam gracili modulatus avena' ('I am he who once modulated my song on a slender reed').

[G1ʳ] For transpose any of those feet in pronouncing, and make short either the two, four, six, eight, ten, twelve syllable, and it will (do what you can) fall out very absurdly.

Again, though our words cannot well be forced to abide the touch of position and other rules of *prosodia*, yet is there such a natural force or quantity in each word, that it will not abide any place but one without some foul disgrace; as for example, try any verse, as this:[188]

⏑ — ⏑ — ⏑ ⏑ — ⏑ — ⏑ ⏑ — —
Of shapes transformed to bodies strange I purpose to entreat[cxxvi][189]

Make the first syllable long, or the third, or the fifth and so forth. Or, contrariwise, make the other syllables to admit the shortness of one of them places, and see what a wonderful defacing it will be to the words, as thus:

— ⏑ — ⏑ — ⏑ — ⏑ — ⏑ — ⏑
Of strange bodies transformed to shapes purpose I to entreat

So that this is one special thing to be taken heed of in making a good English verse: that by displacing no word be wrested against his natural propriety,[190] whereunto you shall perceive each word to be affected, and may easily discern it in words of two syllables or above, though some there be of indifferency that will stand in any place.[191] Again, in couching°[cxxvii] the whole sentence, the like regard is to be had: that we exceed not too boldly in placing the verb out of his order and too far behind the noun, which the necessity of rhyme may oftentimes urge. For, though it be tolerable in a verse to set words so extraordinarily as other speech will not admit, yet heed is to be taken, lest by too much affecting that manner, we make both the verse unpleasant and the sense obscure.[192] And sure

---

[188] Again, though [...] this] Latin *prosodia* was a compulsory discipline in Elizabethan education; its rules determined the quantity of Latin syllables. For the Elizabethans, the rule of position counted over other rules like vowel length or diphthong. See Attridge, *Well-Weighed Syllables*, p. 72. On the controversy about the convenience to apply Latin rules to English words see note 16 above.
[189] Of shapes [...] entreat] Arthur Golding, *Metamorphoses*, 1; Ovid, *Metamorphoses*, 1-2: 'In nova fert animus mutatas dicere formas/corpora;' ('My mind is bent to tell of bodies changed into new forms').
[190] that by [...] propriety] Gascoigne, *Certain Notes* 4, p. 239: 'And in your verses remember to place every word in his natural emphasis or sound'.
[191] though some [...] place] Webbe assumes the Elizabethan idea that English monosyllables could be considered stressed or unstressed and long or short depending on the demands of the occasion. Gascoigne, *Certain Notes* 5, p. 241: 'words of one syllable will more easily fall to be short or long as occasion requireth'. Puttenham, *The Art*, 2.7: 'in words monosyllable, which be for the more part our natural Saxon English, the accent is indifferent, and may be used for sharp or flat and heavy at our pleasure'; see also Puttenham 2.6.
[192] For, though [...] obscure] Gascoigne also recommends moderation in the use of the poetic licence ('*licentiam poeticam*'), which allowed relative syntactic and orthographic flexibility in the benefit of rhyme; see *Certain Notes* 11 and 12, pp. 243-44. Puttenham warns against the abuse of orthographic licence (*The Art*, 2.9).

it is a wonder to see the folly of many in this respect that use not only too much of this overthwart° placing, or rather displacing, of words in their poems and verses, but also in their prose or continued writings, where they think to roll [G1ᵛ] most smoothly and flow most eloquently. There by this means come forth their sentences dragging° at one another'sᶜˣˣᵛⁱⁱⁱ tail as they were tied together with points, where often you shall tarry° (scratching your head) a good space before you shall hear his principal verb or special word, lest his singing grace, which in his sentence is contained, should be less and his speech seem nothing poetical.

The third observation is the rhyme or like ending of verses, which, though it is of least importance, yet hath won such credit among us that of all other it is most regarded of the greatest part of readers. And surely, as I am persuaded, the regard of writers to this hath been the greatest decay of that good order of versifying,[193] which might ere this have been established in our speech. In my judgement, if there be any ornament in the same, it is rather to be attributed to the plentiful fullness of our speech, which can afford rhyming words sufficient for the handling of any matter, than to the thing itself for any beautifying it bringeth to a work, which might be adorned with far more excellent colours than rhyming is. Notwithstanding I cannot but yield unto it (as custom requireth) the deserved praises, especially where it is with good judgement ordered. And I think them right worthy of admiration for their readiness and plenty of wit and capacity who can with facility entreat at large and, as we call it, *extempore* in good and sensible rhyme[194] upon some unacquainted matter.

The ready skill of framing anything in verse, besides the natural promptness which many have thereunto, is much helped by art and exercise of the memory:[195] for, as I remember, I read once among Gascoigne's works a little instruction to versifying, where is prescribed, as I think, this course of learning to versify in rhyme.[196]

---

[193] that good order of versifying] Greek and Latin quantitative metres. Webbe uses the term 'versifying' in references to quantitative metres in order to mark their difference with the English accentual — usually rhyming — verse (which he calls 'rhyme' or 'rhyming'), thus disregarding blank verse.

[194] sensible rhyme] Intelligent or reasonable. Gascoigne, *Certain Notes* 7, p. 242: 'carrying reason with rhyme'.

[195] The ready [...] memory] On the Elizabethan admiration for artificiality ('art') in contrast to inherent talent ('natural promptness') see note 155. Being the fourth part of Ciceronian rhetoric (invention, disposition, elocution, memory and delivery), memory was highly recognized as the faculty of selecting and bringing forth the stored knowledge and commonplaces in the improvised rhetorical speeches; therefore, it was not only related to memorization, but it also implied the ability to choose at the moment the appropriate topics that invention required in the course of the speech. Webbe proposes to make of rhyme a more rhetorical device in order to dignify English versification, aiming at reconciling it with the humanist ideals of 'knowledge and learning', as he points out in the following lines.

[196] I read [...] rhyme] *Certain Notes of Instruction* (1575).

When you have one verse well settled and decently ordered, which you may dispose at your pleasure to end it with what word you will, then, whatsoever the word is, you may speedily run over the other words which are answerable° thereunto (for more readiness through all the letters alphabetically), whereof you may choose that which will best fit the sense [G2ʳ] of your matter in that place. As, for example, if your last word end in *book*, you may straightways° in your mind run them over thus: *brook, cook, crook,° hook, look, nook, pook, rook, forsook, took, awoke*, etc. Now it is twenty to one, but always one of these shall jump with your former word and matter in good sense. If not, then alter the first.[197]

And indeed I think that, next to the art of memory, this is the readiest way to attain to the faculty of rhyming well *extempore*, especially if it be helped with thus much pains. Gather together all manner of words, especially monosyllables,[198] and place them alphabetically in some note, and either have them meetly° perfectly by heart (which is no very laboursome matter), or but look them diligently over at some time, practising to rhyme indifferent often, whereby I am persuaded it will soon be learned, so as the party have withal any reasonable gift of knowledge and learning, whereby he want not both matter and words altogether.

What the other circumstances of rhyming are, as what words may tolerably be placed in rhyme, and what not, what words do best become a rhyme, and what not, how many sorts of rhyme there is, and such like, I will not stay now to entreat. There be many more observations and notes to be prescribed to the exact knowledge of versifying, which I trust will be better and larger laid forth by others, to whom I defer many considerations in this treatise, hoping that some of greater skill will shortly handle this matter in better sort.

Now the sundry kinds of rare devises and pretty inventions which come from the fine poetical vein of many in strange and unaccustomed manner, if I could report them, it were worthy my travel:°[199] such are the turning of verses,[200] the

---

[197] When you [...] the first] Gascoigne, *Certain Notes* 7, p. 242; Webbe's insistence on the need of composing rhyme according to rhetorical procedures ('you may speedily run over the other words' and 'you may straightway in your mind run them over') is his own contribution.

[198] especially monosyllables] In words of more than one syllable the position of the stress restricts the opportunities to match other words for rhyme, whereas, due to the flexibility of monosyllables for being taken as stressed or untressed syllables, they have a high potential for rhyme. Gascoigne warns against using too many polysyllables in rhyme (*Certain Notes* 5, p. 241); Puttenham observes that 'for this purpose serve the monosyllables of our English Saxons excellently well' (*The Art*, 2.6). On monosyllables see note 191 above.

[199] Now the [...] travel] Webbe is likely recalling the variety of experimental rhyme schemes and formal devices in *The Paradise of Dainty Devises* (1576), as the poem by Hunnis quoted below suggests.

[200] turning of verses] The shaping or fashioning of verses (first quote in *OED*3). Spenser, *SC*, 'August', 191: 'How I admire each turning of thy verse' (Brooks-Davies, p. 138); applied to a

enfolding of words,²⁰¹ the fine repetitions,²⁰² the clerkly° conveying of contraries,²⁰³ and many such like. Whereof, though I could set down many, yet because I want both many and the best kinds of them, I will overpass only pointing you to one or two which may suffice for example.

Look upon the rueful song of Colin sung by Cuddie in *The Shepherds' Calendar*, where you shall see a singular rare [G2ᵛ] device of a ditty framed upon these six words: *woe, sound, cries, part*,^{cxxix} *sleep, augment*, which are most prettily turned and wound° up mutually together, expressing wonderfully the dolefulness° of the song.²⁰⁴ A device not much unlike unto the same is used by some, who taking the last words of a certain number of verses, as it were by the rebound of an echo, shall make them fall out in some pretty sense.

Of this sort there are some devised by John Grange which,^{cxxx} because they be not long, I will rehearse° one:

> If fear oppress, how then may hope me shield?
> Denial says vain hope hath pleased well,
> But as such hope thou wouldst not be thine,
> So would I not the like to rule my heart.
> For, if thou lovest, it bids thee grant forthwith
> Which is the joy whereof I live in hope.²⁰⁵

Here, if you take the last word of every verse, and place them orderly together, you shall have this sentence: 'Shield well thine heart with hope'. But of these echoes I know indeed very dainty pieces of work among some of the finest poets this day in London, who for the rareness of them keep them privily to themselves, and will not let them come abroad.

A like invention to the last rehearsed,° or rather a better, have I seen often practised in framing a whole ditty to the letters of one's name,²⁰⁶ or to the words of some two or three verses, which is very witty, as for example, this is one of William Hunnis, which for the shortness I rather chose than some that are better:

---

kind of stanza built on the repetition of the same six words, quoted by Webbe below. For the etymological pun on 'verse' with the meaning of 'line' (from Latin *vertere*, 'turn') see Brooks-Davies' note to line 191, p. 138.

²⁰¹ enfolding of words] Wrapping (first quote in *OED*); varied ways of enclosing the same word repeatedly in middle positions of lines in a stanza, like for instance the Greek *antistrophe* described in Puttenham, *The Art*, 3.19.

²⁰² fine repetitions] Singular figures of repetition; for instance, Richard Edwards' poem 'May' uses the word 'may' with different meanings along the stanzas (*Paradise*, 1578, sig. B1ᵛ).

²⁰³ clerkly conveying of contraries] Coupling contrary words, like in Puttenham's *syneciosis* or 'Cross-Coupling' (*The Art*, 3.19).

²⁰⁴ Look upon [...] song] Spenser, *SC*, 'August', 151–89 (Brooks-Davies, pp. 136–37).

²⁰⁵ If fear [...] hope] *The Golden Aphroditis* (1577), sig. I1ᵛ; Grange calls this device the 'echo'.

²⁰⁶ framing [...] name] Acrostic verses.

If thou desire to live in quiet rest,
Give ear and see, but say the best.[207]

These two verses are now as it were resolved into diverse other, every two words or syllables being the beginning of another like verse, in this sort [G3ʳ]:

If thou	delight in quietness of life,
Desire to	shun from brawls, debate and strife,
To live	in love with God, with friend and foe,
In rest	shall sleep when others[cxxxi] cannot so.

Give ear	to all, yet do not all believe,
And see	the end and then do[cxxxii] sentence give:
But say	for truth of happy lives assigned
The best	hath he that quiet is in mind.

Thus are there infinite sorts of fine conveyances° (as they may be termed) to be used, and are much frequented by versifiers, as well in composition of their verse as the wittiness of their matter, which all I will refer to the consideration of every pleasant headed poet in their proper gifts. Only I set down these few sorts of their forms of versifying which may stand in stead° to declare what many others may be devised in like sort.

But now to proceed to the reformed kind of English verse,[208] which many have before this attempted to put in practice,[209] and to establish for an accustomed right among English poets, you shall hear in like manner my simple judgement concerning the same.

I am fully and certainly persuaded that if the true kind of versifying in imitation of Greeks and Latins had been practised in the English tongue, and put in ure° from time to time by our poets, who might have continually been mending and polishing the same, every one according to their several gifts, it would long ere this have aspired to as full perfection as in any other tongue whatsoever. For why may I not think so of our English, seeing that among the Romans a long time, yea even till the days of Tully, they esteemed not the Latin poetry almost worth anything in respect of the Greek, as appeareth in the oration *Pro Archia Poeta*, yet afterwards it increased in credit more and more, and that in short space, so that in Virgil's time wherein were they not [G3ᵛ] comparable with the Greeks?[210]

---

[207] If thou [...] best] This couplet is in fact the title of the poem 51 in *Paradise* (1578), sig. G3ʳ; on William Hunnis see note 67 above. Notice that 'quiet' appears in the title but is omitted in the fourth line of the extended version; this omission is reproduced from 1578 and 1585 editions.

[208] reformed kind of English verse] In classical quantitative metre.

[209] which many [...] practice] e.g. Gabriel Harvey, Edmund Spenser or Abraham Fraunce.

[210] seeing that [...] Greeks?] Webbe's general interpretation of Cicero's *Pro Archia Poeta*. Attridge considers Webbe's comparison strongly supported by the fact that quantity seemed not as natural a feature in Latin phonetic structure as in Greek; see *Well-Weighed Syllables*, p. 119.

So likewise, now it seemeth not current° for an English verse to run upon true quantity and those feet which the Latins use because it is strange, and the other barbarous custom, being within compass of every base wit, hath worn it out of credit or estimation. But if our writers, being of learning and judgement, would rather infringe° this curious custom than omit the occasion of enlarging the credit of their native speech and their own praises by practising that commendable kind of writing in true verse, then no doubt, as in other parts of learning, so in poetry should not stoop to the best of them all in all manner of ornament and comeliness. But some object that our words are nothing resemblant in nature to theirs, and therefore not possible to be framed with any good grace after their use. But cannot we then, as well as the Latins did, alter the canon of the rule according to the quality of our word, and where our words and theirs will agree, there to jump with them, where they will not agree, there to establish a rule of our own to be directed by? Likewise, for the tenor of the verse, might we not (as Horace did in the Latin)[211] alter their proportions to what sorts we listed,° and to what we saw would best become the nature of the thing handled, or the quality of the words? Surely it is to be thought that if anyone of sound judgement and learning should put forth some famous work containing diverse forms of true verses, fitting the measures according to the matter, it would of itself be a sufficient authority without any prescription of rules to the most part of poets, for them to follow and by custom to ratify.[212] For sure it is that the rules and principles of poetry were not precisely followed and observed of the first beginners and writers of poetry, but were selected and gathered severally out of their works for the direction and behoof° of their followers. And indeed, he that shall with heedful judgement make trial of the English words shall not find them so gross or unapt, but that they will become anyone of the most accustomed sorts of Latin or Greek verses meetly,° and run thereon somewhat currently.°

I myself, with simple skill, I confess, and far unable [G4ʳ] judgement, have ventured on a few,[213] which notwithstanding the rudeness of them may serve to

---

[211] (as Horace did in the Latin)] Ascham, *Schoolmaster*, p. 224: 'Which verse, bicause, in mine opinion, it was not made at the first, more naturallie in *Greke* by *Homere*, not after turned more aptelie into *Latin* by *Horace*'.

[212] Surely it is [...] ratify] The fact that Webbe appeals to poets in his claim for the reformation of English verse implies that he conceives quantity not as a natural property of language, but as an artifice they should incorporate to their verse in order to increase the sophistication of English poetry; rules of prosody should ideally be derived from the poets' practice and answer the natural requirements of their language. See Attridge, *Well-Weighed Syllables*, pp. 153–54.

[213] I myself [...] few] He offers his own approach to some of the controversial rules of prosody widely debated by the supporters of quantitative verse so as to determine the extent to which Latin rules of prosody fitted the nature of English words. Webbe had read Harvey and Spenser's discussion in *Letters* (1580) on the fittest ways to follow the rules that had been originally dictated by Thomas Drant and, according to Spenser, were being used by Philip Sidney in his quantitative experiments. Webbe's will to make himself known among the

show what better might be brought into our speech if those which are of meet°ability would bestow some travel° and endeavour thereupon. But before I set them down, I will speak somewhat of such observations as I could gather necessary to the knowledge of these kind of verses, lest I should seem to run upon them rashly without regard either of example or authority.

The special points of a true verse are the due observations of the feet and place of the feet. The foot of a verse is a measure of two syllables, or of three, distinguished by time[214] which is either long or short. A foot of two syllables is either simple or mixed, that is, of like time or of diverse. A simple foot of two syllables is likewise twofold, either of two long syllables called *spondeus*, as – – *goodness*, or of two short called *pyrrhichius*, as ᴗ ᴗ *hither*. A mixed foot of two syllables is either of one short and one long called *iambus*, as ᴗ – *dying*, or of one long and one short, called *choreus*, as – ᴗ *gladly*. A foot of three syllables in like sort is either simple or mixed. The simple is either *molossus*, that is of three long, as – – – *forgiveness*, or *tribrachus*,[cxxxiii][215] that is of three short, as ᴗ ᴗ ᴗ *merrily*. The mixed is of six diverse sorts: 1) *dactylus*, of one long and two short, as – ᴗ ᴗ *happily*; 2) *anapaestus*, of two short and one long, as ᴗ ᴗ – *travellers*;[cxxxiv] 3) *bacchius*, of one short and two long, as ᴗ – – *rememb'rers*; 4) *palimbacchius*, of two long and one short, as – – ᴗ *accorded*; 5) *creticus*, of a long, a short, and a long, as[cxxxv] – ᴗ – *dangerous*; 6) *amphibrachus*, of a short, a long, and a short, as ᴗ – ᴗ *rejoiced*.[216]

Many more divisions of feet are used by some, but these do more artificially comprehend all quantities necessary to the scanning of any verse, according to Talaeus in his *Rhetoric*. The place of the feet is the disposing of them in their proper rooms, whereby may be discerned the difference of each verse, which is the right numbering of the same.[217] Now, as for the quantity of our words, therein lieth great difficulty and the chiefest matter in this faculty. For in truth, there being such diversity betwixt our words and the Latin, it cannot stand [G4ᵛ] indeed

---

Cambridge scholars likely motivates his attempt to participate, although modestly, in this controversy.

[214] distinguished by time] It was generally assumed by the Elizabethans that quantity was simply a matter of duration; a long syllable would take twice the time of a short one to be pronounced; however, this approach meets some objections concerning aspects of syllable structure when it comes to ascertaining the quantity of Latin syllables. See Attridge, *Well-Weighed Syllables*, pp. 7–13.

[215] *tribrachus*] In Q *trochaeus*, following Talaeus; 'trochaeus' was another accepted name for the tribrach.

[216] A foot [...] *rejoiced*] From Audomarus Talaeus, *Rhetorica* (1552), 1.16 ('De Metro'). It was a revision of rhetoric that shared the Ramist spirit of educational reformation; first translated into English by Dudley Fenner in 1584. Webbe substitutes Talaeus' examples in Latin for English words of his own choice.

[217] The place [...] same] The distribution of feet in a Latin line determines its rhythmic differences with other lines with the same number of feet.

with great reason that they should frame, we being only directed by such rules as serve for only Latin words. Yet notwithstanding one may well perceive by these few that these kind of verses would well become the speech, if so be there were such rules prescribed as would admit the placing of our aptest and fullest words together.[218] For indeed, excepting a few of[cxxxvi] our monosyllables, which naturally should most of them be long,[219] we have almost none that will stand fitly in a short foot, and therefore, if some exception were made against the precise observation of position and certain other of the rules, then might we have as great plenty and choice of good words to furnish and set forth a verse as in any other tongue.

Likewise, if there were some direction in such words as fall not within the compass of Greek or Latin rules, it were a great help and therefore[cxxxvii] I had great miss° in these few which I made. Such as is the last syllable in these words, *able*, *noble*, or *possible*, and such like. Again for the nature and force of our *w*, of our *th*, of our *oo*, and *ee*, of our words which admit an *e* in the end after one or two consonants, and many other.[220] I, for my part, though (I must needs confess)

---

[218] For in truth [...] together] Some Latin rules of prosody like 'position', 'diphthong' or 'vowel before vowel' could be transferred more or less naturally to English verse, whereas others like 'derivation' posed frequent conflicts. All in all, when applied to certain English words, most of them were susceptible of either incurring in contradictions with other rules or forcing to modify natural pronunciation. Richard Stanyhurst exposed some of these conflicts giving practical examples in *Aeneid* (1582) 'To thee Learned Reader'; e.g. whereas the first syllable of the Latin word *brĕuiter* is short, the first of 'brīefly' has to be long according to the rule of position — as in fact it is by natural pronunciation, therefore implying that the rule of derivation is invalidated by position (sig. B1ʳ). Two years earlier Harvey had also expressed his concerns in this regard, warning of the contradictions between rules like, for instance, those of position and diphthong: 'Nay, haue we not somtime, by your leaue, both the Position of the firste, and Dipthong of the seconde, concurring in one, and the same sillable, which neuerthelesse is commonly and ought necessarily to be pronounced short?' (*Variorum* X, 'Letter' V: 474). Confronting Spenser's claims for the strict transference of Latin rules and the consequent adoption of the changes in pronunciation they may imply, Harvey refuses to accept that in order to fulfil the rule of diphthong, the natural pronunciation of words like 'merchaŭndise', 'suddaĭnly' or 'certaĭnly' were to be modified by turning the second syllable from short to long; or, similarly, that carpĕnter would be modified into carpēnter by position. On the debate about Latin rules of prosody see Attridge, *Well-Weighed Syllables*, chapter 10, pp. 136–62.

[219] For indeed [...] long] Although they could be considered short when required by the circumstances; see notes 191 and 198 above. Ascham, *Schoolmaster*, p. 289: 'wordes of one syllable which commonly be long'.

[220] Likewise [...] many other] The reason for Webbe's doubts about these typically English spellings is that they are not regulated by any of the Latin rules of prosody. For instance, as the final -*e* in *able* is not pronounced but counts orthographically as a syllable, the question is whether to scanse it as short or not to scanse it at all. A similar conflict is presented by words ending in -*e* after consonants. Or, according to the rule 'vowel before vowel', the first vowel in -*oo* and -*ee* should be marked separately as short, when in fact it does not sound independently from its partner. For comments on Webbe's discussion and usage of Latin prosody see S. Tillbrook, *Historical and Critical Remarks upon the Modern Hexametrists*

many faults escaped me in these few, yet took I as good heed as I could, and in truth did rather always omit the best words and such as would naturally become the speech best than I would commit anything which should notoriously impugn the Latin rules, which herein I had only for my direction. Indeed, most of our monosyllables I am forced to make short to supply the want of many short words requisite in these verses. The particle°cxxxviii *a*, being but the English article adjoined to nouns, I always make short, both alone and in composition,²²¹ and likewise the words of one syllable ending in *e* as *the*, when it is an article, *he*, *she*, *ye*, etc.²²² *We* I think should needs be always long because we pronounce continually *wee*.cxxxix *I*, being alone standing for the pronoun *ego*, in my judgement might well be used common,° but because I never saw it used but short, I so observed it. Words ending in *y* I make short without doubt, saving that I have marked in others one difference [H1ʳ] which they use in the same, that is to make it short in the end ⏑ of an adverb, as *gladly*, and long in the end –ᶜˣˡ of an adjective, as *goodly*. But the reason is, as I take it, because the adjective is or should be most commonly written thus, *goodlie*.²²³ *O*, being an adverb, is naturally long: in the end of words, both monosyllables and other, I think it may be used common. The first of polysyllables I directed according to the nature of the word, as I thought most answerable to Latin examples, saving that somewhere I am constrained to strain courtesy with the preposition of a word compounded or such like, which breaketh° no great square, as in *defence* or *depart*, etc.²²⁴ The middle syllables, which are not very many, come for the most part under the precinct° of position, whereof some of them will not possibly abide the touch, and therefore must needs be a little wrested. Such are commonly the adverbs of three syllables, as *mournfully*, *spitefully*, and such like words derived of this adjective *full*. And therefore, if there be great occasion to use them, they must be reformed by detracting only (*l*) and then they stand meetly° current,° as

---

(Cambridge: J. Smith, 1822), p. 21; and T. S. Omond, *English Metrists* (Tunbridge Wells: R. Pelton, 1903), pp. 19–20.

²²¹ The particle […] composition] Although there is a Latin rule that establishes that particles or prepositions that form part of compound words should be long.

²²² and likewise […] etc.] Stanyhurst differs: 'E. common: yf yt bee short, I wryte yt vsualy with a single E. as *the*, *me* yf long with two, as *thee mee*' (ibid. 'To thee Learned Reader', sig. B2ᵛ).

²²³ Words ending […] *goodlie*] Webbe's and Stanyhurst's solutions (see note 222 above) indicate that quantity was for the Elizabethans occasionally related to spelling (written letters) rather than to sound. The convenience of a poetic licence that allowed orthographic modifications so as to favour that English words fitted Latin rules was one of the subjects of the debate about quantitative metres; Stanyhurst accepts it, although with an objection: 'I would not wish thee quantitie of syllables too depend so much vpon thee gaze of thee eye, as thee censure of thee eare' (ibid. sig. B2ᵛ). See Attridge, *Well-Weighed Syllables*, pp. 158–60.

²²⁴ saving that […] etc.] A rule of prosody dictated that the particle *de-* in compound words was counted as long.

mournfuly.²²⁵ The last syllables I wholly directed so near as I could to the touch of common rules.

The most famous verse of all the rest is called *hexametrum epicum*,²²⁶ which consisteth of six feet, whereof the first four are indifferently either spondees or dactyls, the fifth is evermore a dactyl, and the sixth a spondee, as thus:

 ‒ ‿ ‿ | ‒ ‿ ‿ | ‒ ‒ | ‒ ‒ | ‒ ‿ ‿ | ‒ ‒
 Tityrus happily thou liest tumbling under a beech tree.²²⁷

This kind of verse I have only seen to be practised in our English speech, and indeed will stand somewhat more orderly therein than any of the other kinds, until we have some toleration of words made by special rule. The first that attempted to practise this verse in English should seem to be the Earl of Surrey, who translated some part of Virgil into verse indeed, but without regard of true quantity of syllables.²²⁸ There is one famous distich,° which is common in the mouths of all men, that was made by one Master Watson, fellow of [H1ᵛ] St John's College in Cambridge about forty years past, which for the sweetness and gallantness thereof, in all respects doth match^cxli and surpass the Latin copy of Horace, which he made out of Homer's words *qui mores hominum*, etc.²²⁹

---

²²⁵ And therefore [...] *mournfuly*] See note 223 above.
²²⁶ *hexametrum epicum*] Heroic verse or hexameter.
²²⁷ Tityrus [...] tree] Webbe's translation of Virgil, *Eclogue* 1, 1–2: 'Tityre, tu patulae recubans sub tegmine fagi/Silvestrem tenui musam meditaris avena' ('You, Tityrus, lie under your spreading beech's covert').
²²⁸ but without [...] syllables] According to Ascham, both Surrey and Gonsalvo Periz, secretary of the Spanish king, had 'auoyded the fault of Ryming, yet neither of them hath fullie hite perfite and trwe versifying. In deede, they obserue iust number, and euen feete: but here is the fault, that their feete: be feete without ioyntes, that is to say, not distinct by trwe quantitie of sillables' (*Schoolmaster*, p. 291). Like Ascham, Webbe interprets Surrey's innovative unrhymed lines (blank verse) as attempts to compose quantitative verse; he identifies a purposeful distribution of feet, although deprived of the expected regard for quantity. This indicates that neither Ascham nor Webbe were aware of the accentual potential of English lines, tending therefore to associate the absence of rhyme with quantitative metre. In fact, William Owen's title to his edition of Surrey's translation of the fourth book of *Aeneid* (1554) described its blank verse as 'a Strange Meter', suggesting the extent to which its previous manuscript versions had disconcerted Elizabethan readers; on the reception of the first instances of blank verse see R. B. Shaw, *Blank Verse: A Guide to Its History and Use* (Athens: Ohio University Press, 2007), p. 34.
²²⁹ There is [...] etc.] Ascham, *Schoolmaster*, pp. 224–25; Ascham hails Thomas Watson's translation of these lines from Homer's *Odyssey* as the perfect example of English hexameter, comparing them with the Greek original and with Horace's Latin version (*Ars Poetica*, 141–42): 'dic, mihi, Musa, virum, captae post tempora Troiae/qui mores hominum multorum vidit et urbes' ('Sing, Muse, for me the man who on Troy's fall/Saw the wide world, its ways and cities all'). See also Spenser-Harvey, 'Letter' V (*Variorum* X, p. 474). Thomas Watson was one of the leading masters at St John's in 1553–54, where he had got his B.A. in 1532–33; a close friend of Ascham and John Cheke, he had been dean of Durham from 1553 to 1557 and bishop of Lincoln from 1556 to 1559.

‾ ‿‿ ‾ ‾ ‾ ‿‿ ‾ ‾ ‾ ‿ ‾ ‿ ‾ ‾
  All travellers do gladly report great praise of ^{cxlii} Ulysses:
‾ ‿‿ ‾ ‿‿ ‾ ‾ ‾ ‿‿ ‾ ‿ ‾ ‿ ‾ ‾
  For that he knew many men's manners, and saw many cities.

Which two verses, if they be examined throughout, all the rules and observations of the best versifying shall be found to attain the very perfection of them all. There be two other not much inferior to these which I found in the gloss of E.K. upon the Fifth Eclogue of the new poet, which Tully translated out of Greek into Latin, *Haec habeo*^{cxliii} *quae edi*, etc.

  All that I ate did I 'joy, and all that I greedily gorged;
‾ ‾ ‾ ‾ ‾ ‿ ‿ ‾ ‾ ‾ ‿ ‿ ‾ ‾
  As for those many goodly matters, left I for others.[230]

Which though they will not abide the touch of synaloepha in one or two places,[231] yet perhaps some English rule which might with good reason be established would make them current° enough and avoid that inconvenience which is very obvious in our words. The great company of famous verses of this sort which Master Harvey made is not unknown to any and are to be viewed at all times.[232] I, for my part, so far as those examples would lead me, and mine own small skill afford me, have blundered° upon these few whereinto° I have translated the two first Eclogues of Virgil, because I thought no matter of mine own invention nor any other of antiquity more fit for trial of this thing, before there were some more special direction which might lead to a less troublesome manner of writing.

---

[230] There be two [...] others] Spenser, *SC*, gloss to 'May' ('Tho with them'). Spenser's translation into hexameters of Sardanapalus' epitaph, quoted by E.K.: 'Haec habui quae edi, quaeque exaturata libido/Hausit, at illa manent multa ac praeclara relicta' (Brooks-Davies, p. 97); translated from Greek by Cicero, *Tusculan Disputations*, 5.35.101: 'Haec habeo, quae edi quaeque exsaturata libido/Hausit; at illa iacent multa et praeclara relicta' ('All I have eaten and wantoned and pleasures of love I have tasted, /These I possess but have left all else of my riches behind me'). Spenser alluded to these lines as those 'which I translated you *ex tempore* in bed, the last time we lay togither in Westminster' (*Variorum* X, 'Letter' III: 16). All that] In ibid.: 'That which'.
[231] Which though [...] places] In fact, this is a metrically conflictive line and Webbe prefers to avoid its scansion; the original spelling in Q allows us to figure out the terms on which the personal pronouns and the conjunction cause Webbe's doubts regarding how to cope with the synaloephas: 'All that I eate did I ioy and all that I greedilie gorged', sig. H1^v.
[232] The great company [...] times] Spenser, *SC*, 'Postcript': 'Now I trust, Master Harvey, that upon sight of your special friend's and fellow-poet's doings, or else for envy of so many unworthy *quidams* (which catch at the garland which to you alone is due), you will be persuaded to pluck out of the hateful darkness those so many excellent English poems of yours which lie hid, and bring them forth to eternal light' (Brooks-Davies, p. 25). See also Spenser-Harvey, 'Letter' V (*Variorum* X, p. 463).

[H2ʳ] The Argument of the First *Eclogue*

Under the person of Tityrus Virgil being figured, himself declareth to *Meliboeus*, another[cxliv] neatherd, the great benefits that he received at Augustus'[cxlv] hand, who in the spoil of Mantua gave him his goods and substance° again [H2ᵛ, H3ʳ, H3ᵛ].

> Meliboeus.   Tityrus.
> Tityrus, happily thou lyste° tumbling under a beech tree,
> All in a fine oat pipe these sweet songs lustily chanting.
> We, poor souls, go to wrack, and from these coasts be removed,
> And fro° our pastures sweet: thou, Tityr', at ease in a shade plot
> Mak'st thick groves to resound with[cxlvi] songs of brave Amaryllis.
>
> Tityrus.
> Oh Meliboeus, he was no man but a god who relieved me;
> Ever he shall be my god: from this same sheep-cot, his altars
> Never a tender lamb shall want with blood to bedew° them.
> This good gift did he give to my steers thus freely to wander,
> And to myself (thou seest) on pipe to resound what I listed.°
>
> Meliboeus.[233]
> Grudge thee sure I do not, but this thing makes me to wonder,
> Whence comes all this ado: with grievous pain not a little
> Can I remove my goats: here, Tityre, scant° get I forward
> Poor old crone,° two twins at° a clap i'th' boisterous hazels
> Left she behind, best hope i'my flock, laid hard on a bare° stone.
> Had not a luckless lot possessed our minds, I remember
> Warnings oft fro° the blast burnt oak we saw to be sent us.
> Oft did a left hand crow foretell these things in her hull tree.
> But this god let us hear what he was, good Tityre, tell me.
>
> Tityrus.
> That same city so brave, which Rome was wont to be called,
> Fool did I think to be like this of ours, where we to the pastures
> Wonted were to remove from dams° our young pretty cattle.
> Thus did I think young whelps and kids to be like to the mothers,
> Thus did I wont compare many great things with many little.
> But this above all towns as loftily mounteth her high head,
> As by the low base shrubs tall cypress shooteth above them.
>
> Meliboeus.
> And what did thee move that needs thou must go to see Rome?
>
> Tityrus.
> Freedom, which, though late, yet once looked back to my poor state,
> After time when hairs from my beard did 'gin to be whitish:
> Yet looked back at last and found me out after a long time,

---

[233] Meliboeus] Smith omits the remaining stanzas.

When Amaryll' was once obtained, Galatea departed:
For (for I will confess) whilst as Galatea did hold me,
Hope did I not for freedom, and care had I none to my cattle.
Though many fair young beasts our fold° for the altars afforded
And many cheeses good fro° my press were sent to the city,
Seldom-times did I bring any store of pence fro° the market.

Meliboeus.
Oh Amaryll', wherefore° to thy gods (very much did I marvel)
Heavily thou did pray, ripe fruits ungathered all still:
Tityrus is not at home. These pine trees, Tityre, missed thee,
Fountains long'd for thee, these hedgerows wished thy return home.

Tityrus.
What was then to be done? From bondage could not I wind out:
Neither I could have found such gentle gods anywhere else.
There did I see, Meliboee, that youth whose hests° I by course still
Fortnights whole to observe on the altars sure will I not fail.
Thus did he gently grant to my suit° when first I demanded:
"Keep your herd, poor slaves, as erst,° let bulls to the makes° still".

Meliboeus.
Happy old man, then thou shall have thy farm to remain still,
Large and large to thyself, others nought but stony gravel
And foul slimy rush wherewith their lees° be besprinkled.
Here no unwonted food shall grieve young theaves° who be laded,°
Nor the infections foul of neighbour's[cxlvii] flock shall annoy them.
Happy old man, in shadowy banks and cool pretty places,
Here by the quainted° floods and springs most holy remaining,
Here, these quicksets fresh which lands sever out fro° thy neighbour's,[cxlviii]
And green willow rows which Hyblae bees[234] do rejoice in,
Oft fine whistling noise shall bring sweet sleep to thy senses.
Under a rock side here will pruiner°[cxlix] chant merry ditties.
Neither on high elm trees, thy belovde° doves loftily sitting,
Nor pretty turtles' trim will cease to crook° with a good cheer.

Tityrus.
First, therefore, swift bucks shall fly for food to the skiesward,
And from fish withdrawn broad seas themselves shall avoid hence:
First (both borders broke) Araris shall run to the Parthanes,°
And likewise Tigris shall again run back to the Germanes:°
Ere his countenance° sweet shall slip once out from my heart root.

Meliboeus.
We, poor souls, must some to the land called Africa pack hence.
Some to the far Scythia, and some must to the swift flood Oaxes.
Some to Britannia[cl] coasts quite parted far fro° the whole world.

---

[234] Hyblae bees] Bees from Hybla, the ancient mount in Sicily celebrated for its delicious honey.

Oh! these pastures pure shall I never more chance to behold ye?
And our cottage poor, with warm turves cover'd about, trim?
Oh! these trim tilled lands, shall a reckless soldier have them?
And shall a barbarian have this crop? See what a mischief
Discord vile hath araisde!° For whom was our labor all took?
Now, Meliboee, engraft° peary stocks, set vines in an order!
Now go, my brave flock once that were. Oh! Now go my kidlings.°
Never again shall I now, in a green bower° sweetly reposed,
See you in queachy° briars far aloof clambering° on a high hill.
Now shall I sing no jigs, nor whilst I do fall to my junkets°
Shall ye, my goats, cropping sweet flowers and leaves, sit about me.

Tityrus.
Yet thou mayst tarry° here, and keep me company this night,
All on a leavy couch: good apples ripe I do not lack,
Chestnuts sweet good store, and plenty of curddes° will I set thee.
Mark i'the town how chimney tops do begin to be smoking,
And from the mountains high how shadows grow to be larger.

[H4ʳ] The Second Eclogue Called *Alexis*

The Argument

Virgil, in the person of Corydon as some think, complaineth that he is not so gracious with Augustus as he would be; or else it is to be referred to a youth Alexander, which was given him of *Asinius Pollio*, whom he blameth for the unsteadfastness° of his wit and wandering appetite in refusing the friendly counsel which he used to give him [H4ᵛ, J1ʳ].

That shepherd Corydon did burn in love with Alexis,
All his master's dear, and nought had he whereby to hope for.
Only in beechen groves and dolesome° shadowy places
Daily resorted he; there these rude disordered outcries,
Hills and desert woods throughout, thus mournfully tuned:
"Oh, hard hearted Alex! Hast thou no regard to my sweet song?
Pyttiest me not a whit?° Yea mak'st me now that I shall die.
Yet do the beasts find out fine shades and trim pretty cool plots,
And fro° the sunbeams safe lie lizards under a bush-tuft,
And for workmen tough, with boiling heat so beparched,°
Garlic savory sweet and cool herbs plenty be dressed.
But, by the scorch'd bank sides i'thy footsteps still I go plodding,
Hedgerows hot do resound with grasshops° mournfully squeaking.
Oh, had I not been better abide Amaryllis her anger?
And her proud disdain? Yea better abide my Menalcas,
What though brown did he seem, yea what though thou be so gallant?
Oh! thou fine cherry-cheek'd child, trust not t'much° to thy beauty!
Black violets are took when daisies white be refused.
Me thou dost despise, unknown to thyself yet, Alexis,

What be my riches great in neat, in milk what abundance.
In Sicil' hills be my lambs of which there wander a thousand;
All times cold and hot, yet fresh milk never I wanted;
Such be my music notes as (when his flocks he recalling)
Amphion of Dirce did use on shore Aracynthus.
Much mishap'd I am not, for late in a bank I beheld me,
When still seas were calm, to thy Daphnis need not I^{cli} give place,
No, though thou be the judge, if pictures have any credit.
Oh, were thou content to remain with me by the downs here,
In these lodgings small, and help me props to put under,
And trim kidling° flock with me to drive to the green fields!
Pan in singing sweet with me should'st bravely resemble;
Pan was first the inventor, pipes to adjoin in an order;
Pan poor flocks and shepherds too most duly regardeth,
Those fine lips thou need'st not fear to bruise with a sweet pipe.
What did Amynt' forsake i'this exercise to be cunning?
One pipe, with seven sundry stops match'd sweetly together,
Have I myself, Damoetas which at's° death he bequeath'd° me,
And said: 'here thou art now the second which ever hath ought it',
So said Damoetas, but Amyntas spitefully scorned it.
Also, two pretty small wild kids most goodly bespotted
Have I, that here i'the dales do run scant° safe, I do fear me;
Twice in a day two teats they suck; for thee will I keep them.
Wondrous fain to have had them both was Thestylis of late,
And so she shall, for I see thou scorn'st whatsoever I give thee.
Come hither, oh, thou sweet face boy! See, see, to thyself here
How fair nymphs in baskets full do bring many lilies;
White violets sweet Nais° plucks and blooms fro° the poppies,
Narciss° and dill flowers most sweet that savoreth also,
Cassia, broad marigolds, with pansies, and hyacinthus;
And I myself ripe peaches soft as silk will I gather,
And such chestnuts as Amaryll' was wont to rejoice at;
Plums will I bring likewise, that fruit shall be honored also.
And ye, oh laurel twigs, shall I crop, and myrtle thyself next,
For ye be wont (bound both in a bunch) most sweetly to savour.
Thou art but a clown, Corydon; these gifts esteems not Alexis,
Nor by thy gifts to obtain art meet° to encounter Iollas.
Wretch, alas! What's this that I wish? South blasts to the young flowers,
Or clear crystal streams with loathsome swine to be troubled?
Ah, mad boy! From whom dost run? Why gods i'the woods dwelt,
And Paris erst° of Troy; Pallas most gladly rejoiceth
In these bowers,° and in trim groves we all chiefly delight us.
Grim lioness doth course curs'd wolves, so wolves do the kidlings,°
And these wanton kids likewise these fair cytisus flowers,
Thee Corydon (Oh, Alex!); some pleasure every wight° pulls.
See these yoked steers, fro° the plough now seem to be let loose,
And these shadows large do declare this sun to depart hence;

> Still I do burn in love. What mean in love to be looked for?
> Ah, Corydon, Corydon! What raging fury doth haunt thee?
> Half-cropped down be thy vines and broad-branched elms overhang them.
> Rather about some needful work now busy thyself well,
> Either on osier's tuft or bulrush weave pretty baskets.
> And if Alexis scorn thee still, mayst hope for another.
>
> FINIS.

I durst° not enterprise to go any further with this rude translation, being for the respects aforesaid a troublesome and unpleasant piece of labour; and therefore these shall suffice till further occasion shall serve to employ some profitable pains in this behalf.

The next verse in dignity to the hexameters is the *carmen elegiacum*, which consisteth of four feet and two odd syllables, *viz.* the two first feet, either dactyls or spondees indifferent, the one long syllable, next two dactyls and another long syllable – – – ᴗ ᴗ – – ᴗ ᴗ – ᴗ ᴗ –; some do measure it in this sort (and more truly yet not so readily to all) accounting first two indifferently either dactyls or spondees, then one spondee and two [J1ᵛ] anapests; but it cometh all to one reckoning. This verse is always unseparably adjoined unto the hexameter, and serveth especially to the handling of love and dalliances,° whereof it taketh the name. It will not frame altogether so currently° in our English as the other, because the shortness of the second *penthemimer*° will hardly be framed to fall together in good sense after the Latin rules. I have not seen very many of them made by any, and therefore one or two for example sake shall be sufficient.

This *distich*° out of Ovid:

> *Ingenium quondam fuerat pretiosius auro;*
> *At nunc barbaria est grandis, habere nihil.*[235]

May thus be translated:

> Learning once was thought to be better than any gold was,
> Now he that hath not wealth is but a barbarian.

And this:

> *Omnia sunt hominum tenui pendentia filo,*
> *Et subito casu quae valuere, ruunt.*[236]

> 'Tis but a slender thread, which all men's states do depend on:
> And most goodly things quickly do fall to decay.

---

[235] *Ingenium* […] *nihil*] *Amores* 3.8, 3–4 ('Time was when genius was more precious than gold; but now to have nothing is monstrous barbarism').
[236] *Omnia* […] *ruunt*] *Ex Ponto* 4.3, 35–36 ('All human affairs hang by a slender thread; chance on a sudden brings to ruin what once was strong').

As for the verses *phalaecian*[237] and *iambic*, I have not as yet made any trial in them, but the *Sapphic*[238] I assure you, in my judgement, will do very pretty if the wants which I speak were once supplied; for trial of which I have turned the new poet's sweet song of Elisa into such homely *Sapphic* as I could. This verse consisteth of these five feet, one choree, one spondee, one dactyl, and two chorees, with this addition, that after every third verse be set one *adonic* verse, which consisteth of a dactyl and a spondee. It is more troublesome and [J2ʳ] tedious to frame in our speech by reason they run without difference, every verse being alike in quantity throughout, yet in my judgement standeth meetly° well in the same. I pray look the copy which I have translated in the Fourth Eclogue of *The Shepherds' Calendar*: the song of Colin's making which Hobbinol singeth in praise of the Queen's majesty, under the name of Elisa.

> Ye dainty nymphs, that in this blessed brook
>   Do bathe your breast,
> Forsake your watery bowers,° and hither look
>   At my request.
> And eke[cliii] you virgins that on Parnass' dwell,
> (Whence floweth Helicon, the learned well)
>   Help me to blaze
>   Her worthy praise,
> Which[cliii] in her sex doth all excel.
>
> Of fair Elisa be your silver song,
>   That blessed wight:°
> The flower of virgins, may she flourish long,
>   In princely plight.
> For she is Syrinx' daughter, without spot,
> Which Pan, the shepherds' god, of[cliv] her begot:
>   So sprung her grace
>   Of heavenly race;
> No mortal blemish may her blot.
>
> See where she sits, etc.[239]

---

[237] *phalaecian*] Commonly called Phalaecian hendecasyllable; five foot lines consisting of a spondee, a dactyl and three trochees.
[238] *Sapphic*] So called for its creator, the Greek lyric poetess Sappho (native of Mytilene, c. 630 BC), who appears to have been at the centre of a female literary society and whose poetry was widely admired by ancient writers; her lyric poems formed nine books, but only fragments are extant.
[239] Ye dainty [...] etc.] Lines 37–55.

The Sapphic verse [J2ᵛ, J3ʳ, J3ᵛ]:

$$-\cup---\cup\cup-\cup--$$
$$-\cup---\cup\cup-\cup--$$
$$-\cup---\cup\cup-\cup--$$
$$-\cup\cup--$$

Oh, ye nymphs most fine who resort to this brook,
For to bathe there your pretty breasts at all times:
Leave the wat'rish bowers,° hither and to me come
                              at my request now.

And ye Virgins trim who resort to Parnass',
Whence the learned well Helicon beginneth:
Help to blaze her worthy deserts,° that all else
                              mounteth above far.

Now the silver songs of Elisa sing ye,
Princely wight° whose peer not among the virgins
Can be found: that long she may remain among us,
                              now let us all pray.

For Syrinx' daughter she is, of her begotten
Of the great god Pan; thus of heaven ariseth,
All her ex'lent race: any mortal hard hap°
                              cannot approach her.

See, she sits most seemly in a grassy green plot,
Clothed in weeds meet° for a princely maiden,
Bossed° with ermines white, in a goodly scarlet
                              bravely beseeming.

Decked is that crown that upon her head stands
With the red rose and many daffadillies,°
Bays, the primrose and violets be set by; how
                              joyful a sight is.

Say, behold did ye ever her angelic face,
Like to Phoebe fair? Or her heavenly havour,°
And the princelike grace that in her remaineth,
                              have ye the like seen?

Meddled ist red rose with a white together
Which in either cheek do depeinct° a trim cheer;
Her majesty and eye to behold so comely,° her
                              like who rememb'reth?

Phoebus once peeped forth with a goodly gilt° hue
For to gaze: but when he saw the bright beams
Spread abroad fro' her face with a glorious grace,
                              it did amaze him.

When another sun he beheld below here,
Blushed he red for shame, nor again he durst° look:
Would he durst° bright beams of his own with hers match,
                        for to be vanquished.

Show thyself now, Cynthia, with thy clear rays,
And behold her: never abashed be thou so:
When she spreads those beams of her heavenly beauty, how
                        thou art in a dump dashed?

But I will take heed that I match not her grace
With the Laton seed; Niobe that once did,
Now she doth therefore in a stone repent; to all
                        other a warning.

Pan he may well boast that he did beget her,
Such a noble wight;° to Syrinx is it joy
That she found such lot with a bellibone° trim
                        for to be loaden.

When my younglings first to the dams° do bleat out,
Shall a milk white lamb to my lady be off'red;
For my goddess she is, yea I myself her herd-groom,°
                        though but a rude clown.

Unto that place Calliope doth high her,
Where my goddess shines; to the same the Muses[clv]
After her, with sweet violins about them,
                        cheerfully tracing.

Is not it bay branch that aloft in hands they have,
Even to give them sure to my Lady Elisa?
Oh so sweet they play, and to the same do sing too;
                        heav'nly to hear ist.

See, the Graces'[clvi] trim to the stroke° do foot° it,
Deftly dancing, and merriment do make them
Sing to the instruments to rejoice the more, but
                        wants not a fourth Grace?

Then the dance will be evne,° to my lady therefore
Shall be gevne° that place, for a Grace she shall be
For to fill that place, that among them in heaven she
                        may be received.

This bevy° of bright nymphs, whither ist go they now,
Ranged all thus fine in a row together?
They be ladies all i'the Lake behight° so,
                        they thither all go.

One that is there chief that among the rest goes,
Called is Chloris,[clvii] of olives she bears a
goodly crownet,° meet° for a prince that in peace
                        ever abideth.

> All ye shepherds' maids, that about the green dwell,
> Speed ye there to her grace; but among ye take heed
> All be virgins pure that approach to deck her,
>   duty requireth.
>
> When ye shall present ye before her in place,
> See ye not yourselves do demean too rudely;
> Bind the fillets,° and to be fine the waist gird°
>   fast with a tawdryne.° clviii
>
> Bring the pinks, therewith many gillyflowers sweet,
> And the columbines; let us have the wine-sops°
> With the cor'nation,° that among the love lads
>   wonts to be worn much.
>
> Daffadowndillies° all along the ground strew,
> And the cowslip with a pretty paunce° let here lie.
> Kingcup° and lilies so belovde° of all men,
>   And the deluce° flower.clix

One verse there remaineth untranslated as yet,[240] with some other of this sort, which I meant to have finished, but by reason of some let° which I had I am constrained to defer to some other time, when I hope to gratify the readers with more and better verses of this sort; for in truth, I am persuaded a little pain° taking might furnish our speech with as much pleasant delight in this kind of verse as any other whatsoever.

[J4ᵛ] Here follow the canons or general cautions of poetry, prescribed by Horace, first gathered by Georgius Fabricius Chemnicensis,cl[241] which I thought good to annex to this treatise as very necessary observations to be marked of all poets.

In his 'Epistle ad Pisones', De Arte Poetica

First, let the invention be meet° for the matter, not differing, or strange, or monstrous. For a woman's head, a horse neck, the body of a diverse-coloured bird, and many members of sundry creatures compact together, whose legs ending like a fish's tail, this in a picture is a wonderful deformity. But, if there be such diversity in the frame of a speech, what can be more uncomely° or ill-favoured?

---

[240] One verse [...] yet] Webbe quits without translating the last stanza of the song to Elisa (ll. 145–53, Brooks-Davies, p. 72).
[241] Here follow [...] Chemnicensis] Webbe translates a section from Georg Fabricius' (1516–1571) *De Re Poetica Libri Septem* (first printed in 1565); a concluding section to the sixth book in the enlarged edition (Paris, 1584) included a summary of Horace's main ideas on poetry as taken from *Ars Poetica* (sigs. 300ʳ–305ᵛ).

2. The ornaments or colours must not be too many nor rashly adventured on; neither must they be used everywhere and thrust into every place.

3. The propriety of speech must be duly observed, that weighty and great matters be not spoken slenderly,° or matters of length too briefly. For it belongeth much both to the comeliness and nature of a matter that in big matters there be likewise used boisterous words.

4. In poetical descriptions the speech must not exceed all credit, nor anything feignedly brought in against all course of nature.

5. The disposing of the work must be such that there be no offence committed, as it were by too exquisite diligence. For many things may be oft committed and some thing by too [K1^r] curious handling be made offensive. Neither is it in one part to be well furnished, and in another to be neglected. Which is proved by example of a carver, who expressed very artificially the head and upper part of a body, but the rest he could not make an end of. Again, it is proved thus, that a body should not be in other parts beautiful and yet be deformed in the crooked nose, for all the members in a well-shapen body must be answerable, sound, and well proportioned.

6. He that taketh in hand to write anything must first take heed that he be sufficient for the same, for often unwary fools through their rashness are overtook with great want of ability.

7. The ornament of a work consisteth in words, and in the manner of the words; they[clxi] are either simple or mixed, new or old, proper or translated. In them all good judgement must be used and ready wit. The chiefest grace is in the most frequented words, for the same reason holdeth in words as doth in coins, that the most used and tried are best esteemed.

8. The kind of verse is to be considered and aptly applied to the argument, in what measure is most meet° for every sort. The most usual kinds are four: the heroic, elegiac, iambic, and lyric.

9. One must use one kind of speech alike in all writings. Sometime the lyric riseth aloft, sometime the comical. To the tragical writers belong properly the big and boisterous words. Examples must be interplaced, according fitly to the time and place.

10. Regard is to be had of affections: one thing becometh pleasant persons, another sad, another wrathful, another gentle, which must all be heedfully respected. Three things therefore are requisite in verses: beauty, sweetness, and the affection. Theophrastus saith that this beauty or delectableness is a deceit, and Aristotle calleth it τυραννίδα ὀλιγοχρόνιον, a momentary tyranny. Sweetness retaineth a reader; affection moveth him.

11. Every person must be fitted accordingly, and the speech well ordered, wherein are to be considered the dignity, age, sex, fortune, condition, place, country, etc. of each person.

[K1ᵛ] 12. The persons are either to be feigned by the poets themselves or borrowed of others. If he borrow them, then must he observe τὸ ὅμοιον, that is, that he[clxii] follow that author exactly whom he purposeth to imitate and whereout he bringeth his examples. But if he feign new persons, then must he keep his τὸ ὁμαλόν, that is, equally so bringing them in each place that it be always agreeable, and the last like unto the first, and not make one person now a bold boaster, and the same straightways° a wise wary man, for that is passing absurd. Again, everyone must observe τὸ ἁρμοστόν, which is interpreted *conuenientiam*, fitness; as it is meet° and agreeable everywhere a man to be stout, a woman fearful, a servant crafty, a young man gentle.

13. Matters which are common may be handled by a poet as they may be thought proper to himself alone. All matters of themselves are open to be entreated of by any man, but if a thing he handled of someone in such sort as he thereby obtain great praise, he maketh it his own or proper to himself; as many did write of the Trojan war, but yet Homer made matter which was common to all proper to himself.

14. Where many things are to be taken out of ancienter tongues, as the Latins took much out of the Greeks, the words are not so precisely to be followed but that they be altered according to the judgement and will of the imitator, which precept is borrowed of Tully: *Non verbum pro*[clxiii] *verbo necesse est reddere*.[242]

15. The beginning must not be foolishly handled, that is, strangely or too long.

16. The proposition or narration let it not be far-fetched or unlikely, and in the same forget not the differences of ages and persons.

17. In a comedy it is not[clxiv] needful to exhibit all the actions openly, as such as are cruel, unhonest, or ugly; but [K2ʳ] such things may better be declared by some meet° and handsome words, after what sort they are supposed to be done.

18. If a comedy have more acts than five, it is tedious; if fewer, it is not sufficient.

It fitteth not to bring in the persons of gods but in very great matters. Cicero saith, when the tragedy writers cannot bring their matters to good pass, they run to God.[243] Let not more persons speak together than four for avoiding confusion.

The *chori* must be well garnished and set forth, wherein either men are admonished, or reprehended, or counselled unto virtue. Such matter must be chosen for the *chorus* as may be meet° and agreeable to that which is in hand. As for instruments and singing, they are relics of old simplicity. For the music commonly used at theaters and the licentiousness of their songs, which together

---

[242] *Non verbum [...] reddere*] Cicero, *De Optimo* 5.14–15: 'In quibus non verbum pro verbo necesse habui reddere, sed genus omne verborum vimque servavi' ('And in so doing, I did not hold it necessary to render word for word, but I preserved the general style and force of the language').

[243] Cicero ... God] *De Natura Deorum*, 1.20.53.

with their wealth increased among the Romans, is hurtful to discipline and good manners.

19. In a satire the clownish company and rural gods are brought in to temperate the heaviness of tragedies with some mirth and pastime. In jesting it must be observed that it be not lascivious, or ribald-like, or slanderous, which precept holdeth generally in all sorts of writings.

In a satire great heed is to be taken of the place, of the day, and of the persons, as of Bacchus, Silenus, or the Satyrs. Again, of the unmeetness or inconvenience of the matter, and of the words that they be fitted according to the persons, of *decorum*, that he which represented some noble personage in the tragedy be not some busy fool in the satire. Finally, of the hearers, lest they be offended by mixing filthy matters with jests, wanton toys with unhonest, or noisome with merry things.

[K2ᵛ] 20. The feet are to be applied proper to every kind of verse, and therein a poet must not use too much licence or boldness. The ancient writers in *iambic* verses used at first pure *iambics*; afterwards, spondee was admitted into *locos impares*. But at last such was the licentious custom that they would both spondee where they listed,° and other feet without regard.

21. In compiling of verses great care and circumspection must be used.

Those verses which be made *extempore* are of no great estimation; those which are unartificial are utterly repelled as too foolish. Though many do lightly regard our verses, yet ought the carelessness of the hearers to be no cause in us of error and negligence. Who desireth to make anything worthy to be heard of learned ears,[clxv] let him read Greek authors heedfully and continually.

22. Arts have their increasings even as other things, being natural. So have tragedies, which were first rudely invented by Thespis, at last were much adorned by Aeschylus; at the first they were practised in villages of the country, afterwards brought to stages in great cities.

23. Some arts do increase, some do decay by a certain natural course. The old manner of comedies decayed by reason of slandering, which therein they used against many, for which there was a penalty appointed, lest their bitterness should proceed too[clxvi] far; in place of which, among the Latins, came the satires.

The ancient authors of comedies were Eupolis, Cratinus, and Aristophanes; of the middle sort, Plato Comicus; of the last kind, Menander, which continued and was accounted the most famous.

24. A poet should not content himself only with others' inventions, but himself also by the example of old writers should bring something of his own industry which may be laudable. So did they which writ among the Latins the comedies called *togatae*, whose arguments were taken from the Greeks, and the other which writ the *praetextatae*, whereof the arguments were Latin.

[K3ʳ] 25. Heedfulness and good composition maketh a perfect verse, and that which is not so may be reprehended. The faculty of a good wit exceedeth art.

26. A poet, that he may be perfect, hath need to have knowledge of that part of philosophy which informeth the life to good manners. The other which pertaineth to natural things is less plausible, hath fewer ornaments, and is not so profitable.

27. A poet to the knowledge of philosophy should also add greater experience, that he may know the fashions of men and dispositions of people. This profit is got by travelling,° that whatsoever he writeth he may so express and order it that his narration may be formable.

28. The end of poetry is to write pleasant things, and profitable. Pleasant it is which delighteth by being not too long or uneasy to be kept in memory, and which is somewhat likely and not altogether forged. Profitable it is which stirreth up the minds to learning and wisdom.

29. Certain escapes° are to be pardoned in some poets, especially in great works. A fault may be committed either in respect of his proper art or in some other art. That a poet should err in precepts of his own art is a shameful thing. To commit a fault in another art is to be born withal. As in Virgil, who feigneth that Aeneas coming into Africa slew with his dart certain stags, whereas indeed Africa hath in it none of those beasts. Such errors do happen either by unheedfulness, when one escapeth them by negligence, or by the common fragility of man, because none there is which can know all things. Therefore, this last kind of error is not to be stuck° upon.

30. A good poet should have respect to this, how to retain his reader or hearer. In a picture something delighteth being set far off, something nearer, but a poet should delight in all places as well in sun as shadow.

31. In a poet is no mean to be admitted, which, if he be not the best[clxvii] of all, is the worst of all.

32. A poem if it run not sweetly and smoothly is odious, which is proved by a simile of the two senses, hearing and tasting, [K3ᵛ] as in sweet and pleasant meats. And the poem must be of that sort, that for the sweetness of it may be acceptable and continue like itself unto the end, lest it weary or drive away a reader.

33. He that would write anything worthy the posterity, let him not enterprise anything whereunto his nature is not agreeable. Mercury is not made of wood, as they say, neither doth Minerva favour all studies in everyone. In all arts nature is the best help, and learned men use commonly to say that a poet is as well born as made a poet.

34. Let no man esteem himself so learned, but that he may submit his writings to the judgements of others, and correct and throughly° amend the same himself.

35. The profit of poetry sprang thus: for that the ancient wise men set down the best things that pertained to man's life, manners, or felicity, and, examining and proving the same by long experience of time, when they were[clxviii] aged they published them in writings. The use of poetry, what it was at the first, is manifest by the examples of the most learned men: as of Orpheus, who first builded°

houses; of Amphion, who made cities; of Tyrtaeus, who first made war; of Homer, who writ most wisely.

36. In an artificial poet three things are requisite: nature, art, and diligence.

37. A writer must learn of the learned, and he must not stick to confess when he erreth, that the worse he may learn to avoid, and know how to follow the better.

The confession of an error betoken[clxix] a noble and a gentle mind. Celsus and Quintilian do report of Hippocrates, that lest he should deceive his posterity, he confessed certain errors, as it well became an excellent minded man and one of great credit. For, as saith Celsus, light wits, because they have nothing, will have nothing taken from them.[244]

38. In making choice of such friends as should tell us the truth and correct our writings, heedful judgement must be used, lest either we choose unskilful folk, or flatterers, or dissemblers.° The unskilful know not how to judge; flatterers [K4r] fear to offend; dissemblers,° in not praising, do seem to commend.

39. Let no man deceive himself or suffer himself to be deceived, but take some grave learned man to be judge of his doing, and let him according to his counsel change and put out what he thinketh good.

40. He which will not flatter and is of ability to judge, let him endeavour to nothing so much as to the correction of that which is written, and that let be done with earnest and exquisite judgement. He which doth not thus, but offendeth willfully in breaking his credit too rashly, may be counted for a mad, furious, and frantic fool.

41. The faults commonly in verses are seven, as either they be destitute of art, of facility, or ornament, or else they be superfluous, obscure, ambitious, or needless.

---

[244] Celsus and Quintilian [...] them] Aulus Cornelius Celsus (*c.* 25 BC–*c.* 50 AD), *De Medicina*, 8.4.3–4: 'A suturis se deceptum esse Hippocrates memoriae prodidit, more scilicet magnorum virorum et fiduciam magnarum rerum habentium. Nam levia ingenia, quia nihil habent, nihil sibi detrahunt: magno ingenio, multaque nihilo minus habituro, convenit etiam simplex veri [erroris] confessio praecipueque in eo ministerio, quod utilitatis causa posteris traditur, ne qui decipiantur eadem ratione, qua quis ante deceptus est' ('Hippocrates, with great men's love of truth in great matters, has described how he had been deceived by sutures. For shallow minds, because they have nothing, never belittle themselves; such a sincere confession of the truth befits a great mind which will still have many titles to greatness, and especially in performing the task of handing down knowledge for the advantage of posterity, that no one else may be deceived again by what has deceived him'). Quintilian, *Institutio Oratoria*, 3.6.64: 'Nam et Hippocrates, clarus arte medicinae, videtur honestissime fecisse, quod quosdam errores suos, ne posteri errarent, confessus est' ('For Hippocrates, the great physician, in my opinion took the most honourable course in acknowledging some of his errors to prevent those who came after from being led astray').

Out of the 'Epistles ad *Maecenatem*,^{clxx} *Augustum, et Florum*'.²⁴⁵

42. An imitation should not be too servile or superstitious, as though one durst° not vary one jot from the example; neither should it be so senseless or unskilful as to imitate things which are absurd and not to be followed.

43. One should not altogether tread in the steps of others, but sometime he may enter into such ways as have not been haunted or used of others. Horace borrowed the *iambic* verse of Archilocus,²⁴⁶ expressing fully his numbers and elegantly,^{clxxi} but his unseemly words and prattling taunts he most wisely^{clxxii} shunned.

44. In our verses we should not gape after the phrases of the simpler sort, but strive to have our writings allowable in the judgements [K4ᵛ] of learned men.

45. The common people's judgements of poets is seldom true, and therefore not to be sought after. The vulgar sort in Rome judged Pacuvius to be very learned; Accius to be a grave writer; that Afranius followed Menander, Plautus Epicharmus; that Terence excelled in art, Caecilius in gravity. But the learned sort were not of this opinion.²⁴⁷ There is extant in Macrobius (I know not whether A. Gellius)^{clxxiii} the like verdict concerning them which writ epigrams: that Catullus and Calvus writ few things that were good, Naevius obscure, Hortensius uncomely,° Cinna unpleasant, and Memmius^{clxxiv} rough.²⁴⁸

---

²⁴⁵ Out of [...] *Florum*] *Epistles*, 'To Maecenas', 1.1; 'To Augustus', 2.1; 'To Florus', 2.2.
²⁴⁶ Archilocus] Archilocus of Paros (fl. *c.* 714–676 BC) was the first Greek poet who composed iambic verses following established rules; the invention of the elegy is also ascribed to him.
²⁴⁷ The common ... opinion] Horace's meaning in this passage from his letter to Augustus (*Letters*, 2.1) has been widely discussed; he seems to be challenging the accepted idea that archaic poetry is objectively superior; on the interpretation of this passage see Richard Hunter, *Critical Moments in Classical Literature* (Cambridge: Cambridge University Press, 2009), pp. 90–91. Pacuvius] Born at Brundisium in Calabria (*c.* 220 BC) and nephew of Ennius. Famous as a painter before he began writing tragedies, some of his plays enjoyed great popularity. Accius] Lucius Accius was born at Pisaurum (170 BC); he was Pacuvius' contemporary and successor in Roman tragedy, both producing a play for the same occasion (140 BC), which was the former's last work. *Tereus* was one of his most famous plays. Afranius] Lucius Afranius, a Roman comic poet who lived at the begining of the first century BC, representative of the *fabula togata*. In *De Finibus* 1.3, Cicero states that Afranius followed the Greek comedy writer Menander (*c.* 390–*c.* 341 BC). Plautus Epicharmus] As there are not many similarities in titles or subjects between the comedies of Plautus and Epicharmus, Horace may mean as a common feature the liveliness in dialogues and action. Epicharmus of Kos (*c.* 540–*c.* 450 BC) was known to be the originator of the Doric comedy. On Caecilius and on Ascham's comparison of Roman and Greek comedy writers see note 43 above.
²⁴⁸ There is ... rough] Fabricius adds to Horace's judgement on the authority of the ancient writers the view of either the grammarians Ambrosius Macrobius (5th century AD), author of the *Saturnalia* or of Aulus Gellius (2nd century AD) — erroneously called Agellius by Lipsius. He was the author of *Noctes Atticae*. Fabricius reproduces the mistaken name 'Agellium', and Webbe increases the error with 'Angellius'. Calvus] Licinius Macer Calvus (82–*c.* 47 AD) is supposed to be Catullus' most intimate friend. Naevius] see note 43. Hortensius] Quintus Hortensius Hortalus (150–114 BC) was a Roman orator known for his florid rhetoric and

46. The old writers are so far to be commended as nothing be taken from the new: neither may we think but that the way lieth open still to others to attain to as great matters. Full well said Sidonius to Eucherius: 'I reverence the old writers, yet not so as though I less esteemed the virtues and deserts° of the writers in this age'.²⁴⁹

47. Newness is grateful if it be learned, for certain it is arts are not both begun and perfected at once, but are increased by time and study, which notwithstanding, when they are at the full perfection, do debate and decrease again.

Cicero. De Oratore. 'There is nothing in the world which bursteth out all at once and commeth to light all wholly together'.²⁵⁰

48. No man should dare to practice an art that is dangerous, especially before he have learned the same perfectly; so do guiders of ships, so do physicians, but so did not many Roman poets (yea, so do not too many English writers), who in a certain courageous heat gaped° after glory by writing verses, but few of them obtained it.

49. A poet should be no less skilful in dealing with the affects of the mind than a tumbler or a juggler should be ready in his art. And with such pith° should he set forth his matters that a reader should seem not only to hear the thing, but to see and be present at the doing thereof. Which faculty Fabius calleth ὑποτύπωσιν,²⁵¹ and Aristotle πρὸ ὀμμάτων θέσιν ἢ ποίησιν.

50. Poets are either such as desire to be liked of on stages, [L1ʳ] as comedy and tragedy writers, or such as would be registered in libraries. Those on stages have special respect to the motions of the mind, that they may stir both the eyes and ears of their beholders. But the other, which seek to please privately within[clxxv] the walls, take good advisement in their works that they may satisfy the exact judgements of learned men in their studies.

51. A poet should not be too importunate, as to offend in unseasonable speeches; or ungentle, as to contemn° the admonitions of others; or ambitious, as to think too well of his own doings; or too wayward, as to think reward enough cannot be given him for his desert;° or, finally, too proud, as to desire to be honoured above measure.

---

artificial action and way of wearing his toga; mentioned in Macrobius' *Saturnalia* 3.13.3 Cinna] C. Helvius Cinna, a renown poet friend of Catullus and author of *Smyrna* and of elegiac verses. Memmius] Gaius Memmius (f. 66 BC), a tribune and poet and acquaintance of Catullus; Ovid mentions his impudent poems and classes him with Cinna in *Tristia* 2.433–35.

²⁴⁹ Full well ... age] In Sidonius Apollinaris (5th century AD), *Letters*, 3.8.1.
²⁵⁰ There ... together] Cicero, *De Oratore*, 3.78.317.
²⁵¹ Fabius] Fabius Quintilian, *Institutio Oratoria*, 9.2.40: 'Ab aliis ὑποτύπωσι dicitur proposita quaedam forma rerum ita expressa verbis, ut cerni potius videatur quam audiri' ('Others give the name of ὑποτύπωσι to any representation of facts which is made in such vivid language than they appeal to the eye rather than the ear').

52. The emendations of poems be very necessary, that in the obscure points many things may be enlightened, in the baser parts many things may be throughly° garnished. He may take away and put out all unproper and unseemly words; he may with discretion imitate the ancient writers; he may abridge things that are too lofty, mitigate things that are too rough, and may use all remedies of speech throughout the whole work. The things which are scarce seemly, he may amend by art and method.

53. Let a poet first take upon him as though he were to play but an actor's part, as he may be esteemed like one which writeth without regard. Neither let him so polish his works, but that every one for the baseness thereof may think to make as good. He may likewise exercise the part of gesturer, as though he seemed to meddle in rude and common matters, and yet not so deal in them, as it were for variety sake, nor as though he had laboured them thoroughly, but trifled with them, nor as though he had sweat for them, but practised a little. For so to hide one's cunning, that nothing should seem to be laboursome or exquisite,[clxxvi] when notwithstanding, every part is polished with care and study, is a special gift which Aristotle calleth κρύψιν.

54. It is not[clxxvii] only a point of wisdom to use many and choice elegant words, but to understand also and to set forth [L1ᵛ] things which pertain to the happy end of man's life. Whereupon the poet Horace calleth the art poetical, without the knowledge of learning and philosophy, a 'prating vanity'. Therefore a good and allowable poet must be adorned with words, plenteous in sentences and, if not equal to an orator, yet very near him, and a special lover of learned men.

FINIS.

Epilogus

This small travel,° courteous reader, I desire thee take in good worth, which I have compiled not as an exquisite censure° concerning this matter, but, as thou mayst well perceive, and in truth to that only end, that it might be an occasion to have the same throughly° and with greater discretion taken in hand and laboured by some other of greater ability, of whom I know there be many among the famous poets in London, who, both for learning and leisure, may handle this argument far more pithily° than myself. Which, if any of them will vouchsafe to do, I trust we shall have English poetry at a higher price in short space, and the rabble of bald° rhymes shall be turned to famous works comparable, I suppose, with the best works of poetry in other tongues. In the meantime, if my poor skill can set the same anything forward, I will not cease to practise the same towards the framing of some apt English *prosodia*, still hoping and heartily wishing to enjoy first the benefit of some others' judgement, whose authority may bear greater credit, and whose learning can better perform it.

TEXTUAL NOTES

The Epistle

i Master] Ma. Q, Arb, Hasl. 'Epistle' omitted in Smith.
ii more] missing in Hasl.
iii lovely] missing in Arb.
iv (even this summer evenings)] Hasl, Arb, Sm; euen thys Summer Eueninges) Q.
v William Webbe] VV.VV. Q, Hasl, Arb.

A Preface

i at the least] at least Arb, Sm.
ii poetry] Poerry Hasl.
iii renowned] renowmed Q, Hasl, Arb, Sm.
iv our] your Smith, Arb.
v William Webbe] VV: VV: Q, Arb; VV.VV. Hasl, Sm.

A Discourse

i De Arte Poetica] de arte Poetica Q, Hasl, Arb, Sm.
ii *Panegyrica*] *Panegeryca* Q, Hasl, Arb, Sm.
iii *'ρυθμός*] ρ'ιθμοσ Q.
iv hearers' ears] hearers eares Q, Hasl, Arb, Sm.
v *γοητεία*] λοητεια Q.
vi Tusculan Questions] *Tusculane* questions Q, Hasl, Arb, Sm.
vii calescimus] callescimus Q, Hasl, Arb.
viii besides] Beside Hasl.
ix renowned] renowmed Smith
x make houses, and keep] made houses, and kept Q, Hasl, Arb.
xi *Iliads*] *Iliades* Q, Arb, Sm; Iliades Hasl.
xii Plato Comicus] *Plato, Comicus* Q, Hasl, Arb; *Plato (Comicus)* Sm.
xiii Phocylides] *Phocitides* Q, Arb; Phocitides Hasl.
xiv Theagenes] *Theagines* Q, Arb, Smith; Theagines Hasl.
xv Aeschylus] *Aeschitus* Q; Aeschitus Hasl; Aeschilus Arb, Sm.
xvi shepherds'] Shéepeheards Q, Hasl, Arb, Sm.
xvii Turpilius] *Turpitius* Q, Arb; Turpitius Hasl; *Turpilius* Sm.
xviii Lucius] *Luscius* Q, Arb, Smith; Luscius Hasl.
xix renowned] renowmed Smith.
xx maius] magis Q, Hasl, Arb, Sm.
xxi with] and Smith.
xxii Palingenius] *Pallengenius* Q, Hasl, Arb, Sm.
xxiii *Fairclough*] *Fayreclowe* Q, Arb, Sm; Fayreclowe Hasl.
xxiv diverse] diuer Q, Hasl; diuer[s] Arb; diuers Sm.
xxv Piers Plowman] *Pierce Ploughman* Q, Arb, Sm; Pierce Ploughman Hasl.
xxvi Eighth] eyght Q, Hasl, Arb, Sm.

xxvii eleventh] ninth Q, Hasl, Arb, Sm.
xxviii albeit] Q; albee it Q1, Q2, Q3, Brooks.
xxix of Norton of Bristol] of Norton, of Bristow Q, Hasl, Arb; of Norton of Bristow Sm.
xxx Heywood] *Haiwood* Q, Arb, Sm; Haiwood Hasl.
xxxi Thomas Phaer] *D. Phaer* Q, Arb, Sm; D. Phaer Hasl.
xxxii many respects] many respests Hasl.
xxxiii Palingenius' *Zodiac*] *Pallengenius. Lodiac* Q, Arb; Pallengenius. Lodiac Hasl; *Pallengenius Zodiac* Sm.
xxxiv skill] skyl Q, Hasl, Arb; styl Sm.
xxxv for] nor Arb.
xxxvi or] of Arb.
xxxvii jig] Jygge Q, Hasl; Iygge Sm; lygge Arb.
xxxviii whereof] wherof Q₁; missing in Q, Hasl, Arb, Sm.
xxxix foam] fome Q₁,Q₂, Q₃; fume Q, Hasl, Arb, Sm.
xl middest] midst Q, Hasl, Arb, Sm.
xli either] missing in Q, Hasl, Arb, Sm.
xlii vices] vice Arb.
xliii people's] peoples Q, Hasl, Arb, Sm.
xliv historical] Historicall Q, Hasl; Histori[c]all Arb; Historiall Smith.
xlv as] is Arb, Smith.
xlvi two, do] two, [which] doo Sm.
xlvii *Lectorem*] *Lectorum* Q, Hasl, Arb.
xlviii figurat] fugitat Q, Hasl, Arb.
xlix tender] stable Q, Hasl, Arb, Sm.
l Pulling] Gulling Q, Hasl, Arb, Sm.
li and things] missing in Gov1531, 1580.
lii The] To Q, Hasl, Arb, Sm.
liii ought] aught Hasl.
liv vices] vices? Q, Hasl, Arb.
lv and] or Q, Hasl, Arb, Sm.
lvi things] thing Gov1531, 1580.
lvii wits, their] wits and Q, Hasl, Arb, Sm.
lviii the] missing in Q.
lix is a medicine] is in medicine Gov1531; is medicine Gov1580.
lx A] and Arb, Sm; missing in Gov1531, 1580.
lxi if he prohibit] if be prohite Gov1531; he be prohibite Gov1580.
lxii alway] euer Q, Hasl, Arb, Sm.
lxiii gnawing] annoyance Q, Hasl, Arb. Sm.
lxiv wholly] holy Gov1531.
lxv The less mayst thou joy] the lesse ioy shalt you have Gov1531; the less shalt thou ioy Gov1580.
lxvi the] missing in Gov1580.
lxvii their] the Hasl.
lxviii pathetical] pathecall Q, Hasl; pathe[ti]call Arb, Sm.
lxix *Aeneidos*] *Æn.* Q, Hasl, Arb, Sm.
lxx enim] missing in Q, Hasl, Arb.
lxxi sonantis] sonantes Q, Hasl, Arb, Sm.
lxxii Cyclopia] cyclopea Q, Hasl, Arb; Cyclopea Sm.
lxxiii Scylla's] Sylla Q, Hasl, Arb, Sm; Scylla Phaer1573, 1584.
lxxiv fear and care] thought and fear Phaer1573, 1584.
lxxv with] By Q, Hasl, Arb, Sm.
lxxvi Italy] Italia Phaer1573, 1584.

Textual Notes 143

lxxvii kingdom] kingdome Q, Hasl, Arb, Sm; kindoms Phaer1573, 1584.
lxxviii hearts] selfs Phaer1573, 1584.
lxxix when] while Q, Hasl, Arb, Sm.
lxxx him had] had him Q, Hasl, Arb, Sm.
lxxxi Flaventisque] Flauentesque Q, Hasl, Sm.
lxxxii inluserit] illuserit Q, Hasl, Sm.
lxxxiii four] thrée Q, Hasl, Arb, Sm.
lxxxiv kingdoms] kingdome Q, Hasl, Arb, Sm.
lxxxv peoples] people Q, Hasl, Arb, Sm.
lxxxvi or] and Q, Hasl, Arb, Sm.
lxxxvii all] vp Q, Hasl, Arb, Sm.
lxxxviii attemptings] attempting Q, Hasl, Arb; attempting[s] Sm.
lxxxix then] than Q.
xc ship] shyps Q, Hasl, Arb, Sm.
xci This] Thus Q, Hasl, Arb, Sm.
xcii unrevenged] vereuenged Q, Hasl.
xciii But] And Sm.
xciv acris] acries Q, Hasl, Arb.
xcv scuta] scutae Q, Hasl, Arb.
xcvi aspera] asper Q, Hasl, Arb.
xcvii winds] wind Q, Hasl, Arb, Sm.
xcviii beats] gets Phaer1573, 1584.
xcix Winter's] winter Phaer1573, 1584.
c vigiles] vigilos Q, Hasl, Arb.
ci A] missing in Arb, Smith.
cii or gates, or towns] or gates of Townes Q, Hasl, Arb, Sm.
ciii falshed] falshood Q, Hasl, Arb, Smith.
civ speak] spaake Q, Hasl.
cv of] missing in Arb, Smith.
cvi Eighth] eight Q, Hasl, Arb, Sm.
cvii E.K.] E,K. Q, Hasl, Arb.
cviii seasons] season Q, Hasl, Arb; season[s] Smith.
cix rhyme's] Rymes Q, Hasl, Arb, Sm.
cx hill] hils Googe1576.
cxi the] to Q, Hasl; to [the?] Arb.
cxii hill] hils Googe1561; hylles Googe1565.
cxiii you] your Q, Hasl.
cxiv shepherd's boys] Shéepheardes boyes Q, Hasl, Arb, Sm.
cxv nigheth] nighest Q_1 Q_2 Q_3.
cxvi shall alegge] wyll allay Q, Hasl, Arb, Sm.
cxvii Winter's] Winters Q_1; Winter Q, Hasl, Arb, Sm.
cxviii that] which Q, Hasl, Arb, Sm.
cxix which] that Q, Hasl, Arb, Sm.
cxx fourteen] twelue Q, Hasl, Arb, Sm.
cxxi now] Thus Q, Hasl, Arb, Sm.
cxxii this] our Q, Hasl, Arb, Sm.
cxxiii thou] the Q_2 Q_3, Q, Hasl, Arb, Sm.
cxxiv rueful] mournfull Q, Hasl, Arb, Sm.
cxxv now shalt thou] now thou shalt Brooks-Davies.
cxxvi to entreat] for to treate Gold1584.
cxxvii couching] chouching Q, Hasl, Arb, Sm.
cxxviii another's] Authors Q, Hasl, Arb; anothers Sm.

cxxix *part*] pact Q, Hasl, Arb.
cxxx which] [of] which Sm.
cxxxi others] other Q, Hasl, Arb, Sm [this poem is not in *Paradise* 1576].
cxxxii do] thy Q, Hasl, Arb, Sm [this poem is not in *Paradise* 1576].
cxxxiii tribrachus] Trochaeus Q.
cxxxiv travellers] tauelers Q, Hasl; t[r]auelers Arb, Sm.
cxxxv as] missing in Arb; [as] Sm.
cxxxvi of] if Q, Hasl.
cxxxvii therefore] thereof Q, Hasl.
cxxxviii particle] Participle Q, Hasl, Arb, Sm.
cxxxix wee] vve Q, Hasl, Arb, Sm.
cxl –] ‿ Q, Hasl.
cxli match] math Q, Hasl; mat[c]h Arb, Smith.
cxlii of] to Sm.
cxliii habeo] habui Q, Hasl, Arb, Sm, Q_1, Q_2, Q_3, Brooks-Davies.
cxliv another] an nother Q, Hasl, Arb ['Argument' missing in Sm].
cxlv Augustus's] Augustus Q, Hasl, Arb ['Argument' missing in Sm].
cxlvi with] vvith Q, Hasl, Arb; from now on Webbe writes w as vv, likely because it is convenient to adapt his lines to the Latin rule of position.
cxlvii neighbour's] neighbours Q, Hasl, Arb.
cxlviii neighbour's] neighbours Q, Hasl, Arb.
cxlix pruiner] proyner Q, Hasl, Arb.
cl Britannia] the Britannia Hasl.
cli not I] I not Hasl.
clii eke] onely Q, Hasl, Arb, Sm.
cliii which] that Q, Hasl, Arb, Sm.
cliv of] on Q, Hasl, Arb, Smith.
clv Muses] Muser Q, Hasl, Arb.
clvi Graces'] Graces Q, Hasl, Arb, Sm.
clvii Chloris] Chores Q, Hasl, Arb.
clviii tawdryne] tawdrie lace Q_1, Q_2, Q_3; tawdry lace Brooks-Davies.
clix deluce flower] deluce flowre Q, Hasl, Arb, Sm; flowre Delice Q_1, Q_2, Q_3; flower de lis Brooks-Davies.
clx Chemnicensis] Cremnicensis Q, Hasl, Arb.
clxi they] missing in Q, Arb, Hasl.
clxii he] missing in Hasl.
clxiii pro] missing in Q.
clxiv not] missing in Q, Hasl, Arb.
clxv ears] missing in Hasl.
clxvi too] to Smith.
clxvii not the best] not [t]he [best] Smith, not he Q, Hasl, Arb.
clxviii were] are Arb.
clxix betoken] betoken[eth] Sm.
clxx Maecenatem] Mecænatem Q, Hasl, Arb.
clxxi elegantly] eleganty Q, Hasl.
clxxii wisely] wyshlye Q, Hasl, Arb.
clxxiii A. Gellius] Angellius Q, Hasl, Arb, Sm.
clxxiv Memmius] Mummius Q.
clxxv within] with[in] Arb, Sm; with Q, Hasl.
clxxvi exquisite] equisite Hasl.
clxxvii not] missing in Q, Hasl, Arb.

GLOSSARY

This Glossary contains obsolete, archaic, or uncommon words and meanings in Webbe's text, Spenser quotes and Webbe's hexameters. It also includes some terms from versification when they are not explained by Webbe. Most definitions are grounded on *OED*, with a special mention to sense numbers or order of citation when Webbe's meanings occur as examples. For words used in different grammatical forms the uninflected form is listed. When needed, the sources of terms are given in brackets. Superscript circles in the text have been used to indicate glossary entries.

A

abiding: dwelling place.
amiss: out of course.
anon: straightway.
answerable: proportional.
araisde: araised.
at a clap: at once.
at leastwise: at least.
at's: at his.

B

bald: meagrely simple.
bane: destruction.
bare: v. disclose; adj. uncovered.
bedew: v. wet by drops.
behight: named.
beholding: indebted.
behoof: benefit.
bellibone: fair lass (Fr. *belle et bonne*).
belovde: beloved.
beparched: parched all over; unique cit. in *OED*: beparch, v.
bequeath'd: entrusted.
bevy: company of maidens.
bewaileth: laments.
bickerments: skirmishes; first cit. in *OED*.
blundered: performed blindedly.
blunt: unpolished.
bossed: ornamented; first cit. in *OED*3b.
bower: abode.
breaketh no great square: makes not a big difference.

builded: built.
bulwark: fortification; fig. defence.

C

callings: occupations.
careful: mournful.
caveat: admonition.
cavils: quibbling objections.
censure: judgement.
clambering: v. climbing.
clerkly: skilfully.
cogitations: meditations.
comely: decorous; pretty.
commendation: recommendation; compliment.
commodity: benefit.
common: *Lat. pros.* applied to syllables, those that may be pronounced either long or short at the poet's choice.
conference: comparison.
contemn: v. disdain.
contentions: disputes.
conveyance: ingenious device.
cor'nation: carnation, clove-pink (from *Lat. Betonica coronaria*).
couching: framing; second cit. in *OED15a*.
countenance: estimation; face.
crone: female sheep.
crook: v. coo as a dove; first cit. in *OED2*.
crownet: coronet.
curddes: curds.
curiosity: nicety.
current: fluent.
currentness: fluency; first cit. in *OED*.

D

daffadillies: daffodils.
daffadowndillies: daffodils.
dalliance: amorous toying.
dams: female parents of animals.
debarred: excluded; cit. in *OED*.
delectation: enjoyment.
deluce flower: anglicized form of old *Fr. fleur-de-lys*; second cit. in *OED*.
depeinct: depict.
desert: merit.
diets: ways of living.
disport: amusement.
dissemblers: deceivers.
distich: *pros.* couplet (*Lat. distichon*).

doleful, dolesome: sorrowful.
dolefulness: sorrow.
dragging: v. pulling.
draught: sketch.
durst: dare.

E

eft: again.
engraft: v. implant.
entrappings: stratagems.
erst: formerly.
escapes: mistakes.
evne: even.

F

fardels: bundles.
fell: adj. cruel; n. bitterness.
fillets: hair ribbons.
flout: mock.
fold: enclosure for domestic animals.
foot it: dance.
foresaid: aforesaid.
fro: from.

G

gainsay: deny.
gall: vex.
gaped after: were eager to obtain.
Germanes: Germans.
gevne: given (*yeven* in SC, 'April', l. 114)
gilt: guilded.
gird: v. gibe; fasten.
gnawing: pang.
grasshop: grasshopper.

H

hap: fortune; chance.
harkening: adj. that listen with attention.
hatched up: brought to maturity.
havour: haviour.
hearse: obsequy.
herd-groom: shepherd-lad.
hests: vows.

I

illecebrous: alluring; second cit. in *OED* (previous cit. from Elyot's *Gov.*: 'the illecebrous dilectations of Venus' (1.7, p. 40).
ill-willers: who harbour hostile feelings towards someone.
inconveniences: improprieties, unseemly behaviour.
indifferent: undetermined.
indued: endowed.
infringe: break.
instinction: inspiration.
intituled: dedicated.
inveigh: censure.

J

junkets: picnic meals.

K

kidling: a little kid; first cit. in *OED*.
kingcup: Marsh Marigold.

L

laded: fig. burdened oppressively (with sorrow, for instance).
leering: adj. looking with side glances.
lees: shelters.
let: hindrance.
lewd: foolish, wicked.
line: stock, race.
list: desire.
lyste: v. 2nd sing. lie (ME form; 16th cent. liest).

M

makes: n. breeding partner of animals.
meet: adj. suitable.
meetly: fairly; suitably.
miss: doubt.

N

Nais: Naiad.
narciss: narcissus; first cit. in *OED*.
naughty: wicked.
nice: absurd.

O

original: origin.
otherwhile: at other times; cit. in *OED2*.

outwrestle: to escape by wrestling. Phaer's is the only cit. in *OED1*.
overthwart: crosswise.

P

pain taking: painstaking; fourth cit. in *OED2*.
painful: diligent.
Parthanes: Parthians.
particle: function word (*OED6a*)
pathetical: pathetic.
past: v. passed.
paunce: pansy.
pensiful: thoughtful.
penthemimer: *pros.* metrical unit consisting of two and a half feet of a pentameter or hexameter; first cit. in *OED*.
pestered: infested.
phalaecian: *pros.* a line consisting of a spondee, a dactyl, and three trochees.
pith: substance, force.
policy: political cunning.
pottical: inspired by alcohol; first cit. in *OED*. A jest with 'poetical'.
precinct: n. limit.
pruiner: pruner.

Q

quainted: familiar; second cit. in *OED*.
queachy: thickly wooded; third cit. in *OED*.

R

rakehelly: adj. of a dissolute nature.
rank: adj. violent.
ransacketh: searches.
rehearsal: catalogue.
rehearse: mention, describe at length.

S

scant: adv. hardly, scarcely; fourth cit. in *OED*.
scoffing: ridiculing irreverently.
silly: simple.
sith: seeing that, since (expressing cause).
slenderly: poorly.
society: cooperation; assistance. Unique cit. in *OED*.
sore: adv. to a great extent; adj. sorry, painful.
stead, in my: instead of me.
stead, stand in: serve.
steven: noise.
straightways: inmediately.

strake: v. struck.
stroke: a touch on a stringed instrument, a tune; third cit. in *OED*8a.
strowed: scattered.
stuck upon: lingered or dwelt on; second cit. in *OED*6c.
substance: possessions.
suit: kind.
sway: authority.

T

tarry: keep waiting; remain.
tawdryne: tawdry lace (from *St Audrey's lace*); a silk lace or necktie worn by women in 16th century.
theaves: female young sheep.
tho: then.
through: thoroughly.
throughly: all through; fully.
tinkerly: adj. unskilful, clumsy; first cit. in *OED*.
t'much: too much.
toward: promising, willing to learn.
travel: n. and v. labour.

U

uncomely: improper.
unsteadfast: inconstant.
uprightly: adv. straightforwardly.
ure: practice.
urged: brought forward.

V

victuals: animals serving for food.

W

wags: stirs.
wasteful: that causes devastation.
wellaway: alas.
wherefore: why.
whereinto: into which.
whit: bit; no whit: adv. not at all.
wight: creature.
wine-sops: sops-in-wine, gillyflowers (*Fr. soup en vin*).
wound up: bound, joined.
wried: turned aside.

Y

yore, of: adv. of old, anciently.

BIBLIOGRAPHY

The following reference list contains items mentioned or quoted in this edition, or works consulted for general reference. I have divided this list into four sections: 1) William Webbe's editions for *A Discourse* (First Edition and Modern Editions); 2) Pre-1586 Primary Sources; 3) Post-1586 Editions of Primary Sources; 4) Secondary Sources. Abbreviations of frequently quoted sources follow each reference in square brackets.

William Webbe's editions of *A Discourse of English Poetry*

First Edition

WEBBE, WILLIAM, *A Discourse of English Poetrie. Together, with the Authours iudgment, touching the reformation of our English Verse* (London: John Charlewood for Robert Walley, 1586): [Q] [*A Discourse*]

Modern Editions

ARBER, EDWARD, ed., *A Discourse of English Poetrie. Together, with the Authours iudgment, touching the reformation of our English Verse* (London: English Reprints, 1815): [Arb]
HASLEWOOD, JOSEPH, ed., *Ancient Critical Essays Upon English Poets and Poësy*, 2 vols (London: T. Bensley for Robert Triphook, 1815), II, pp. 13–95: [Hasl]
MAGNUS, LAURIE, ed., *Documents Illustrating Elizabethan Poetry by Sir Philip Sidney, George Puttenham and William Webbe* (London: George Routledge and Sons Ltd.; New York: E. P. Dutton and Co., 1906)
SMITH, G. GREGORY, ed., *Elizabethan Critical Essays*, 2 vols (London: Oxford University Press, 1904), I, pp. 226–302: [Smith, Sm]

Pre-1586 Primary Sources

A Handefull of Pleasant Delites, ed. by Clement Robinson (London: Richard Ihones, 1584)
AELIAN, *A Registre of Hystories*, trans. by Abraham Fleming (London: for Thomas Woodcocke, 1576)
ASCHAM, ROGER, *The Scholemaster, or Plaine and Perfite Way of Teachyng Children* (London: John Daye, 1570)
BALE, JOHN, *Scriptorum Illustrium Maioris Bryttanniae, quam nunc Angliam and Scotiam uocant: Catalogus* (Basel: Johannes Oporinus, 1557–59)
CHURCHYARD, THOMAS, *The thre first bookes of Ouids De tristibus, translated into Englishe* (London: Thomas Marshe, 1572)

——, *The Firste Parte of Churcheyeards Chippes, containing twelve severall Labours* (London: Thomas Marshe, 1578)
DONATUS, AELIUS, 'De tragoedia et comoedia', in Thomas Marsh, *Pub. Terentii Afri Comoediae Sex* (London, 1583) sigs. A7^r–A7^v
ELYOT, THOMAS, *The Boke Named the Gouernour* (London: Thomas Berthelet, 1531. 2nd edn London: Thomas East, 1580) [*Governour, Gov*]
FABRICII CHEMNICENSIS, GEORGII (Georg Fabricius), *De Re Poetica Libri Septem* (Parisiis: Hieronymun de Marnef, 1584; 1st edn 1565)
FLEMING, ABRAHAM, *The Bucolikes of Publius Virgilius Maro* (London: John Charlewood for Thomas Woodcocke, 1575)
FOXE, JOHN, *Acts and Monuments*, 2 vols (London: John Day, 1583; 1st edn 1563), I
GOOGE, BARNABY, *The firste six bokes of the mooste Christian Poet Marcellus Palingenius, called the Zodiake of Life* (London: John Tildale, 1561)
——, *Eclogs, Epytaphs and Sonettes* (London: Thomas Colwell, 1563)
——, *The Zodiake of Life* (London: Henry Denham, 1565; 2nd edn London: Raufe Newberie, 1576; 3rd edn London: Richard Watkins, 1577)
——, *Foure Bookes of Husbandry, collected by M. Conradus Heresbachius, counseller to the high and mighty prince, the Duke of Cleue: conteyning the whole arte and trade of husbandry, with the antiquitie, and commendation thereof. Newly Englished, and increased, by Barnabe Googe, Esquire* (London: Richard Watkins, 1577)
GOLDING, ARTHUR, *The xv. Bookes of P. Ouidius Naso, entytuled Metamorphosis, translated oute of Latine into English meeter* (London: Willyam Seres, 1567)
GRANGE, JOHN, *The Golden Aphroditis* (London: Henry Binneman, 1577)
HARVEY, RICHARD, *An Astrological Discourse upon the great and notable Conjunction of two Superiour Planets, Saturne and Jupiter, which shall happen on the 28 day of April 1583* (London: Henrie Bynneman, 1583)
HEYWOOD, JASPER, *The sixt tragedie of the most graue and prudent author Lucius Anneus, Seneca, entituled Troas* (London: by Thomas Powell, for George Bucke, 1559)
——, *The seconde tragedie of Seneca entituled Thyestes faithfully Englished by Iasper Heywood* (London: Thomas Berthelettes, 1560)
HUNNIS, WILLIAM, *Certayne Psalmes chosen out of the Psalter of David and drawen furth into English Meter* (London: by the widow of John Herforde, 1550)
LYLY, JOHN, *Euphues and his England* (London: for Gabriell Cawood, 1580)
MARSH, THOMAS, ed., *Pvb. Terentii Afri Comoediae Sex* (London, 1583)
MUNDAY, ANTHONY, *The Mirrour of Mutabilitie* (London: John Allde, 1579)
PHAER, THOMAS, *The whole xii Bookes of the Aeneidos of Virgill* (London: William How, 1573): [Phaer1573]
——, *The xiii Bookes of Aeneidos* (London: William How, 1584): [Phaer1584]
SCALIGER, JULIUS CAESAR, *Poetices Libri Septem* (Geneva, 1561)
SPENSER, EDMUND, *The Shepheardes Calender Conteyning Twelue Aeglogues Proportionable to the Twelue Monethes* (London: Hugh Singleton, 1579; 2nd edn London: Thomas East for John Harrison, 1581; 3rd edn London: John Wolf for John Harrison, 1586): [Q_1, Q_2, Q_3]
STANYHURST, RICHARD, *Thee first foure bookes of Virgil his Aeneis* (Leiden: John Pates, 1582)

SURREY, EARL OF (Henry Howard), *The fourth boke of Virgill, intreating of the love betwene Aeneas and Dido, translated into English, and drawne into a strange metre by Henrye late Earle of Surrey, worthy to be embraced* (London: John Day, for William Owen, 1554)
TALAEUS, AUDOMARUS (Omer Talon), *Rhetorica* (Paris: Matthaei Davidis, 1552)
The Paradyse of Daynty Deuises (London: Henry Disle, 1576; 2nd edn 1578; 3rd edn 1580; 4th edn London: Robert Waldegrave, for Edward White, 1585) [*Paradise*]
TUSSER, THOMAS, *Fiue Hundreth Good Pointes of Husbandrie* (London: Henrie Denham, 1557)
WHETSTONE, GEORGE, *The Rocke of Regard* (London: H. Middleton, 1576)
——, *A Remembraunce of the Wel Imployed Life, [and] Godly End, of George Gaskoine Esquire* (London: for Edward Aggas, 1577)
——, *Promos and Cassandra* (London: John Charlewood, 1578)
YATES, JAMES, *The Castell of Courtesie* (London: John Wolfe, 1582)

Post-1586 Editions of Primary Sources

ALEXANDER, GAVIN, ed., *Sir Philip Sidney's 'The Defence of Poesy' and Selected Renaissance Literary Criticism* (London: Penguin, 2004)
AELIAN, *Historical Miscellany*, ed. and trans. by Nigel G. Wilson, The Loeb Classical Library, vol. 486 (Cambridge, Massachusetts; London, England: Harvard University Press, 1997)
ARBER, EDWARD, ed., *Tottel's Miscellany. Songes and Sonettes* (Westminster: A. Constable and Co., 1903)
ARISTOTLE, *The Poetics. 'Longinus'*, trans. by W. Hamilton Fyfe. *Demetrius*, trans. by W. Rhys Roberts, The Loeb Classical Library, vol. 199 (Cambridge, Massachusetts: Harvard University Press; London: William Heinemann, 1982; 1st edn 1927)
ARISTOPHANES, *The Peace. The Birds. The Frogs*, trans. by Benjamin Bickley Rogers, The Loeb Classical Library, vol. 488 (London: William Heinemann; New York: G. P. Putnam's Sons, 1924).
ASCHAM, ROGER, *The Scholemaster*, in *English Works*, ed. by William Aldis Wright (Cambridge: Cambridge University Press, 1904), pp. 171–302: [*Schoolmaster*]
CAMPION, THOMAS, *Observations in the Arte of English Poesie* (1602), in *Elizabethan Critical Essays*, ed. by Gregory Smith, 2 vols (London: Oxford University Press, 1904), II, pp. 327–55
CELSUS, *De Medicina*, trans. by W.G. Spencer, The Loeb Classical Library, vol. 336, 3 vols (Cambridge, Massachusetts: Harvard University Press; London: William Heinemann, 1938), III
CICERO, *Leters to Atticus*, trans. by E.O. Winstedt, The Loeb Classical Library, vol. 8, 3 vols (London: William Heinemann; New York: The Macmillan Co., 1913), II
——, *De Finibus Bonorum et Malorum*, trans. by H. Rackham, The Loeb Classical Library, vol. 40 (London: William Heinemann; New York: The Macmillan Co., 1914)
——, *Leters to Atticus*, trans. by D. R. Shackelton Bailey, The Loeb Classical Library, vol. 97, 3 vols (London: William Heinemann; Cambridge: Massachusetts, 1962), III

——, *De Natura Deorum. Academica*, trans. by H. Rackham, The Loeb Classical Library, vol. 268 (Cambridge, Massachusetts: Harvard University Press; London: William Heinemann, 1967)

——, *Tusculan Disputations*, trans. by J. E. King, The Loeb Classical Library, vol. 141 London: William Heinemann; Cambridge, Massachusetts: Harvard University Press, 1971; 1st edn 1927)

——, *De Inventione. De Optimo Genere Oratorum; Topica*, trans. by H. M. Hubbel, The Loeb Classical Library, vol. 386 (London: Heinemann; Cambridge, Massachusetts: Harvard University Press, 1968)

——, *Pro Archia Poeta. Post Reditum ad Quirites. Post Reditum in Senatu. De Domo Sua. De Haruspicum Responsis. Pro Plancio*, trans. by N. H. Watts, The Loeb Classical Library, vol. 158 (Cambridge, Massachusetts: Harvard University Press; London: William Heinemann, 1979)

——, *Brutus, Orator*, trans. by G. L. Hendrickson and H. M. Hubbell, The Loeb Classical Library, vol. 342 (Cambridge, Massachusetts: Harvard University Press; London: William Heinemann, 1988; 1st edn 1939)

DONATUS, AELIUS, *Vitae Vergilianae*, ed. by Iacobus Brummer (Leipzig: Teubner, 1912)

DRANT, THOMAS, *Horace his arte of poetrie, pistles and satyrs Englished* (London: Thomas Marshe, 1567)

ELYOT, THOMAS, *The Boke Named The Gouernour*, ed. by Henry Herbert Stephen Croft, 2 vols (London: Kegan Paul, Trench, and Co, 1883): [*Governour*]

FRAUNCE, ABRAHAM, *The Lamentations of Amyntas* (London: John Wolfe, 1587)

——, *The Lawiers Logike exemplifying the praecepts of logike by the practice of the common law* (London: William How, for Thomas Hubbin, and T. Newman, 1588)

GASCOIGNE, GEORGE, *Certayne Notes of Instruction* (1575), in *Elizabethan Critical Essays*, ed. by Gregory Smith, 2 vols (London: Oxford University Press, 1904), I, pp. 46–57: [*Certain Notes*]

——, *Certain Notes of Instruction* (1575), in *Sidney's 'The Defence of Poesy' and Selected Renaissance Literary Criticism*, ed. by Gavin Alexander (London: Penguin Books, 2004), pp. 237–47

HARVEY, GABRIEL, *The Works of Gabriel Harvey*, ed. by Alexander B. Grosart, 3 vols (London: Hasel, Watson and Viney, 1884): [*Grosart*]

——, *Foure Letters, and Certaine Sonnets*, in *The Works of Gabriel Harvey*, ed. by Alexander B. Grosart, 3 vols (London: Hasel, Watson and Viney, 1884), I, pp. 151–254 [*Foure Letters*]

HOLINSHED, RAPHAEL, *The First and Second Volumes of Chronicles. Now newlie augmented and continued by John Hooker and others*, 2nd edn (London: Henry Denham, 1587; 1st edn 1580)

HORACE, *Satires. Epistles. Ars Poetica*, trans. by H. Rushton Fairclough, The Loeb Classical Library, vol. 194 (London: William Heinemann; Cambridge, Massachusetts: Harvard University Press, 1926)

LODGE, THOMAS, *Defence of Poetry* (1579), in *Elizabethan Critical Essays*, ed. by Gregory Smith, 2 vols (London: Oxford University Press, 1904), I, pp. 61–86

MARTIAL, *Epigrams*, trans. by Walter C. A. Kerr, The Loeb Classical Library, vol. 95, 3 vols (London: William Heinemann; New York: G.P. Putnam's Sons, 1920), II

MACROBIUS, *Saturnalia*, ed. and trans. by Robert A. Haster, The Loeb Classical Library, vol. 511, 3 vols (Cambridge, Massachusetts; London: Harvard University Press, 2011), II
MERES, FRANCIS, *Palladis Tamia* (1598), in *Elizabethan Critical Essays*, ed. by Gregory Smith, 2 vols (London: Oxford University Press, 1904), II, pp. 308–24
MUSTARD, WILFRED P., ed., *The Eclogues of Baptista Mantuanus* (Baltimore: The Johns Hopkins Press, 1911)
NECKAM, ALEXANDER, *De Naturis Rerum. Libri Duo. With the poem of the same author, The Laudibus Divinae Sapientiae*, ed. by Thomas Wright (London: Longman, Roberts, and Green, 1863)
OVID, *Heroides and Amores*, trans. by Grant Showerman, The Loeb Classical Library, vol. 41 (London: William Heinemann; New York: The Macmillan Co., 1914)
——, *Tristia. Ex Ponto*, trans. by Arthur Leslie Wheeler, The Loeb Classical Library, vol. 151 (Cambridge, Massachusetts: Harvard University Press; London: William Heinemann, 1939)
——, *Metamorphoses*, trans. by Frank Justus Miller, The Loeb Classical Library, vol. 42, 2 vols (London: William Heinemann; Cambridge, Massachusetts: Harvard University Press, 1951), I
——, *The Art of Love, and other poems*, trans. by John Henry Mozley, The Loeb Classical Library, vol. 232 (London: William Heinemann; Cambridge, Massachusetts: Harvard University Press, 1957)
——, *Fasti*, trans. by James G. Frazer, The Loeb Classical Library, vol. 253 (London: William Heinemann; Cambridge, Massachusetts: Harvard University Press, 1959)
PLATO, *The Republic*, trans. by Paul Shorey, The Loeb Classical Library, vol. 41 (London: William Heinemann; Cambridge, Massachusetts: Harvard University Press, 1942; 1st edn 1935)
PLAUTUS, *Amphitryon. The Comedy of Asses. The Pot of Gold. The Two Bacchises. The Captives*, ed. and trans. by Wolfgang de Melo, The Loeb Classical Library, vol. 60 (Cambridge, Massachusetts: Harvard University Press, 2011)
PLINY, *Natural History*, trans. by H. Rackham, The Loeb Classical Library, vol. 352 (Cambridge, Massachusetts: Harvard University Press; London: William Heinemann, 1961).
PLUTARCH, *Lives. Demosthenes and Cicero. Alexander and Caesar*, trans. by Bernadotte Perrin, The Loeb Classical Library, vol. 99 (Cambridge, Massachusetts; London, England: Harvard University Press, 1919)
PROPERTIUS, *Elegies*, trans. by H. E. Butler, The Loeb Classical Library, vol. 18 (London: William Heinemann; New York: G. P. Putnam's Sons, 1918)
PUTTENHAM, GEORGE, *The Art of English Poesy*, ed. by Frank Whigham and Wayne E. Rebhorn (Ithaca: Cornell University Press, 2007)
QUINTILIAN, *Institutio Oratoria*, trans. by Harold Edgeworth Butler, The Loeb Classical Library, vols. 126, 127, 4 vols (London: William Heinemann; New York: G. P. Putnam's Sons, 1920–1922), III, IV
ROLLINS, HYDER EDWARD, ed., *The Paradise of Dainty Devices* (Cambridge: Harvard University Press, 1927)
SIDNEY, PHILIP, *A Defence of Poesy* (1595), in *Sidney's 'The Defence of Poesy' and Selected Renaissance Literary Criticism*, ed. by Gavin Alexander (London: Penguin Books, 2004): [*Defence*]

SIDONIUS, *Letters 3–9*, trans. by W. B. Anderson, The Loeb Classical Library, vol. 420 (Cambridge, Massachusetts: Harvard University Press; London: William Heinemann, 1965)
SPENSER, EDMUND, *Selected Shorter Poems*, ed. by Douglas Brooks-Davies (London: Longman, 1995): [Brooks-Davies]
——, *The Works Of Edmund Spenser: A Variorum Edition. The Minor Poems, Part One*, ed. by Edwin Greenlaw and others, 11 vols (Baltimore: The Johns Hopkins University Press, 1943), VII
——, *The Works Of Edmund Spenser: A Variorum Edition. The Prose Works*, ed. by Edwin Greenlaw and others, 11 vols (Baltimore: The Johns Hopkins University Press, 1949), X: [*Variorum X*]
TERENCE, *P. Terenti Comoediae cum Scholiis Aeli Donati et Eugraphi Commentariis*, ed. by Reinholdus Klotz, 2 vols. (Lipsiae: E.B. Schwickert, 1838–40)
——, *Phormio. The Mother-in-law. The Brothers*, trans. by John Sargeaunt, The Loeb Classical Library, vol. 23 (London: William Heinemann; New York: Putnam's Sons, 1920)
——, *The Woman of Andros. The Self-Tormentor. The Eunuch*, ed. and trans. by John Barsby, The Loeb Classical Library, vol. 22 (Cambridge, Massachusetts: Harvard University Press, 2001; 1st edn 1912)
The Paradise of Dainty Deuices, ed. by Samuel Egerton Brydges (London: Robert Triphook and William Sancho, 1810): [*Paradise*]
TURBERVILLE, GEORGE, *The heroycall epistles of Publius Ouidius Naso* (London: Henry Denham, 1567)
——, *The eglogs of the poet B. Mantuan Carmelitan* (London: H. Bynneman, 1572)
VARRO, *On the Latin Language*, trans. by G. Kent Roland, The Loeb Classical Library, vol. 333, 2 vols (London: William Heinemann; Cambridge, Massachusetts: Harvard University Press, 1938), I
VIRGIL, *Eclogues. Georgics. Aeneid 1–6*, trans. by H. Rushton Fairclough; rev. by G. P. Goold, 3rd edn, Loeb Classical Library, vol. 63 (Cambridge, Massachusetts; London, England: Harvard University Press, 1999; 1st edn 1916)
——, *Aeneid 7–12. Appendix Vergiliana*, trans. by H. Rushton Fairclough; rev. by G. P. Goold, 3rd edn, Loeb Classical Library, vol. 64 (Cambridge, Massachusetts; London, England: Harvard University Press, 2000; 1st edn 1918)
WILMOT, ROBERT, *The Tragedie of Tancred and Gismund. Newly reuiued and polished according to the decorum of these daies. By R.W.* (London: Thomas Scarlet, 1592)

Secondary Sources

AMES, JOSEPH, *Typographical Antiquities: Being a Historical Account of Printing in England* (London: by W. Faden, 1749)
ANDERSEN, JOHANNES C., *The Laws of Verse* (Cambridge: Cambridge University Press, 2014; 1st edn 1928)
ANDERSON, JUDITH H., DONALD CHENEY and DAVID A. RICHARDSON, eds, *Spenser's Life and the Subject of Biography* (Amherst: University of Massachusetts Press, 1996)

BIBLIOGRAPHY

ARBER, EDWARD, ed., *A Transcript of the Registers of the Company of Stationers of London, 1554-1640*, 5 vols (London: F.S.A., 1875)

ATTRIDGE, DEREK, *Well-Weighed Syllables: Elizabethan verse in classical metres.* (Cambridge: Cambridge University Press, 1974)

AUSTEN, GILLIAN, *George Gascoigne* (Cambridge: D. S. Brewer, 2008)

BELOE, WILLIAM, *Anecdotes of Literature and Scarce Rare Books*, 2 vols (London: F. C. and J. Rivington), I

CANTOR, A., 'Aristotle and the History of Tragedy', in David Perkins, ed., *Theoretical Issues in Literary History* (Cambridge, Mass.: Harvard University Press, 1991), pp. 60-84

CAREY, JOHN, *The Latin Prosody Made Easy* (London: Longman, Hurst, Rees and Orme, 1808)

Catalogue of a Further Selection of Extremely Rare and Valuable Books in Early English Poetry and other Literature from the Renowned Library formerly at Britwell Court, Burnham, Bucks (London: Dryden Press, 1922)

CLARK, DONALD LEMEN, *Rhetoric and Poetry in the Renaissance: A Study of Rhetorical Terms in English Renaissance Literary Criticism* (New York: Columbia University Press, 1922)

COOPER, CHARLES HENRY and THOMPSON COOPER, *Athenae Cantabrigienses 1586-1609*. 2 vols (Cambridge: Deighton, Bell and Co.; and Macmillan and Co. London: Bell and Daldy, 1861), II

CURTIUS, ERNST ROBERT, *European Literature and the Latin Middles Ages* (Princeton: Princeton University Press, 1990; 1st edn 1953)

EDWARDS, ANTHONY, *John Skelton: The Critical Heritage* (Abingdon: Routledge, 1999; 1st edn 1981)

FOWLER, ALASTAIR, 'The Beginnings of English Georgic', in B. K. Lewalski, ed., *Renaissance Genres: Essays on Theory, History and Interpretation* (Cambridge: Harvard University Press, 1986), 105-25

HADFIELD, ANDREW, *Edmund Spenser: A Life* (Oxford: Oxford University Press, 2012)

HAMILTON, A. C., ed., *The Spenser Encyclopaedia* (London: Routledge, 1996; 1st edn Toronto: University of Toronto Press, 1990)

HEALE, ELIZABETH, 'William Webbe', in *Oxford Dictionary of National Biography*, ed. by Leslie Stephen, 60 vols (Oxford, Toronto: Oxford University Press, 2004; 1st edn 1885), vol. 57, pp. 865-66

HELGERSON, RICHARD, *Forms of Nationhood. The Elizabethan Writing of England* (Chicago: The University of Chicago Press, 1992)

HENDRICKSON, G. L., 'Elizabethan Quantitative Hexameters', *Philological Quaterly*, 28.2 (1949), 237-60

HERBERT, WILLIAM, *Typographical Antiquities: Being a Historical Account of Printing in England. Begun by the late Joseph Ames. Considerably augmented both in the Memoirs and the Number of Books*, 3 vols (London, 1785), II

HUNTER, RICHARD, *Critical Moments in Classical Literature* (Cambridge: Cambridge University Press, 2009)

JOHNSON, BARBARA A., *Reading Piers Plowman and The Pilgrim's Progress: Reception and the Protestant Reader* (Carbondale: Southern Illinois University Press, 1992)

KINNEY, ARTHUR F., *Humanist Poetics: Thought, Rhetoric and Fiction in Sixteenth-century England* (Amherst: The University of Massachusetts Press, 1986)
KOLLER, KATHRINE, 'Abraham Fraunce and Edmund Spenser', *ELH*, 7.2 (1940), 108–20
MAY, STEPHEN W., 'Marlowe, Spenser, Sidney and –Abraham Fraunce?', *The Review of English Studies*, New Series 62 (2010), 30–63
MONFASANI, JOHN, 'The Ciceronian controversy', in *The Cambridge History of Literary Criticism*, ed. by Glyn P. Norton, 9 vols (Cambridge: Cambridge University Press), III, 395–401.
NORTON, GLYN P., ed., *The Renaissance. The Cambridge History of Literary Criticism*, 9 vols (Cambridge: Cambridge University Press), III
OLDYS, WILLIAM, *The British Librarian* (London: for T. Osborne in Grays's Inn, 1738)
OMOND, THOMAS STEWART, *English Metrists* (Tunbridge Wells: R. Pelton, 1903)
PINCOMBE, MICHAEL, 'William Webbe', in *Dictionary of Literary Biography* (Detroit, Mi.: Gale, 1993), pp. 329–32.
——, *Elizabethan Humanism* (Harlow: Longman, 2001)
RHODES, NEIL, *The Power of Eloquence and English Renaissance Literature* (New York: St Martin's Press, 1992)
——, *Shakespeare and the Origins of English* (Oxford: Oxford University Press, 2004)
——, Gordon Kendal and Louise Wilson, eds, *English Renaissance Translation Theory* (London: Modern Humanities Research Association, 2013)
RITSON, JOSEPH, *Robin Hood. A Collection of all the Ancient Poems, Songs and Ballads, now extant, Relative to that Celebrated English Outlaw* (London: T. Egerton, Whitehall, and J. Johnson, 1795)
ROLLINS, HYDER E., 'William Elderton: Elizabethan Actor and Ballad-Writer', *Studies in Philology*, 17.2 (1920), 199–245
SCHUMAN, SHARON, 'Sixteenth-Century English Quantitative Verse: Its Ends, Means, and Products', *Modern Philology*, 74.4 (May, 1977), 335–49
SHAW, ROBERT BURNS, *Blank Verse: A Guide to Its History and Use* (Athens: Ohio University Press, 2007)
SHUGER, DEBORA, 'Conceptions of Style', in *The Cambridge History of Literary Criticism*, ed. by Glyn P. Norton, 9 vols (Cambridge: Cambridge University Press, 1999), III, pp. 176–86.
TILLBROOK, S., *Historical and Critical Remarks Upon the Modern Hexametrists* (Cambridge: J. Smith, 1822)
TIMPERLEY, CHARLES HENRY, *History of Printers and Printing* (London: H. Johnson, 1839)
VENN, JOHN and J. A. VENN, *Alumni Cantabrigienses*, Part 1, 4 vols (Cambridge: Cambridge University Press; London: Peter Lane, 1927), IV
WARTON, THOMAS, *The History of English Poetry*, 2nd edn, 4 vols (London: for Thomas Tegg, 1824; 1st edn 1774–81)
White Knights Library. Catalogue (London: W. Bulmer and Co., 1819)
WILLCOCK, GLADYS, 'Passing Pitefull Hexameters', *Modern Language Review*, 29.1 (1934), 1–19
WILSON-OKAMURA, DAVID SCOTT, *Spenser's International Style* (Cambridge: Cambridge University Press, 2013)

Dictionaries

A Dictionary of Greek and Roman Biography and Mythology, ed. by William Smith, 3 vols (London: John Murray, 1872)

A New Classical Dictionary of Greek and Roman Biography, Mythology and Geography, ed. by William Smith (New York: Harper, 1884)

Oxford English Dictionary (online version)

Universal Pronouncing Dictionary of Biography and Mythology, ed. by Joseph Thomas, 2 vols (Philadelphia: J. B. Lippincott and Co., 1870)

Dictionary of National Biography, ed. by Leslie Stephen and Sidney Lee (Oxford University Press, 2004), http://onlinebooks.library.upenn.edu/webbin/metabook?id=dnb

INDEX

Accius 138
Achates 58
Achilles 68, 69
Aelian 57, 151, 153
Aeneas 15, 58, 74, 96, 98, 99, 136, 153
Aeschylus 72, 135, 141
Afranius 138
Alexander, Gavin vii, 1, 50, 105, 108, 110, 113, 153, 154, 155
Alexander, Prince 58, 68, 69, 70
Amphion 69, 127, 137
Andronicus, Livius 71
Arber, Edward vii, 3, 4, 49, 151, 153, 156
Archilocus 138
Aristophanes 70, 71, 72, 88, 135, 153
Aristotle 63, 66, 67, 69, 70, 71, 72, 87, 133, 139, 140, 153, 157
Ascham, Roger viii, 1, 6, 9, 10, 11, 12, 13, 14, 15, 16, 17, 18, 19, 21, 23, 26, 27, 34, 35, 38, 39, 40, 61, 62, 63, 68, 73, 77, 78, 80, 81, 82, 87, 89, 91, 95, 102, 103, 105, 106, 107, 118, 120, 122, 138, 151, 153
Atilius, Marcus 73
Attridge, Derek 40, 42, 43, 44, 46, 48, 62, 63, 65, 66, 79, 105, 106, 107, 113, 117, 118, 119, 120, 121, 157
Ausonius 75, 76

Bacchus 135
Bale, John 79, 151
Bewe, Master 84
Boethius 75, 76

Caecilius Statius 49, 73, 75, 76, 138
Caesar 75, 82, 152, 155
Calvin, John 82
Campion, Thomas 42, 44, 65, 153
Catullus 74, 76, 91, 138, 139
Celsus 137, 153

Charlewood, John vii, 2, 3, 104, 151, 153
Chaucer, Geoffrey 13, 25, 27, 38, 78, 79, 90, 101
Cheke, John 11, 26, 40, 78, 122
Churchyard, Thomas 26, 28, 80, 81, 83, 151
Cicero, Tully 19, 63, 66, 71, 96, 138, 153, 155
  De Orator 62, 139
  Tusculan Disputations 49, 67, 73, 123, 141, 154
  Pro Archia Poeta 37, 46, 67, 69, 117, 154
  De Optimo 73, 134, 154
Cinna 138, 139
Claudian 75, 76
Cratinus 71, 135
Corydon 102, 126, 127, 128
Croft, Henry H. S. 13, 50, 66, 154

Darius, King 69
Darrel, ? 84
Dekker, Thomas 83
Demosthenes 15, 96, 155
Donatus, Aelius 72, 74, 88, 89, 152, 154
Drant, Thomas 23, 40, 41, 44, 45, 46, 47, 83, 118, 154
Drayton, Michael 83

E.K. 24, 27, 30, 33, 34, 35, 36, 38, 66, 67, 68, 69, 80, 84, 102, 123, 143
Edwards, Richard 80, 81, 116
Elderton, William 39, 86, 158
Elyot, Thomas vii, 7, 8, 10, 13, 19, 20, 21, 22, 50, 51, 66, 67, 69, 70, 74, 75, 78, 82, 90, 91, 92, 93, 96, 148, 152, 154
  The Governour 7, 8, 10, 13, 19, 20, 22, 50, 51, 66, 67, 69, 70, 74, 75,

78, 82, 91, 92, 93, 94, 96, 152, 154
 and Webbe 13, 19, 20, 21, 22, 50
 as source of examples 67, 69, 70, 74, 75, 78, 82, 90, 91, 92, 93, 96
Empedocles 71
Ennius 47, 69, 71, 73, 76, 138
Epicharmus 138
Eucherius 139
Eupolis 71, 135
Euripides 72

Fabricius, Georg 7, 10, 132, 138, 152
Flaccus, Valerius 75, 76
Fleming, Abraham 28, 29, 57, 82, 104, 105, 152
Foxe, John 77, 152
Fraunce, Abraham 11, 67, 83, 117, 154, 157, 158
 and Webbe 4, 22, 23, 24, 25, 28, 29, 30, 31, 33, 43
 The Lamentations of Amyntas 28, 43, 83, 127
 The Arcadian Rhetorike 43, 67

Gascoigne, George 27, 29, 35, 83, 84
 Certain Notes vii, 1, 8, 10, 28, 63, 80, 106, 107, 109, 111, 112, 113, 114, 115, 154
 instructions on versifying 10, 39, 106, 107, 109, 111, 112, 113, 114, 115
 as a source for Webbe 8, 28, 39, 63, 107, 114
Gellius, Aulus 138, 144
Golding, Arthur 16, 26, 33, 51, 82, 101, 108, 113, 152
Googe, Barnaby 5, 28, 51, 76, 82, 104, 108, 109, 111, 143, 152
Gothians 77, 107
Gower, John 13, 78, 108
Grange, John 84, 116, 152
Greeks 15, 37, 46, 47, 63, 94, 95, 102, 106, 109, 117, 134, 135
Greville, Fulke 84

Hadfield, Andrew 4, 31, 62, 48, 157
Hannibal 74

Harvey, Gabriel vii, 1, 4, 5, 8, 11, 23, 24, 27, 28, 29, 30, 31, 32, 40, 41, 42, 43, 44, 45, 46, 47, 48, 49, 50, 61, 63, 78, 80, 84, 85, 106, 117, 118, 120, 122, 123
 Foure Letters 86, 96, 154
Harvey, John 5, 32, 78, 85
Harvey, Richard 5, 32, 78, 85, 152
Haslewood, Joseph vii, 2, 4, 49, 151
Hector 68
Henry VIII, King 80
Henry I, King 13, 58, 78
Heresbach 5, 82, 104, 152
Hesiod 49, 72, 72, 74, 104
Heywood, Jasper or John 26, 80, 81, 83, 142, 152
Hill, Richard 80, 81
Hippocrates 137
Homer 15, 20, 47, 68, 69, 70, 71, 73, 74, 87, 89, 95, 105, 118, 122,
 Iliad 49, 74, 88, 89, 141
 Odyssey 49, 70, 88, 122, 134, 137
Horace 7, 12, 26, 69, 70, 74, 75, 76, 78, 83, 89, 90, 91, 118, 122, 132, 138, 140
 Ars Poetica 7, 10, 65, 71, 72, 83, 90, 122, 154
 Satires 71, 154
 Epistles 73, 90, 91, 138, 154
Humanism 7, 10, 67, 75, 158
 and Ciceronianism 11
 and matter and form 11
 and translation 16, 17
 and imitation 14, 15, 16, 17
Hunnis, William 25, 26, 80, 81, 115, 116, 117, 152
Huns 18, 77, 107

Inns of Court 29, 41
 Gray's Inn 27, 29, 43, 81, 84, 158

Juvenal 75, 76

Kindlemarsh or Kinwelmarsh, Francis 84
Knight, Edward? 84
Koller, Kathrine 23, 24, 25, 30, 33, 67, 157

Licinius 73, 138
Lodge, Thomas 67, 69, 70, 71, 73, 154
Lucan, Annaeus 74, 75, 76
Lucian 94
Lucius 73, 138, 141
Lucretius 49, 75, 76
Lydgate, John 79
Lyly, John 63, 81, 95, 152

Macrobius 138, 139, 155
Magnus, Laurie 68, 76, 152
Manilius 75, 76
Mantuan, Baptista 28, 76, 83, 101, 155, 156
Martial 20, 75, 76, 91, 93, 94, 154
Matter 9, 11, 13, 14, 15, 16, 17, 20, 35, 36, 37, 61, 77, 78, 79, 86, 87, 88, 89, 91, 93, 96, 98, 101, 102, 103, 105, 110, 114, 115, 117, 118, 132, 134, 139
    Moral or serious 19, 21, 57, 66, 70, 71, 85, 111, 133, 134, 137, 139
    Wanton or light 21, 66, 71, 74, 79, 90, 101, 135, 140
May, Steven 28, 29, 41, 43, 44, 83, 158
Meliboeus 124, 125
Memmius 138, 139, 144
Memory 39, 62, 73, 78, 106, 114, 115, 136
Menander 71, 135, 138
Mercury 136
Meres, Francis vii, 24, 67, 73, 74, 75, 76, 79, 80, 82, 83, 87, 96, 104, 155
Middleton, Thomas 83
Minerva 136
Munday, Anthony 28, 83, 84, 152

Naevius 73, 138
Nemesianus 101
Norton of Bristol 80, 81, 142

Ocland, Christopher 76
Orpheus 19, 66, 69, 70, 136
Osborne, Peter 104
Ovid 20, 74, 75, 83, 93,
    Metamorphoses 16, 22, 75, 82, 101, 113, 155
    Fasti 34, 67, 75, 155
    Tristia 49, 74, 83, 139, 155
    Remedia Amoris 93, 155
    Amores 128, 155
Owen, William 153

Pacuvius 73, 138
Palingenius 76, 82, 141, 142, 152
Paradise of Dainty Devices vii, 25, 26, 51, 62, 80, 81, 83, 84, 115, 116, 117, 144, 153
Periz, Gonsalvo 122
Persius 75, 76
Phaer, Thomas vii, 16, 26, 51, 80, 82, 96, 97, 98, 99, 100, 112, 142, 152
Phocylides 72, 141
Piers Plowman 79, 141, 157
Pincombe, Michael 1, 5, 7, 10, 68, 158
Plato 65, 66, 67, 71, 87, 103, 155
Plato Comicus 71, 135, 141
Plautus 138, 155
Pliny 49, 57, 69, 70, 155
Plutarch 69, 155
Pompey 75
Propertius, Sextus 49, 74, 155
Puttenham viii, 58, 61, 65, 66, 67, 69, 70, 72, 74, 78, 79, 80, 82, 83, 95, 101, 106, 107, 108, 109, 112, 113, 115, 116, 151, 155

Quantitative verse 1, 2, 6, 10, 17, 26, 27, 31, 32, 33, 38, 39, 40, 41, 43, 44, 45, 46, 51, 62, 65, 66, 82, 83, 95, 105, 106, 114, 117, 122, 157, 158
    as reformed versification 6, 8, 11, 37
    and rules of prosody 8, 9, 17, 37, 40, 41, 42, 44, 45, 46, 47, 48, 51, 63, 113, 118, 120, 121, 122, 123, 128, 138
    hexameter 2, 17, 23, 25, 29, 31, 40, 43, 122, 128
Quintilian 16, 63, 96, 137, 139, 155

Index

Raleigh, Walter 81
Rhodes, Neil 66, 79, 87, 158
Rhyme, English 6, 9, 25, 28, 37, 38, 39, 62, 66, 77, 78, 79, 80, 95, 105, 106, 107, 108, 109, 11, 112, 113, 114, 115, 122
  extempore 39, 114, 115, 135
  as barbarous device 8, 11, 13, 14, 17, 23, 26, 33, 34, 35, 38, 39, 40, 66, 86, 106,
  origin of 18, 106
Rollins, Hyder E. 81, 86, 155, 158
Romans, Latins 37, 46, 47, 48, 62, 63, 73, 94, 95, 102, 106, 117, 118, 134, 135

Sannazaro, Jacopo 68
Scaliger, Joseph 89, 152
Scipio 69, 74, 75
Seneca 75, 76, 83, 152
Sidney, Philip 7, 11, 29, 40, 41, 42, 43, 45, 47, 58, 62, 66, 67, 68, 69, 70, 71, 72, 73, 81, 83, 84, 89, 92, 95, 105, 118, 151, 155, 158, 159
Sidonius 139, 156
Silenus 135
Silius 74, 75
Simias Rhodius 106
Skelton, John 38, 80, 157
Smith, Thomas 84
Sophocles 72, 73
Spenser, Sp. vii, viii, 1, 5, 8, 11, 15, 23, 24, 27, 28, 29, 30, 31, 32, 34, 39, 40, 41, 42, 44, 45, 46, 50, 61, 62, 63, 65, 66, 67, 68, 69, 70, 78, 79, 80, 83, 84, 85, 86, 96, 101, 102, 103, 106, 115, 116, 117, 118, 122, 123, 145, 152, 156, 157, 158
  and Webbe 3, 5, 10, 21, 23, 33, 34, 35, 36, 39, 43, 102, 110
  published works
    The Shepherds' Calendar, SC 4, 5, 8, 9, 10, 21, 22, 23, 24, 27, 28, 30, 32, 33, 34, 35, 36, 38, 39, 41, 50, 61, 62, 65, 66, 67, 68, 69, 70, 73, 76, 79, 80, 83, 84, 85, 86, 94, 101, 102, 103, 109, 115, 116, 123, 129, 147
    Letters vii, 1, 8, 30, 31, 40, 41, 42, 45, 46, 47, 48, 61, 63, 85, 106, 118, 120, 122, 123
  unpublished works
    The English Poet 31, 34, 68, 85
    Dreams 31, 68, 85
    Legends 31, 68, 85
    Court of Cupid 31, 68, 85
    Dying Pellicane 85
Stanyhurst, Richard 42, 82, 96, 120, 121, 152
Statius 49, 73, 75, 76
Staff, staves 65, 109, 110, 112
Studley, John 83
Sulyard, Edward 4, 5, 6, 9, 57, 58
Surrey, Earl of 26, 27, 40, 80, 122, 153, 197

Talaeus, Audomarus 8, 16, 119, 153
Terence 20, 49, 65, 73, 91, 92, 93, 138, 156
Theagenes 72, 141
Theocritus 15, 34, 68, 72, 73, 74, 101, 102
Theophrastus 133
Thespis 72, 135
Tibullus 74, 91
Titus Calphurnius 101
Tityrus 79, 122, 124, 125, 126
Trabea 73
Trismegistus, Hermes 85
Turpilius 73, 141
Tusser, Thomas 80, 81, 104, 153
Twyne, Thomas 82
Tyrtaeus 69, 70, 137

Ugoletus, Angelus 101
Ulysses 70, 123
University
  Cambridge 4, 5, 7, 8, 11, 12, 18, 19, 22, 23, 24, 25, 26, 27, 28, 29, 31, 32, 34, 40, 41, 42, 43, 44, 80, 81, 82, 83, 104, 105, 119, 122
  Christ's College 82, 84
  of Oxford 2, 49, 80, 81, 82

Index

Pembroke Hall 4, 30, 34, 84, 85, 105
Queen's College 82
St John's College 4, 5, 26, 29, 40, 41, 43, 83, 122
Trinity College 27, 80
Trinity Hall 30, 81, 85

Vaux, Lord 26, 80
Vinsauf, Geoffrey de 65
Virgil 6, 10, 15, 20, 29, 33, 34, 35, 37, 49, 58, 68, 73, 74, 76, 78, 80, 82, 96, 101, 102, 104, 105, 107, 122, 124, 126, 136
  Aeneid vii, 8, 10, 16, 21, 27, 42, 49, 51, 58, 75, 82, 86, 95, 96, 108, 112, 120, 142, 152, 156
  Eclogues 2, 5, 10, 15, 24, 25, 29, 51, 73, 82, 102, 104, 122, 123, 156
  Georgics 5, 6, 21, 29, 57, 58, 82, 104, 156
  Webbe's translation of Eclogues I and II 5, 10, 24, 25, 122, 124, 126

Walley, Robert vii, 2, 3, 4, 55, 151
Warton, Thomas 2, 3, 57, 105, 158
Watson, Thomas 11, 26, 28, 40, 43, 78, 96, 122
Wyatt, Thomas 7, 26, 80
Webbe, William
  and classical or quantitative metre 2, 6, 7, 9, 10, 11, 17, 26, 27, 31, 37, 39, 40, 43, 46, 47, 51, 63, 64, 107, 114, 117, 122, 123
  and imitation 9, 14, 15, 16, 19, 33, 36, 46, 47, 63, 66, 88, 95, 102, 104, 117, 138
  and rhyme 6, 8, 9, 11, 13, 14, 17, 18, 23, 25, 26, 28, 33, 34, 37, 38, 39, 61, 66, 77, 78, 79, 86, 105, 106–09, 111, 113, 114, 115, 121, 139
  and translation 2, 5, 6, 8, 10, 16, 19, 24, 25, 28, 42, 43, 48, 57, 58, 82, 90, 96, 101, 104, 128
Webster, John 83
Whetstone, George 3, 27, 28, 82, 83, 153
Whigham, Frank and Wayne A. Rebhorn viii, 1, 50, 155
Whitgift, John 105
William, Duke of Normandy 18, 58, 76
Wright, William Aldis viii, 50, 61, 153
Wilmot, Robert 6, 7, 84, 156

MHRA Critical Texts

This series aims to provide affordable critical editions of lesser-known literary texts that are not in print or are difficult to obtain. The texts will be taken from the following languages: English, French, German, Italian, Portuguese, Russian, and Spanish. Titles will be selected by members of the distinguished Editorial Board and edited by leading academics. The aim is to produce scholarly editions rather than teaching texts, but the potential for crossover to undergraduate reading lists is recognized. The books will appeal both to academic libraries and individual scholars.

Malcolm Cook
Chairman, Editorial Board

Editorial Board

Professor Malcolm Cook (French) (Chairman)
Professor Guido Bonsaver (Italian)
Dr Tyler Fisher (Spanish)
Professor David Gillespie (Slavonic)
Professor Justin Edwards (English)
Dr Stephen Parkinson (Portuguese)
Professor Ritchie Robertson (Germanic)

www.criticaltexts.mhra.org.uk

www.ingramcontent.com/pod-product-compliance
Lightning Source LLC
Chambersburg PA
CBHW071501150426
43191CB00009B/1398